The Politics of Labor Reform in **Latin America**

The Politics of Labor Reform in

Latin America

Between Flexibility and Rights

MARIA LORENA COOK

THE PENNSYLVANIA STATE UNIVERSITY PRESS
UNIVERSITY PARK, PENNSYLVANIA

Library of Congress Cataloging-in-Publication Data

Cook, Maria Lorena.
    The politics of labor reform in Latin America : between flexibility
    and rights / Maria Lorena Cook.
        p.   cm.
Includes bibliographical references and index.
ISBN-13: 978-0-271-02929-0 (cloth : alk. paper)
ISBN-10: 0-271-02929-3 (cloth : alk. paper)
    1. Labor policy—Latin America—Case studies.
I. Title.

HD8110.5.C667 2006
331.12′042098—dc22
2006019848

The Pennsylvania State University Press is a member of the
Association of American University Presses.

It is the policy of
The Pennsylvania State University Press
to use acid-free paper. This book is printed on Natures Natural,
containing 50% post-consumer waste, and meets the minimum
requirements of American National Standard for Information
Sciences—Permanence of Paper for Printed Library Material,
ANSI Z39.48–1992.

For Lance

Contents

Tables

Acknowledgments

This book has been a long time coming, and I have had a lot of help along the way. I was lucky to work with a number of highly capable and enthusiastic research assistants at Cornell University, some of whom have long since moved on to other pursuits and fruitful careers of their own: Gabriela Alvarez, Mark Anner, Jack Cognetta, Carlos Mallén, Sergio Mukherjee, Alice Nash, Michael Ristorucci, and Michaela Rosenholz. Alan Michael Benson worked closely with me during the last two years of this research and deserves special mention. Alan's contributions to the project far surpassed anything I would have expected when he first dropped into my office as a freshman student looking for a research opportunity. His assistance has been invaluable, from tracking down obscure pieces of legislation to providing insightful interpretations of his own. This book is all the better for his part in it.

Cornell University has been a generous academic home, and much of my research would not have been possible without the assistance of the following programs for undergraduate and graduate student research: the Undergraduate Research Fellows Program at the School of Industrial and Labor Relations; the Cornell Presidential Research Scholars Program; and the Cornell Institute for Public Affairs Distinguished Faculty Program. In addition, my fieldwork was funded by a Summer Faculty Research Grant from the Latin American Studies Program, a grant from the International Program of the Center for Advanced Human Resource Studies, and a Special Faculty Grant from the School of Industrial and Labor Relations, all at Cornell University.

Many people were interviewed for this study. I am grateful to them all for taking the time to share their expertise and perspectives with me. In addition, the following individuals provided orientation, contacts, documents, ideas, or helpful suggestions on parts of the manuscript: Mark Anner, Carlos Arze, Graciela Bensusán, Teri Caraway, Adolfo Ciudad, Ruth Collier, David Collier, Lance Compa, Ericson Crivelli, Stan Gacek, Louise Haagh, Wesley Hiers, Roberto Izquierdo, Thomas Kruse, Jorge Mattosso, Ana Virgínia Moreira Gomes, Emilio Morgado

Valenzuela, Oscar Olivera, Hugo Perosa, Maria Silvia Portella de Castro, José Luís Robinson, Cecilia Senén González, Alexandre Sgreccia, Jim Shea, José Francisco Siqueira Neto, George Strauss, Francisco Tapia Guerrero, Karen Travis, Carlos Tomada, and Marisa von Bülow. Katrina Burgess and Paul Drake provided incisive comments on the manuscript and pointed out areas for improvement. I thank them both for their close and supportive reading. Sandy Thatcher of Penn State Press made the publication process as painless as possible. Of course, none of these individuals bears any responsibility for the errors of fact or interpretation that remain.

Finally, I thank those on the home front who may not always understand what I am up to but who make my life better nonetheless: my mother, Fernanda Galván Vargas; my sister, Pamela Nakashima, her husband, Ken, and my nephews Esteban and Sebastián; my stepdaughters Katie and Beth Compa, and my husband's family in East Rochester, New York. In Ithaca my constant companions have been Petiso and my husband, Lance Compa. For close to ten years I have had the good fortune to share my life with Lance, which means that I have watched him write, study, teach, strategize, and conspire to advance workers' rights. It is a small thing by comparison to dedicate this book to him.

Acronyms

ADN	Acción Democrática Nacionalista (Bolivia)
AFL-CIO	American Federation of Labor-Congress of Industrial Organizations
AFPS	Administradores de Fondos de Pensiones
ANEPC	Acuerdo Nacional para la Elevación de la Productividad y la Calidad (Mexico)
APRA	Alianza Popular Revolucionaria Americana (Peru)
CAFTA	Central American Free Trade Agreement
CARICOM	Caribbean Community
CCE	Consejo Coordinador Empresarial (Mexico)
CDES	Conselho de Desenvolvimento Econômico e Social (Brazil)
CEACR	Committee of Experts on the Application of Conventions and Recommendations
CEDAL	Centro de Asesoría Laboral del Perú
CEDLA	Centro de Estudios para el Desarrollo Laboral y Agrario (Bolivia)
CGT	Confederación General del Trabajo (Argentina)
CGT	Confederação Geral dos Trabalhadores (Brazil)
CGTP	Confederación General de Trabajadores del Perú
CI	Comunidad Industrial (Peru)
CLT	Consolidação das Leis do Trabalho (Brazil)
CNT	Confederación Nacional de Trabajadores (Peru)
CNT	Consejo Nacional del Trabajo (Peru)
COB	Central Obrera Boliviana
COMIBOL	Corporación Minera de Bolivia
COPARMEX	Confederación Patronal de la República Mexicana
CPC	Confederación de la Producción y del Comercio (Chile)
CT	Congreso del Trabajo (Mexico)
CTA	Central de los Trabajadores Argentinos
CTM	Confederación de Trabajadores de México
CTP	Confederación de Trabajadores del Perú

CTP	Confederación de Trabajadores Peruanos
CTRP	Central de Trabajadores de la Revolución Peruana
CUT	Central Unitaria de Trabajadores (Chile)
CUT	Central Unica dos Trabalhadores (Brazil)
DL	Decreto Ley
ECLA	Economic Commission for Latin America
FAT	Frente Auténtico del Trabajo (Mexico)
FGTS	Fundo de Garantia do Tempo de Serviço (Brazil)
FNT	Fórum Nacional do Trabalho (Brazil)
FREPASO	Frente País Solidario (Argentina)
FS	Força Sindical (Brazil)
FSTMB	Federación Sindical de Trabajadores Mineros de Bolivia
GNP	Gross National Product
GSP	Generalized System of Preferences
ICFTU	International Confederation of Free Trade Unions
IADB	Inter-American Development Bank
IFI	International Financial Institution
ILCCR	International Labour Conference Committee
ILO	International Labor Organization
IMF	International Monetary Fund
ISI	Import Substitution Industrialization
LABOR-AOS	Centro de Estudios Laborales-Ayuda Obrera Suiza
MIR	Movimiento de Izquierda Revolucionaria (Bolivia)
MNR	Movimiento Nacionalista Revolucionario (Bolivia)
MTA	Movimiento de Trabajadores Argentinos
NAALC	North American Agreement on Labor Cooperation
NAFTA	North American Free Trade Agreement
NGO	Non-Governmental Organization
NPE	Nueva Política Económica
OECD	Organisation for Economic Co-operation and Development
OIT	Organización Internacional del Trabajo
ORIT	Organización Regional Interamericana de Trabajadores
PAN	Partido Acción Nacional (Mexico)
PIR	Partido de Izquierda Revolucionaria (Bolivia)
PJ	Partido Justicialista (Argentina)
PMDB	Partido do Movimento Democrático Brasileiro
PND	Plan Nacional de Desarrollo
POR	Partido Obrero Revolucionario (Bolivia)

PRD	Partido de la Revolución Democrática (Mexico)
PRI	Partido Revolucionario Institucional (Mexico)
PT	Partido dos Trabalhadores (Brazil)
SINAMOS	Sistema Nacional de Apoyo a la Movilización Social (Peru)
SME	Sindicato Mexicano de Electricistas
SOFOFA	La Sociedad de Fomento Fabril (Chile)
UCR	Unión Cívica Radical (Argentina)
UDAPE	Unidad de Análisis de Políticas Sociales y Económicas
UNT	Unión Nacional de Trabajadores (Mexico)
UP	Unidad Popular (Chile)
USTR	U.S. Trade Representative
WTO	World Trade Organization
YPFB	Yacimientos Petrolíferos Fiscales Bolivianos

1

The Politics of Labor Reform in Latin America

The reform of national labor laws is one of the most widely implemented recent policy changes in the world.[1] Since the early 1990s, countries as varied as South Korea, Chile, Russia, and South Africa have changed their labor laws. Labor reforms have also provoked massive protests, including general strikes in Argentina, Italy, and Portugal. Labor law reform is both widespread and contentious, yet as a political process it remains understudied.[2]

These changes in labor laws occurring on a global scale are themselves a response to the pressures of globalization. In most na-

1. Unless otherwise specified, I use the term "reform" to mean change in labor laws, regardless of the orientation of that change.

2. Until recently, most studies of labor reform were limited to technical assessments by analysts linked to multilateral funding agencies. See, for example, Lora and Pagés (1997); IADB (1998); and Gill, Montenegro, and Dömeland (2002). Analytical surveys of labor reform in the region include Bronstein (1995, 1997), Ciudad (2002), Cook (1998), and Vega Ruíz (2000). Comparative studies include Frundt (1998), Cook (2002), Etchemendy (2004), Murillo (2005), and Murillo and Schrank (2005). Among the national case studies are Córdova (1996) on Brazil; Haagh (2002), Frank (2002), and Barrett (2001) on Chile.

tions, labor legislation was originally crafted to reflect government-employer-worker relationships embedded in more protected national economies. In recent years, trade liberalization and greater global competitiveness have created new challenges for employers and workers. Pressures for legal and institutional change have naturally followed. Yet labor reform remains among the most difficult changes to implement. Reform advocates have puzzled over why governments delay in passing labor reforms, and they have lamented the reforms' partial nature and limited outcomes.[3]

Why study labor law reform? First, labor laws structure the inevitable and recurring conflicts of employment relations. They define the balance of power among government, employers, workers, and unions. The redrafting of a country's labor laws typically reflects a shift in these power relations and may carry unfavorable consequences for the laws' former beneficiaries. Even if workers have suffered from lax enforcement or inefficient labor markets, labor laws often hold symbolic value, serving as a reminder of a time when workers' organizations were more powerful. For unions, relinquishing laws that protect rights may mean accepting an indefinite institutional disadvantage and forfeiting future power. In many countries, labor law reform has become a focal point in the debate over organized labor's future under globalization. Labor reform, therefore, provides a good lens through which to view conflicts over political and institutional change. As the Colliers put it, "Labor law is a highly visible and concrete policy statement around which political battles are fought, won, and lost, and around which political support is attracted, granted, and withheld . . . labor law thus provides a valuable point of reference for analyzing the larger political context" (Collier and Collier 1979, 971).

Second, labor laws are not only about a country's ability to operate in a global market—a common justification for labor reform. Labor law also spans the arenas of rights and citizenship. Laws establish protection for workers' voice in the workplace and in society. National labor laws are the vehicle for safeguarding internationally recognized human rights of association, organization, and collective bargaining, which have received heightened attention in global trade debates of recent years. Finally, because labor laws affect representative organizations of workers—i.e., unions—they help determine the extent to which fuller

3. See Gill, Montenegro, and Dömeland (2002); Lora and Pagés (1997); Birdsall, Graham, and Sabot (1998).

versions of democracy and deeper expressions of citizenship are present and possible. Labor law is also, therefore, a good gauge of a country's prospective ability to meet social justice claims.

This book is about the role of Latin American labor organizations in shaping the design and implementation of labor law reforms at the end of the twentieth century. Despite similar initial prescriptions for change in the direction of greater flexibility, the outcomes of labor law reforms differed throughout Latin America. This study examines why that is by analyzing labor reform processes of the 1990s in six countries: Argentina and Brazil, where moderate flexibility reforms were implemented; Chile and Peru, where changes in labor law were extensive; and Mexico and Bolivia, where labor law reform did not occur despite extensive economic liberalization.

I argue that labor's efforts to influence reform account in large part for this diversity in outcomes in the region. To make this case, I look at labor's strategic interests in labor law and at its ability to pursue those interests during specific rounds of reform. Labor's strategic interests in labor law are derived, in turn, from the legal and institutional framework of labor relations, which is often inherited from an earlier period of legal and political incorporation of labor.[4] I refer to this inherited complex of labor laws, institutions, and political alliances as the "political legacy." This legacy may confer legal, institutional, and political resources to labor organizations, or it may constrain labor's access to resources. In this way, the political legacy helps to define the relative strength of labor organizations to defend or promote specific labor law initiatives. Clearly, those labor movements that benefit from more legal and institutional resources are in a better position to resist adverse reforms and to shape the outcome, even when their political alliances weaken or other unfavorable conditions dominate.

Yet the relative strength of labor does not dictate a specific outcome. Instead, it is labor's use of resources in interaction with other factors that explains outcomes. One of these factors is the degree of government resolve or political will to see reform through. Government resolve is shaped by the pressure for reform that it faces from international actors or domestic constituencies. International pressure can be oriented toward expanding labor rights or labor market flexibility.

A second important factor for both government and labor is the

4. On the political incorporation of labor in Latin America, see Collier and Collier (1991).

"transition context." Most countries in the region have undergone dual transitions: a transition toward democracy and another toward economic opening. The nature of the transitions as well as their timing affects the political environment for labor reform. Democratic transitions tend to favor rights-based reforms and strengthen unions, while market-oriented economic transitions tend to favor labor flexibility and weaken unions. Moreover, the sequence of these transitions—whether democratization comes before economic liberalization, for example— can affect the relative power of labor to shape reform.

The next section looks more closely at the political dynamics of labor reform in the region, examining the role of labor, government, and transition contexts in turn. This is followed by a discussion of the political legacies that give rise to distinct contemporary legal frameworks, which in turn shape labor's ability to influence reforms. The final section presents the country cases and the method of paired comparisons by which I analyze labor reform processes in the region.

POLITICAL DYNAMICS OF LABOR REFORM

The political dynamics of labor reform differ from those of economic or other institutional reforms. These differences have been insufficiently studied in the political economy of reform literature, yet they help to explain the contentiousness of labor reform and the relative influence that labor unions wield in this policy arena, despite an overall decline in bargaining power.

During the 1990s, studies of Latin American political economy focused on the implementation of market-oriented economic reforms and on accompanying institutional or "second-stage" reforms of health, education, justice, and pension systems. Although most of these studies were concerned with policymakers' ability to implement reforms, they also addressed the role of nonelite social actors, insofar as these obstructed or facilitated elites' reform goals.[5]

The portrayal of these actors in each of these literatures differed. The economic reform literature tended to see both labor and business

---

5. Recent market reform studies that discuss labor yet focus on elite formulation and/ or implementation of reform include M. Williams (2001), Murillo (2001), Madrid (2003b), and Teichman (2001). A study that focuses on social movement strategic choices and responses to reform is H. Williams (2001).

groups as relatively weak. Business groups were regarded as weak for failing to provide the strong base of support governments wanted in order to implement economic reform, and for being uncooperative or indifferent toward reforming governments (Haggard and Kaufman 1995; Nelson 1994). Labor unions were portrayed as weak because they failed to prevent economic reforms that harmed their interests, such as privatization and market opening, and because they failed to propose alternative policies (Geddes 1995).[6] The institutional reform literature, by contrast, tended to portray unions as effective and powerful challengers to reform. Analysts emphasized unions' confrontational responses to reforms and their frequent ability to stall changes (Haggard and Kaufman 1995).

This perception of unions as potentially powerful opponents was further evident in the attention paid in the institutional reform literature to how elites managed opposition by affected groups, posing what Mark Williams has called the "reformer's dilemma."[7] Most approaches discussed in the literature aimed either to gain support for reform or to diminish opposition to it. One approach was to build a positive consensus for reform by constructing pro-reform coalitions (Nelson 1994). A second approach was consultation, whether through legislative channels or directly with affected groups via bipartite or tripartite pacts (Nelson 1994, 190–91; Haggard and Kaufman 1995). A third approach was compensation, or giving actors a stake in the reform (Graham 1998, 336; M. Williams 2001, 27).[8]

Yet these approaches downplayed the degree of coercion often required to overcome opposition to reforms. While each of these approaches implied some degree of negotiation and compromise, policymakers who saw standardized solutions (privatization, flexibilization, decentralization) to institutional problems were unlikely to find compromise satisfying. Not only did compromise go against the grain of technocratic problem solving, but it risked distortion of the original reform design or, worse, led to the scuttling of reform. Some pro-reform

6. But see Remmer (2002), who argues that unions continue to influence economic policy even in a context of globalization and international economic pressures.

7. The reformer's dilemma involves having to overcome the short-term resistance to policy shifts by beneficiaries of current policies, in order to implement reforms that policymakers believe to be beneficial for most people in the long run (M. Williams 2001, 26–27).

8. One example of the compensation approach was to allow trade unions to buy privatized state enterprises as a way of securing their support for privatization (Murillo 1997; Levitsky and Way 1998).

elites tried to circumvent this problem by avoiding any forum requiring compromise with affected actors. Actions ranged from repression and coercion to division and political isolation. Consensus, consultation, and compensation were rare (Teichman 2001, 191; M. Williams 2001, 27).

Indeed, market reform advocates often constructed their perceptions of trade unions in ways that justified strategies that marginalized (and repressed) labor. One common characterization of unions was that they were powerful "insiders" who resisted efforts to implement reforms that would benefit weaker "outsiders" (informal-sector workers, the unemployed, women, and youth) (Cortázar et al. 1998; Lora and Pagés 1997). Labor reforms were seen as a zero-sum game in which unions' gains cost unorganized workers and business. The implication was that trade unions' resistance to reform must be overcome. At a minimum, these portrayals complicated any consultative process. They also provided justification for avoiding negotiations with trade unions, and even for promoting reforms that weakened trade union power. These dynamics account in part for the especially contentious character of most labor reform in the region.

Labor's Role: A Strategic Approach

Studies of reform have paid relatively little attention to what factors make labor a more or less formidable opponent. Characterizations of labor as weak vis-à-vis economic reform and strong with regard to institutional changes do not get at the underlying strategic interests and motivations or at the larger contextual issues likely to shape labor's effective resistance. Some scholars have argued that the nature of the reforms themselves determines a greater propensity for resistance. For instance, Madrid (2003a) argues that unions' opposition to labor reform is more intense, and so more able to delay or stall changes, because labor reform affects union organization, leadership, and membership all at once.[9] Compared with other reforms, labor reforms have the effect of unifying diverse factions of workers and therefore of

9. Murillo (2001) also points to the concentrated effects of labor reforms on organized labor but suggests that labor-based parties in government are more likely to give unions favorable terms because political costs are relatively low, in that such concessions do not harm the average voter. Yet this argument underestimates the struggle labor unions often face to wrest concessions from government when party allies are in power.

strengthening an organization's ability to act in defense of its interests. Battles that form around labor reform initiatives may also reinforce a class cleavage, thus placing the issue into more traditional and familiar territory for trade unions (Etchemendy 1995; Etchemendy and Palermo 1997).

Yet the impact of labor reform is not felt equally across all groups of workers, and the unity of worker organizations should not be over-stated. The effects of reforms aimed at individual workers and at collective interests are different, and unions forced to choose which to defend are more likely to safeguard collective provisions over changes in individual or employment legislation. Moreover, the divisive tactics governments employ in other arenas to pressure groups to make concessions are also found here. Labor unity can dissolve when some unions are allowed to retain restrictions on freedom of association, such as monopoly rules that put competing unions at a disadvantage.

While labor unions may respond more forcefully to labor reforms than to other kinds of reform, this still does not explain why unions in some countries are more successful than others in shaping reform outcomes. Nor does it help in understanding labor's varied responses to different reform initiatives or to the timing of those initiatives. Rather, how labor responds—what and when it resists—depends not only on labor's capacity for mobilization or negotiation, but also on labor leaders' strategic assessments of what matters most. Which provisions in labor law are labor leaders most likely to defend? Which are they willing to concede? How do unions choose to make trade-offs or to expend resources during rounds of reform? Answers to these questions call for greater attention to labor's strategic interests in labor reform.

One fruitful approach is to focus on trade unions' identification and defense of their core interests. Core interests are linked to the group's organizational survival. They are the issues that an organization will defend most forcefully, being willing to bargain or trade on other matters outside the core. Labor's identification of core interests and its perception of threat to this core shape where and when it assigns limited resources and when it assumes risks and costs. This focus on core interests makes it is easier to understand why unions may cooperate on some reforms and resist others. For example, unions tend to defend established policies, laws, or provisions that grant them power and resources, such as representational mechanisms that establish union monopolies in given sectors.[10] We gain a better understanding of a group's behavior by viewing how it behaves—what it trades off—in order to defend these interests.[11]

This strategic approach also calls for a more disaggregated view of labor policy than has appeared in much of the literature. By looking at both individual and collective labor laws and at how they are packaged in reform rounds, we can better evaluate labor's strategic interests and choices.[12] Studying these rounds of reform enables us to understand the trade-offs that take place among pieces of legislation in a reform package, as well as the political and economic influences that shape bargaining over reforms. These trade-offs may in turn explain the contradictory outcomes of many labor reforms. They also provide a good indication of what matters most to labor leaders.

Government Resolve

Labor movements that seek to influence the reform process must contend with the intensity of government commitment to reform, or government "resolve." This resolve entails government's willingness to confront resistance to reform, which may involve political costs. One of the most important factors shaping a government's commitment to labor reforms is the degree of international pressure brought to bear on it. In many instances, international pressure may be more effective than domestic pressure because of the high costs of noncompliance. For instance, international financial institutions like the International Monetary Fund and the World Bank have conditioned loans on flexible reforms of the labor market. International pressure can also function in support of labor rights. To secure a country's enjoyment of preferential trade status under the U.S. Generalized System of Preferences (GSP), Central American governments were pressured to push for improved

10. Employer organizations are likely to defend laws that guarantee employers' discretionary authority in managing their workforce.

11. Core interests will not be identical across countries or even within a country over time, since they depend on specific historical, political, and legal developments. Yet it is possible to compare group behavior around core interests cross-nationally by identifying analogous issues in each case (Locke and Thelen 1995).

12. Proposals for changes in labor law are often bundled together and considered in a single "round" of reform. Such rounds begin when the issue of labor reform is first raised and consist of the ensuing proposals and the negotiations and efforts to influence those proposals. Reform rounds typically center on a few critical changes with a predominant substantive orientation.

legal protections for labor rights (Frundt 1998; Compa and Vogt 2001). The International Labor Organization has also acted as a source of pressure for labor rights.

Domestic pressure also shapes a government's commitment to labor reform. In recent years employers have been the key domestic group pushing for flexibility of employment regulations. The strength of employers will depend on the unity of employer organizations, their political alliances, the degree of consistency in their demands, the business orientation of the government or party in power, and the ability of employers to pose a credible threat to economic or political stability if reform is not achieved. Like trade unions, employer organizations may also identify and defend core interests in labor law.

The strength of employer pressure may also depend on structural factors that force employers to reduce labor costs and to respond more rapidly to market demands. These factors include the overall degree of trade liberalization and the percentage of the economy affected by trade. Related to how employers respond to these pressures is the degree of protection (often labeled "rigidity" by pro-reform forces) of existing legislation, and the ease with which these laws are evaded (Bensusán 2006). Clearly, where protective laws are easily evaded, employers are less driven to demand reform, although the call for reform may still be there.

Finally, structural economic conditions can influence both international and domestic demands for reform. In the classical literature on labor markets, a high unemployment rate is usually evidence of excessively rigid rules and high labor costs. The neoliberal policy response is to ease protective legislation governing the hiring and dismissal of workers, especially requirements that employers make long-term commitments to employees. These ideas can shape perceptions of the need for labor reform to address unemployment.[13]

A similar link is drawn between protective labor legislation and high levels of informality, yet informal-sector employment does not seem to elicit strong domestic demand for flexibility the way that high unemployment does. Informality indicates a good deal of flexibility in the labor market. It is often a condition that employers can exploit because

13. During the 1990s the link between protective legislation and unemployment was rarely contested in policy circles, yet scholarly studies of both Latin American and European countries failed to show conclusively that flexible reforms reduced unemployment (Marshall 1996; Blank and Freeman 1994).

of the lower costs involved and the flexibility of employment relationships. Informality does, however, present high costs to governments in the form of lost revenues due to the failure to pay taxes and other social charges. It remains a concern of international financial institutions and other international agencies, and is often cited as a reason to adopt reforms aimed at introducing more labor market flexibility.

Government resolve is typically most intense when strong international pressure is involved, or where strong domestic and international pressures converge in favor of flexibility reform. This may be counterbalanced, however, by domestic resistance that is politically timed, as in the period leading up to important elections.

Implementation Mechanisms

Governments typically pursue one of three mechanisms for implementation of labor reforms: executive decrees, legislative action, or concertation (social dialogue). These mechanisms can be combined, as when concertation over reform proposals becomes the basis for legislation. The government's choice of mechanism may offer a good indication of its commitment to reform. Decrees may be the most direct route to reform but are often limited. By sending proposals to its legislative branch, the executive may indicate a serious commitment to reform, or it may signal others, especially multilateral lending institutions, that the government has made an effort to change labor regulations in good faith. Concertation mechanisms may, but often do not, indicate that priority is being granted to serious reform, although they may serve other important political purposes. I examine each of these mechanisms in turn below.

In political systems that make such action feasible, executive decrees have been used to set specific legislation.[14] The advantage of decrees—from the perspective of the executive—is that the issue is not first submitted to the Congress for discussion and a vote; hence, it can be implemented relatively quickly and with minimal disruption. Although in most systems such decrees are supposed to be reserved for matters of "urgency and necessity" and therefore limited to crisis measures, they have often been used for labor reform. Governments may consult be-

---

14. In Argentina, Brazil, and Colombia, presidents have the ability to issue new laws by decree in practically any policy arena. Even in systems without this wide-ranging decree power, presidents may use decrees to shape legislation (Mainwaring and Shugart 1997, 45).

forehand with business or labor groups about such decrees, but in many instances they act quickly to thwart opposition prior to implementation.

In democracies, however, the reform of labor markets and industrial relations cannot be wholly executed by decree. Legislative initiatives sent by the executive branch to Congress typically involve the most comprehensive pieces of labor legislation, and therefore also those that are the most contentious and risk being significantly reformulated. The prevalence of presidentialist systems and divided legislatures in Latin America means that passing reform legislation can be a complex process, since opposition parties can dominate one or both houses of Congress. Legislative proposals are also vulnerable to opposition by affected groups, especially if labor or business has strong ties to legislators. Even if political alignments are in the executive's favor, labor reform bills can run into opposition in legislative labor committees, which tend to be dominated by labor deputies or their allies. The politics of the legislature, executive-legislative relations, and national party politics all play a role in determining the fate of labor reform legislation. Labor reform that travels this path typically takes a long time. A period of several years is not uncommon, and the end product may look very different from the initial proposal.

Governments may also place a reform proposal before the affected parties, or even request that they arrive at a compromise. Bipartite or tripartite "concertation" arrangements have been used quite often in Latin America as a means to shape labor reform. Typically the stated goal is for business and labor groups to reach a consensus on reform terms. The belief is that, once sent to Congress, an initiative shaped by consensus will weaken any objections of legislators and limit the conflict that could result from interest group pressure. This process has rarely resulted in significant labor reform, however, since agreement among the parties is difficult to achieve. Indeed, sometimes the best way for a government to look like it is trying to move on labor reform while ensuring that no real reform occurs is to toss the task into a bipartite or tripartite negotiation. Successful dialogue very much depends on political context and political will.

Given the relative difficulty of passing labor reform legislation, it is remarkable that governments repeatedly expend enormous effort to push reform. One way to understand what may seem like a futile exercise is to note the powerful "signaling" effect of labor reform efforts.

Considering the tremendous pressure from international and domestic actors that some governments face, these governments may attempt to pass reforms even when their expectation of success is low. Even a failed effort to reform can signal to investors, international institutions, or domestic constituencies that the government is at least taking steps toward a shared goal. Whether a given executive adopts decrees, goes through the legislature, or seeks consensus, therefore, provides some indication of its commitment.

The mechanisms that the government uses will also shape labor's response. Decrees, where trade unions are not consulted beforehand, leave them little option but to mobilize in protest or refuse cooperation if it is needed for effective implementation. Even when labor leaders are consulted, workers or unions that are left out may still resort to protest. Since the ability to mobilize effectively is costly and limited to relatively few labor organizations, decrees are an efficient way of implementing reform, although one that often lacks the legitimacy of legislation passed by Congress.

Reform initiatives sent to Congress provide another range of possible action by labor unions. Depending on their party ties and the presence of legislative allies, unions can lobby representatives and flex their electoral muscle to press their interests and either defeat or modify the legislation. Finally, concertation or social-dialogue mechanisms enable those unions that are invited to sit at the table to present their positions on reform. But, as noted, this more "participatory" method may be the one least likely to yield significant changes.

Sequencing of Dual Transitions

Labor's strategic calculations on how to respond to reforms, as well as government resolve to reform, will also be shaped by political and economic transition contexts.[15] The countries studied here underwent two distinct transitions: democratic transitions from periods of authoritarian rule, and market-oriented economic transitions under pressures of globalization (see Table 1.1). Both democratic and economic transitions often give rise to reform efforts and present distinct constraints and opportunities for unions. Moreover, these contexts shape the substance and direction of labor reforms. For example, labor reforms that

---

15. The following discussion draws on Cook (2002).

TABLE 1.1   Timing of Democratic Transition and Economic Reform in Selected Latin American Countries

Country	Timing of Democratic Transition	Initiation of Economic Reform
Argentina	1983	1989
Bolivia	1982	1985/1990s
Brazil	1985	1994
Chile	1990	1976
Colombia	—	1990
Ecuador	1980	1990
Mexico	2000	1985/1990s
Paraguay	1989	1991
Peru	1980	1992
Uruguay	1985	1991
Venezuela	—	1989

coincide with democratization tend to enhance rights and protections, whereas reforms that respond to market policies tend to increase flexibility. This helps us to understand contradictory reform sequences in many countries: periods of protective or rights-based reforms followed by a move toward flexibility a few years later.

Reforms undertaken during democratic transition periods have tended to reinforce or extend protections to individual workers and to restore or bolster collective rights, such as the right to strike, organize, and bargain collectively (Bronstein 1995; Cook 1998).[16] These reforms typically took place during "first-round" democratic governments, those that followed authoritarian regimes. Scholars have argued that first-round democratic governments enjoyed multiple advantages in implementing a wide range of policies—including tough stabilization measures—because of the value society places on peaceful democratic transition (Haggard and Kaufman 1995; Nelson 1994; Geddes 1995).

Yet while transition governments attempted stabilization measures, the experience of Brazil, Argentina, and Spain shows that these were more successful during "second-round" governments that followed the transition regime. In the Spanish case, Nancy Bermeo argues that this was because the core task of the first-round government was the establishment and consolidation of democracy, which took precedence over orchestrating economic recovery (Bermeo 1994, 606). Since it was unable to resolve economic crisis, the transition administration became

---

16. This expansion of legal labor rights during democratic transitions occurred to varying degrees in Argentina, Brazil, Chile, Paraguay, Uruguay, Guatemala, and El Salvador.

"sacrificial," leading to the election of a new government headed by the opposition. This government, in turn, was better situated to address economic recovery through stabilization and economic liberalization because it was no longer burdened by the task of democratic consolidation. The result was an "unintentional sequencing of tasks" between the first two ruling parties after the end of authoritarian rule (Bermeo 1994, 602).

Bermeo's analysis of the sequencing of core tasks during democratic and economic transitions is useful for understanding the similar sequencing of labor reform. Democratic consolidation involved rebuilding democratic institutions, securing political stability, and restoring civil and political rights to citizens. First-round democratic governments found themselves under pressure to restore collective labor rights and protective employment laws that were removed during antilabor military regimes, or else to extend new rights and protections. Even where democratic governments might have resisted implementing labor-friendly reforms, they were often confronted by the relative social and political strength of organized labor.[17] In general, trade unions enjoyed greater legitimacy in this period due to their persecution under the military and their role in the transition to democracy (Valenzuela 1989). Governments faced a social consensus that saw favorable policy reforms as labor's due. This combination of factors often had a stronger bearing on labor reform outcomes than did strictly partisan concerns, in which labor-based ruling parties would play to their labor constituencies. During democratic transitions, nonlabor governments also implemented labor-friendly policies.

The premium governments placed on political stability and accommodation during democratic transition produced a generally favorable political context for labor, even when the economy was unfavorable. Governments were less likely to use repression in response to worker mobilizations, and interest in stability meant a higher likelihood that labor would receive concessions. Indeed, strike activity increased

17. Even where unions were weak, democratic transitions still brought pressures for the expansion of labor rights. Stronger individual employment protections and collective rights were incorporated into the new labor code and constitution of Paraguay in the early 1990s despite the weakness of the labor movement. Pressure from the International Labor Organization and the United States (through the Generalized System of Preferences) compensated for the weakness of labor movements in Guatemala and El Salvador (Frundt 1998).

throughout the region during democratic transitions, and labor protest against structural adjustment policies was common (Cox Edwards 1997, 135). Labor was able to engage in a traditional sectoral strategy—strike activity—but it was also able to operate in a number of arenas made available by the return of democracy: political party activity; working through congressional allies to defend labor interests; participating in demonstrations with other sectors of civil society; engaging in tripartite accords or direct negotiations with the state; and even collective bargaining. In this context, organized labor was not only better able to advocate for labor rights, it was also free to protest economic policies, such as austerity measures, that it would later find more difficult to resist.

Economic transitions presented a different set of challenges to labor and imparted a different tenor to labor reform. Although market-oriented economic reforms may have been initiated or attempted by first-round governments, they were usually deepened and consolidated in second- and third-round democratic governments (Nelson et al. 1994; Haggard and Kaufman 1995). By this time the core task of democratic consolidation had been achieved or was well under way, ceding to a more pressing concern for the implementation and consolidation of economic reforms, which in Latin America typically occurred during the late 1980s and 1990s.

With the more systematic implementation of market-oriented economic reforms, the favorable political and economic environment disappeared for unions. Most economic reforms generated higher levels of unemployment and income inequality. Even if not accompanied by legal reform, employment generally became more precarious. For instance, the number of people working in the informal sector increased throughout the region in the 1990s (International Labor Office 1999). These structural economic changes and their effects on the labor market weakened labor organizations by reducing union membership, increasing workforce segmentation, and creating an adverse environment for strikes. The strengthening of business actors, who were often favored by trade liberalization, privatization, and flexible labor market policies, also diminished unions' relative power in society.

The political environment during economic transitions was also unfavorable for workers and unions. Market rationality and efficiency rather than rights and democracy became the watchwords of government. Unions were often portrayed as privileged special interests that sought to protect union leaders' access to sources of wealth and corruption, or as market-distorting institutions that pushed up wages at the expense of the vast majority excluded from the formal labor market.[18] This portrayal of unions in turn legitimated policies and legal reforms that aimed to remove or reduce unions' sources of power.

Where economic transition *preceded* democratic transition, labor was often placed at a special disadvantage. In these instances, unions generally moved into the democratic transition weakened by structural economic reforms as well as by legal-institutional changes imposed during dictatorship, as in the Chilean case. In addition, a core task of first-round democratic governments was complicated by a commitment to preserve economic reforms implemented earlier, which often conflicted with the expansion of labor rights. While democratization may have generated a public debate about labor rights, as in Mexico, and even led to movement in this direction, as in Chile, the constraints on expansion of labor rights tended to be greater.

In sum, during democratic transitions that preceded market reforms, labor could both resist economic policies and attain and defend organizational gains. During economic transitions that followed democratization, labor was more likely to be forced onto the defensive and to concentrate its resources on organizational survival. The nature of the transition context and its sequencing are important for understanding the strategic options of both government and labor in labor law reform.

LEGAL FRAMEWORKS AND POLITICAL LEGACIES

The creation of early labor legislation in these countries represented a critical watershed in the relationship between the state and labor. The drafting of an initial labor code often reflected labor's level of mobilization and political alliances, and the state's attempts to limit conflict, secure political support, and establish control over labor. In many cases, these early labor codes also reflected nationalist political and economic alliances that underlay the import-substitution industrialization model of economic development. The initial labor law frameworks, therefore, had a substantial bearing on labor's capacity to organize, bargain, and

18. See Cortázar, Lustig, and Sabot (1998, 195); Birdsall, Graham, and Sabot (1998, 5); Cox Edwards (1997, 130); Edwards and Lustig (1997, 20); Márquez and Pagés (1998); IADB (1998).

mobilize. They also defined which organizational, financial, and even political resources accrued to labor.

Where labor was sufficiently strong to require inducements to cooperate with the state, these were reflected in labor law. Provisions in trade union legislation that stipulated monopoly representation, a role for labor in tripartite structures, automatic dues check-off, and direct subsidies reflected reasonably strong labor movements allied with parties in power. In contrast, weak collective protections signaled weak labor, authoritarian government, or a powerful industrial or landowning class.

These foundational labor codes, like most institutions, were difficult to change. This difficulty was even more salient in those cases in which labor provisions were incorporated into national constitutions (Bronstein 1995). The wholesale revision of labor laws was rare; generally this occurred only in cases of revolution or dictatorship, when a radical break with the previous regime made possible the creation of new institutions that would reflect a new balance of power. More commonly, however, legal frameworks produced enduring legacies.

Legal frameworks followed one of three distinct historical patterns or trajectories in each of the six countries I examine in this book. Each of these was initially defined by the combined legal/labor relations/political regime established during a critical juncture in each country. Each in turn generated its own legacy, which in some cases resulted in a very different legal and institutional labor relations framework in the contemporary period:

1. State corporatist → State corporatist (Argentina, Brazil)
2. Radical (pro-worker) → Flexible (radical pro-employer) (Chile, Peru)
3. Revolutionary-state → Parallel (nonenforcement) regime (Mexico, Bolivia)

State Corporatist

The first historical pattern is state corporatist. The initial legal framework originated during the key period of labor incorporation and at the height of import-substitution industrialization in the 1930s and 1940s. The characteristics of this pattern were an initial incorporation of labor by the state through labor and social legislation that combined protection and control. The early state corporatist pattern involved control of labor organizations through laws that set the terms of union organization and representation in ways that permitted a significant degree of state oversight and intervention. Competition among labor organizations was circumscribed by clearly defined jurisdictions, and entry by new groups was restricted. Along with these controls, laws provided for direct subsidies to labor organizations through a variety of mechanisms. This was another means of tying labor to the state and of enabling the state to channel resources to unions with official recognition. Political parties might or might not have been part of this arrangement; the key factor was the structuring of labor-state relations through legislation.

What were the implications of this initial pattern for labor strength and influence in later decades? What was its political legacy? We find relatively unified and large labor organizations that were protected from competition by newcomers, held a privileged seat in dealings with the state, and depended strongly on state subsidies. Because of regulations that called for compulsory membership or broad coverage through collective agreements, these unions represented large numbers of workers and therefore wielded some power. Corporatist provisions were difficult to get rid of because of their benefits to dominant labor groups and others with vested interests in the system. Labor was therefore most likely to defend those provisions that granted collective rights and powers (including those that ensured predominance of some groups over others), and those that provided financial resources to organizations and their leadership. Because of the difficulty in changing these laws, and because of the relative stability they engendered, this pattern exhibits a significant degree of continuity between early legislation and the contemporary period. Argentina and Brazil best represent this pattern.

Radical (Pro-Worker) → Flexible (Pro-Employer)

This pattern originated in a political regime that overhauled labor laws to install radical pro-worker legislation and policy. Such legislation included expanded employment protections, improved working conditions, and greater tolerance of union organizing and strikes. To qualify as radical, these regimes also enacted regulations that increased worker control at the workplace. The immediate result was greatly expanded mobilization among workers.

These changes were profoundly threatening to foreign and national business elites and usually generated a strong reaction. Radical pro-worker regimes were therefore short-lived. The reaction involved not only a change of regime but also a change of labor laws. Since these contexts were politically polarized, the result was not accommodation with the radical regime but rather its defeat. This was reflected, in turn, in the new laws and policies pursued by the victors. Implementation of new regulations had to overcome resistance by the workers who bene-fited from the previous regime, and the new laws institutionalized the relatively weak position of defeated workers' organizations. Radical pro-worker legislation gave way, then, not only to flexible employment relations and reduced costs to employers, but also to strong restrictions on collective power and rights.

This pattern's legacy was that labor had the most limited influence over labor reforms. Not only were unions too weak to stop flexibiliza-tion and curbs on their collective activities, they could not amass the political resources required to recover basic labor rights. It was more difficult to mobilize for new rights than to defend rights already en-shrined in law, especially when the broader economic and political envi-ronment was not amenable. International pressure in support of labor rights may be most needed in these cases and could lead to a better equilibrium in industrial relations. Chile and Peru both represent in-stances of this trajectory, and exhibit the greatest discontinuities in our set of countries.

Revolutionary-State → Parallel (Nonenforcement) Regime

In the revolutionary-state pattern the foundational labor legislation was associated with a regime that assumed the mantle of the "revolution." This was not necessarily a revolution that came from below but rather a regime that claimed to rule in the name of popular classes, even though its origins may have been part of a struggle among elite factions. Here labor was allied with the political party in power that claimed revolutionary origins.

Labor law contained many provisions favorable to unions. In con-trast to the radical regime, however, these legal concessions to labor did not pose a threat in terms of creating an autonomous, mobilized labor movement. This was because labor in this revolutionary-state pattern was allied with the ruling party, such that those ties served to moderate and constrain labor action.

The revolutionary-state legacy produced a strong disjuncture between law and practice. Labor relations operated in a "parallel realm" of nonenforcement or selective enforcement of pro-worker legislation. In our cases this took two forms. In one, labor laws were favorable to labor organizations, but the actions of labor were comparatively moderate, since they were constrained by alliances and commitments to the ruling party. The result was a form of collaboration, even collusion, between labor organizations, the state, and employers to maintain stability and labor peace. This collaboration extended to the creation of a "parallel" labor regime that violated the favorable dispositions of labor laws. This was the case in Mexico. In the other form, seen in Bolivia, the constraining commitments to the "revolutionary" party were weaker since the party was not sustained in power, yet the original legislation stood. Protective labor legislation was tolerated by employers owing in large part to the fact that legal enforcement was weak.

Under this pattern, labor organizations were relatively strong in exerting their influence to halt reform of labor laws. This was because of their alliance with prominent political parties and/or their mobilization potential. There was also relatively less pressure to reform the laws because of the limited enforcement or parallel containment arrangements described above. The result was no reform (or greatly delayed reform) of labor legislation despite its strongly protective nature.

Labor Strength

Political legacies and legal frameworks also shape the relative strength of labor movements. To the extent that these extend and protect trade unions' organizational resources, those unions are more likely to defend their interests in potentially antagonistic rounds of labor reform. As noted earlier, however, "strength" and "weakness" do not by themselves explain specific labor reform outcomes. In order to understand how labor's capacity is deployed—whether it is "strong enough" to shape the reform process—we have to look at other factors discussed here: labor's strategic or core interests, government resolve, and transition contexts.

I draw on characterizations of labor strength here to assist in devising the pairings of cases. To do this I use several data indicators to assess labor strength in Argentina, Brazil, Mexico, Bolivia, Chile, and Peru during the 1990s (Table 1.2). The focus is on national confederations, since labor law reform negotiations typically involve national organizations rather than local unions.

The indicators include two measures of union density, union structure, degree of political unity among peak organizations, and political-strategic orientation of the largest peak organization. Although each one of these measures presents drawbacks, together they combine features of membership, structure, and politics suitable to assessing peak organization bargaining power on national policy issues. The final designations of labor strength also coincide with most assessments found in the secondary literature on labor in these countries.

Union density is a common measure of labor strength, but a problematic one. While reliable data on union density exist for advanced industrial countries, in developing countries data collection has often been difficult (McGuire 1997, 267). Moreover, high density in some countries, such as Mexico, may reflect involuntary or compulsory union membership and is therefore less meaningful as an indication of member commitment or mobilization capacity. Nonetheless, taken together with other measures, union density can signal the relative strength of organized labor.

Two other measures of labor strength relate to union structure and the degree of political unity where multiple central organizations exist.[19] The assumption is that more centralized structures—a system based on national industrial unions rather than on provincial, municipal, craft, or enterprise-level unions—both reflect and confer a greater degree of labor power. Likewise, the number of peak confederations and competition among centrals or within these can indicate the degree of labor influence. Simply put, labor is stronger where there is a single peak labor confederation and where internal political or ideological divisions are limited, so that labor speaks with one voice.[20] A single or a

19. See McGuire (1997, 265) for a discussion of these criteria of union power.
20. Murillo (2001) argues, however, that limited competition among unions but partisan competition for leadership within unions leads to a greater degree of effective militancy, at least in regimes where labor-based parties are in power. This is because governments will want to make concessions to their party allies when there is internal competition, yet they cannot exploit divisions in the labor movement as a whole in order to undermine labor militancy.

TABLE 1.2 Indicators of Organized Labor Strength in Selected Latin American Countries (1990s)

Country	Union Members as % of Nonagricultural Labor Force	Union Members as % of Formal-Sector Wage Earners	Dominant Union Structure	Number of Peak Confederations	Political-Strategic Orientation of Largest Peak Org.	Strength of Organized Labor
Argentina	25.4	65.6	Industry	Dominant	Conciliatory/militant (split)	High
Brazil	32.1	66.0	Local	Multiple	Militant	High
Mexico	31.0	72.9	Industry/Local	Multiple	Conciliatory	Medium
Bolivia	16.4	59.7	Firm	Single	Militant	Medium
Chile	15.9	33.0	Firm	Single	Conciliatory	Low
Peru	7.5	18.3	Firm	Multiple	Militant	Low

SOURCES: Union density data are from International Labor Organization (1997), table 1.2. Data for Argentina are from 1995; Brazil, 1991; Mexico, 1991; Bolivia, 1994; Chile, 1993; Peru, 1991. Dominant union structure information is from McGuire (1997, 268, table 10). Number of peak organizations is from ICFTU (2003).

dominant peak organization usually indicates greater unity and hence greater negotiating power than multiple confederations, from which the government may pick its allies.[21]

A final indicator is the political-strategic orientation of peak organizations. This measure refers to the largest peak organization's primary policy orientation and response to government initiatives. This measure tries to capture both the extent to which peak organizations engage in general strikes and other forms of collective action and protest, and their political party alliances.[22] In this formulation, "conciliatory" peak organizations had ties to ruling parties during most of the 1990s, whereas those with opposition party ties were "militant."[23] Militancy here is weighted more heavily as an indicator of labor strength: "Moderately strong" movements (as measured by density and union structure) may be able to compensate for a weaker structural position with militancy, whereas otherwise "strong" labor movements that are conciliatory toward government initiatives can be weaker actors when faced with unfavorable reforms, given a lesser propensity to confront their allies. Political-strategic orientation defines why, for example, Brazilian labor appears as "strong" in Table 1.2 despite "lower" measures in the areas of union structure and political unity among peak confederations, whereas Mexican labor is listed as moderate in strength, despite high scores on other indicators. The final determination of degree of labor strength (high, medium, or low) combines this political-strategic dimension with measures of structure and density.

Table 1.3 shows countries paired according to political legacy, labor

21. Exceptions to this claim include Brazil, which has multiple peak organizations, including one, Força Sindical, that aligned with the government on flexible reforms. Yet during the 1980s and 1990s, the oppositional stance of the Central Unica dos Trabalhadores (CUT) and close ties between leaders and the rank and file enabled it to wield considerable mobilizational power.

22. Mobilization capacity is also a common indicator of strength, often measured by strike activity. I do not directly employ this measure here because strike data are problematic, since rules and conditions for strikes vary considerably among countries. Protests that fall short of strikes, such as marches, rallies, or work stoppages, are arguably a better measure of capacity and are typically missing from strike data. General strikes may also reflect considerable strength, given the degree of unity and mobilization of resources required to carry them out. Yet data on general strikes are difficult to obtain as they are rarely distinguished from other strikes.

23. This characterization differs from that of some other scholars, who assume that labor's alliance with a ruling party is an indicator of greater strength. As Burgess (2004) has pointed out, labor's alliance with a ruling party can generate a greater degree of subordination and less room for maneuver.

TABLE 1.3   Country Pairings by Legacy, Labor Strength, and Reform Outcome

Country	Legacy	Labor Strength	Flexible Reform
Argentina/Brazil	State Corporatist	Strong	Moderate
Chile/Peru	Radical	Weak	Extensive
Mexico/Bolivia	Revolutionary	Moderate	None

strength, and reform outcomes. The last is presented in terms of degree of flexibility.[24] One would expect stronger labor movements to exert the greatest influence over labor reform outcomes. Likewise, since unions resist flexible reforms that shift power to management, those cases with the greatest degree of flexibility ("extensive" reform outcome) should reflect the weakest labor influence. However, the puzzle evident in this table is that "strong" labor movements—those of Argentina and Brazil—present cases of moderate or mixed reform outcomes, while "moderately strong" labor in Mexico and Bolivia is linked to retention of protective legislation with no reform. Weak unions have the least influence over reform outcomes, which is consistent with expectations.

This puzzle suggests that there is not a simple linear relationship between labor strength and reform outcomes. While labor strength is certainly important insofar as it relates to labor's capacity to influence outcomes, other variables also matter. For instance, legal frameworks establish the terrain on which battles over reform are played out, and they shape labor's identification of its core interests. Government commitment to reform, as determined by international and domestic pressure, indicates the degree of intensity with which government actors will pursue reform against labor opposition. As noted, this can affect the mechanisms governments employ to design and implement reforms, another factor that can disadvantage labor unions. Finally, transition contexts and sequencing can create more or less favorable political environments for labor organizations in their efforts to influence labor law reform.

---

24. I assess the extent of flexibility reform by looking at the overall number of decrees and laws that promote greater flexibility passed in the 1990s (see Chapters 2–5 for specific legislation), including the extent to which collective as well as individual laws were affected. In the case of Chile, outcome is based on the degree of flexibility from earlier changes under the dictatorship of Augusto Pinochet (1973–90), plus the reforms of the 1990s.

APPROACH OF THE BOOK: PAIRED COMPARISONS

This book analyzes labor law reform in six countries: Argentina, Brazil, Chile, Peru, Mexico, and Bolivia. These countries were selected because of similarities on several key dimensions: Since the 1990s they have all been democracies;[25] labor has been a historically important force in national politics in each case; and each has pursued extensive economic liberalization.[26] Despite these similarities, the countries vary on labor reform outcomes, as defined by degree of flexible reform at the end of the 1990s (see Table 1.3).[27]

By the end of the 1990s, Argentina's and Brazil's labor laws included flexible reforms, which mostly affected the individual employment relationship. Yet they also retained significant protections in collective legislation that benefited unions, despite government efforts to change those laws. These countries experienced a moderate flexibility of labor regulation overall. Chile and Peru had the greatest degree of flexibility, giving significant power to employers in their dealings with individual workers and unions. This was so even after the expansion of protections in Chile during the democratic governments of the 1990s. Mexico and Bolivia are the only cases in this set that did not significantly change labor laws despite strong economic liberalization.

How do we account for these varied outcomes in the face of similar pressures for flexible reforms? By pairing countries that are quite different on a range of variables yet similar on reform outcome, we can isolate common features that are important determinants of labor reform.[28] For instance, Argentina and Brazil are very different in terms

25. While there may be some debate about Mexico's status as a democracy during the early 1990s, by 1994 presidential elections were substantially free and fair, even though the PRI won.

26. All six countries implemented a range of structural reforms in the 1980s–90s, including privatization, financial reforms, and reduction of average tariffs to below 20 percent (Lora 1997). Revenues from privatization were highest (as percentage of GDP) in Mexico and Argentina. Also see Remmer (2002, 3).

27. Since transition sequence differs within two of our three pairings, it does not emerge as a significant factor in explaining similar outcomes within those pairings. Yet an examination of transitions as a contextual variable still yields important insights for most of these cases in the 1980s, 1990s, and even into the 2000s.

28. The paired comparison allows me to probe for differences in contexts and strategies among pairs and for similarities and differences within pairs. This paired comparison reflects the use of the Most-Similar-Systems (MSS) design across the pairs, and of a Most-Different-Systems (MDS) approach within pairs. See Collier and Collier (1991, 12–18), and P. Smith (1995, 4–8) for a discussion of these approaches.

of political party system, party ties with labor, and historical incorporation of labor.[29] Until the early 2000s they also had different socioeconomic characteristics, with higher inequality and lower per capita
income in Brazil. Yet their labor laws exhibit similar features of state
corporatism, and their labor movements rank the highest of the six
cases in terms of strength.

Chile and Peru differ even more starkly in terms of the stability and
size of their economies, histories of labor incorporation (state vs. party/
movement), and orientation of their respective military regimes in the
1970s. Yet both countries share a more recent period of radical policy
change under a pro-worker regime, which in turn produced a backlash
reflected in subsequent governments' antiworker policies. In both countries labor also appears in the weakest position.

Mexico and Bolivia differ in stability of political regime and size of
the economy. While Mexico's PRI ruled for seventy-one years, Bolivia
suffered multiple military interventions in politics during the second
half of the twentieth century. Mexico's large and dynamic economy also
contrasts with that of Bolivia, one of the poorest countries in the region.
Yet in both cases labor ranks as moderate in strength and labor legislation derives from similar revolutionary-state origins.[30] Mexico also
shares features of state corporatism, but the mobilizational nature of
labor incorporation due to the revolutionary experience in Mexico dis-
tinguishes it from Argentina and Brazil and places it alongside Bolivia.
Despite similar revolutionary legacies, however, Mexico and Bolivia
differ in closeness of labor's alliance with the revolutionary party. This
alliance was much stronger in Mexico than in Bolivia, where labor and
the party split in the mid-1980s, and where the labor movement was an
autonomous source of political power, often rivaling that of its party
allies (Malloy 1970).

ORGANIZATION OF THE BOOK

Chapter 2 gives the context for labor reforms in Latin America, indicates the range and direction of reforms throughout the region, and

29. Collier and Collier (1991) identify Argentina as a case of party or movement incorporation of labor, and Brazil as an example of state incorporation.

30. Different combinations of features lead to a common characterization of "moderate" labor strength in the cases of Mexico and Bolivia. Mexico's labor movement is so
designated because of its higher union density levels and its strong party/state alliance,
which, however, also accounts for labor's subordination and lack of mobilization capacity.

outlines the theoretical and ideological bases for reform during the 1990s. It provides background on types of reforms proposed and implemented in the 1990s, on the influences and agencies pushing for reform, and on trends and patterns that have emerged in the region. It contains a detailed explanation of labor flexibility, discusses the role of international financial institutions in promoting flexibility policies, and looks at where labor rights fit into this policy debate.

Chapters 3 through 5 analyze and compare labor reform dynamics in each of the three country pairs. Chapter 3 examines Argentina and Brazil, similar cases with relatively strong labor movements and a state corporatist legacy that explains many of the features of their contemporary labor laws. Both countries also experienced democratic transitions from military rule in the 1980s, followed by a market reform period in the 1990s. In both cases labor flexibility was introduced in the 1990s, but the labor movement managed to stall or defend against changes in collective law even as flexibility reforms proceeded in employment law. The mixed outcome points to the negotiating capacity of strong labor organizations in a context of intense pressure for reform. Although the chapter focuses on the 1980s and 1990s, it also analyzes the labor reforms implemented in Argentina in the early 2000s and reform proposals in Brazil under President Luis Inácio Lula da Silva between 2003 and 2005.

Chapter 4 compares the labor reform experiences of Chile and Peru. Both countries have labor movements that were once strong and politicized but which have weakened considerably since the 1970s. In both countries a radical pro-worker regime (Allende in Chile and Velasco in Peru) instituted policies favorable to labor, and unionization flourished. In reaction, subsequent regimes (Pinochet in Chile and Fujimori in Peru) imposed extreme flexibility and antiworker policies together with market reforms. Worker protections in the 1990s were among the weakest in the region. Yet in both cases, partly as a result of international pressure, recent efforts have turned toward more equilibrium in labor law and industrial relations, including closer attention to labor rights.

Mexico and Bolivia are regional anomalies, given that they display some of the strongest features of economic liberalization but are among

---

Bolivian labor, on the other hand, compensates for lower union density and the lack of a strong and lasting labor party/state relationship with its autonomy and militancy throughout much of the twentieth century.

the few countries in the region (along with Honduras and Uruguay) that have not reformed their labor laws. Chapter 5 explores why. It examines the national revolutionary legacy of both countries and the subsequent development of a parallel labor-relations regime that permitted flexibility in spite of protective laws. In Mexico this occurred via collusion of labor with the state and employers. In Bolivia nonenforcement and labor's veto power stalled reform. Although labor laws have not changed, domestic and international pressures to reform persist. The chapter analyzes several reform proposals, providing a unique view into policy debates prior to implementation and an indication of what type of labor reform is likely to emerge in the future.

The final chapter explores the lessons of this comparison of Latin American countries, assesses the reasons for the failure of reform efforts in the 1990s, and examines prospects for more balanced reform that incorporates labor rights, based on initial developments in the 2000s.

Directions in Labor Reform:
A Regional Overview

This chapter provides a brief background on the role of political and economic change in labor legislation in Latin America, as well as an overview of trends and patterns in labor law reform that have occurred in the region since the late 1980s. It examines the context that gave rise to the most important trend in this period, labor flexibility. What events triggered labor reform initiatives? What accounts for the policy diffusion throughout the region? To what extent can we identify other directions in regional reform patterns, such as enhanced worker protection or increased liberalization? Where do labor rights fit in this reform environment?

The earliest labor legislation in Latin America grew out of government efforts to address increasing social conflict associated with the emergence of an urban industrial workforce in the early twentieth century. The state's role gradually moved from one primarily defined by repression of workers to one of worker protection.[1] In adopting this role, states prodded workers to look to the government rather than to unions to defend their interests, since unions were often linked to radical political ideologies that sought to undermine state authority (Bronstein 1997, 6–7; Hall and Spalding 1986). The labor legislation that developed in this period reflected this mistrust of unions. Although protective of individual workers, labor laws typically ensured a strong state role in overseeing union activities.

Protective legislation and state intervention in labor relations coincided in many countries with an import-substitution phase of industrialization (ISI) that began in the 1930s and 1940s and lasted through the 1960s.[2] ISI involved protection of the domestic market and heavy state involvement in the economy, and the industrial working class was brought into an alliance with the state and national industrialists. Government or political party efforts to bring labor into the political life of the country—through state and party alignments—often coincided with ISI as well. Governments often used labor legislation to secure the political support of trade unions as well as to enhance state control over labor. In Brazil General Getúlio Vargas used corporatist labor legislation during the Estado Novo (1937–45) in an effort to achieve harmonious capital-labor relations via the state's strong mediation.[3] In other countries incorporation of labor into the political system took different forms, and was often reflected in labor law (Collier and Collier 1991). In most cases the state acquired a key role in overseeing industrial relations and in controlling trade union activities.

Labor laws also reflected the belief that the state should intervene to protect the individual worker against employers. In this way governments acknowledged the power imbalance that existed between labor and capital. Legislation contained disincentives for employers to dismiss workers by requiring substantial severance payments. The idea that

---

1. This protection should not be overstated. It consisted of social and labor legislation that was not always enforced, and its objective in many cases was to separate workers from the "harmful" influence of unions and radical thought.

2. In smaller countries that did not industrialize early, the ISI period began much later, if at all, and had different political consequences (Conaghan 1988).

3. Corporatist legislation was also included in the Chilean labor laws of 1924, and was established by the Liberal Party in Colombia in 1944, by the Acción Democrática Party in Venezuela in 1947, and in Argentina under Juan Domingo Perón in 1945. Mexico's federal labor law of 1931 had similar features, and President Lázaro Cárdenas brought labor directly to the ruling party in 1938.

workers' gains were irrevocable also found expression in several national constitutions. Labor legislation was highly detailed with regard to working conditions, benefits, leaves, holidays, and compensation; some provisions were even incorporated into constitutions as social rights. Article 123 of the 1917 Mexican constitution, which was drafted shortly after the Mexican Revolution, contained some of the most progressive language on workers' rights known at the time.[4] This document, together with the founding of the International Labor Organization (ILO) in 1919, served as an important influence on other countries as they drew up their own labor codes (Bronstein 1997).

Eventually the breakdown of the import-substitution model and the economic strains it generated produced a crisis of democratic regimes throughout the region. Almost every country on the continent was under authoritarian rule through the 1970s and into the 1980s. The authoritarian regimes of Brazil, Argentina, Chile, Uruguay, Guatemala, and El Salvador in particular were marked by extreme violence and extensive human rights abuses. Trade unionists were persecuted, and collective rights to organize, bargain, and strike were suppressed. In some countries, authoritarian governments adapted existing labor legislation,[5] while in others, such as Chile, the military government implemented a new labor code in an effort to redesign industrial relations (Ruíz-Tagle 1985).[6]

In the 1980s most countries returned to civilian democratic government, as support for military governments crumbled under the pressure of the debt crisis, human rights violations, and even military failures, such as the Argentine military's defeat in the Falkland Islands/Islas Malvinas war with Britain. The return to democratic rule brought a restoration of collective labor rights and even an extension of worker protections in some cases. Yet democratic transitions occurred in the

4. Besides guaranteeing freedom of association, the right to organize, and the right to strike, the Mexican constitution set terms for minimum wages, hours of work and work shifts, overtime pay, maternity leave, vacations and holidays, profit sharing, job training, safety and health and workers' compensation, just cause for discharge, seniority in promotions, and other working conditions.

5. In Brazil legislation dating from the Estado Novo provided military rulers with ample opportunities to control labor activities. The labor code remained largely intact, with the addition of several decree-laws restricting the right to strike and facilitating dismissals (Mericle 1977; Pastore and Skidmore 1985).

6. Chile represented one of the earliest cases of flexibilization in the region, along with Argentina, whose military rulers implemented labor law changes in 1976 (Córdova 1996, 318.)

context of severe economic crisis, so that restored legal rights for labor did not always translate into material gains.

Most countries in the region responded to the economic crisis by shifting from ISI to export-oriented economic strategies. This shift was a result of the exhaustion of the ISI model of development and the debt crisis of the 1980s, when many Latin American countries were forced to adopt structural adjustment plans under the supervision of the International Monetary Fund (IMF). Although some nations experimented with economic opening in the 1970s and 1980s, it was not until the late 1980s or early 1990s that most countries began systematically to adopt neoliberal policies.[7] Labor reform was seen as the logical next step (Lora and Pagés 1997; Edwards 1995).

LABOR FLEXIBILITY: THE DOMINANT TREND OF THE 1990S

Since the mid-1980s, the most important trend in labor reform has been the flexibility of labor markets through changes in labor legislation. Given the high degree of regulation characteristic of employment and labor relations in most of Latin America, governments, employer groups, and multilateral funding agencies such as the IMF and World Bank have pushed hard to "flexibilize" the terms of employment, particularly with regard to hours of work, overtime, dismissal costs, and employment contracts.

This push to flexibilize was associated with the widespread adoption of market-oriented economic and institutional reforms in the 1990s. In the case of labor law, the arguments for "deregulating" included eliminating "rigidities" in labor markets to improve productivity, increase employment, and attract investment; lowering employers' costs to raise their ability to compete, especially in the context of opening of the economy; and lowering the state's costs in order to obtain greater efficiency, in the case of public administration. For employers, flexibility also meant establishing greater control over the workforce (Córdova 1996, 319). The growth of the informal sector in many Latin American countries has also led policymakers to view flexibility as a way to decrease

7. *Latin American Special Report* [SR-96-03], http://www.latinnews.com. The well-known exception to this pattern was Chile, where the military dictatorship implemented market reforms in the mid-1970s and consolidated them throughout the 1980s.

the barriers between formal and informal employment. The *timing* of labor reform initiatives in the region, therefore, can be explained in large part by the pressures of market reform and by the policy recommendations of international financial institutions (IFIS).

Despite broad consensus among policymakers in the 1990s that labor flexibility was both desirable and necessary, flexibility initiatives have been controversial in most of the countries where they have been introduced. Part of the controversy has stemmed from the fact that flexible labor policies were associated with economic reforms and business practices that contributed to weakening unions and to the decline of legal protections for workers. For instance, extensive privatization has led to dismissals of public-sector employees, many of whom have not been able to find alternative employment in the formal private sector. Competitive pressures on employers have led to labor-saving technologies that also decrease employment opportunities. Trade opening and the ensuing competition have produced a decline in industrial-sector employment in most countries, and hence a decline in union membership. Neoliberal economic reforms have coincided with (and some would say they have caused) growing unemployment and increased income inequality (IADB 1998; International Labor Office 2002). Since most Latin American labor legislation has traditionally included provisions aimed at protecting workers from dismissal, reforms of labor laws have typically involved lowering levels of protection. These are among the many factors that have led trade unions and workers to resist flexibility policies.

Moreover, labor flexibility is rarely seen in value-neutral terms. The phrase itself suggests a positive value. After all, its opposite is "rigidity," which is hard to defend. The most neutral meaning of this term refers to a system's capacity to adapt to change (Meulders and Wilkins 1987; Boyer 1987). The more common understanding of labor flexibility refers to measures that expand an employer's discretionary capacity to manage his or her workforce to meet the needs of the enterprise. Flexible labor markets can expand or contract employment to meet the demand for labor. This would imply minimal legal or statutory constraints, as in laws that make dismissing an employee costly or difficult. Some forms of flexibility may benefit workers, particularly if they are involved in decisions to improve productivity or product or service quality. However, this "negotiated" flexibility is less common in Latin

America than are flexible policies that have been imposed on the work-force, sometimes through force (de la Garza 1993).

Critics of the concept have suggested replacing the term "labor flex-ibility" with others that more accurately reflect existing labor market conditions for many workers: precariousness, informality, instability, or insecurity (Hirata 1998). Others see the move to "flexibility" in the region as part of an ideological shift linked to neoliberalism (Bronstein 1997; Ermida Uriarte 1995). Many observers have also rejected the term "deregulation," which is commonly employed to refer to contem-porary economic and labor reforms. These analysts argue that little ac-tual deregulation (lessening of regulation) occurred in Latin America (Córdova 1996). Instead there was a "re-regulation" of markets in terms that were generally more favorable to capital and employers, to-gether with a decline in workers' security in areas of employment, rep-resentation, and income (Standing 1997).

Although labor reform outcomes have varied across the region, ini-tial policies were often similar. This was due to the key role that IFIS such as the IMF, World Bank, and Inter-American Development Bank played in shaping policy by linking loans and development assistance with calls for labor market reform. This led to a wave of like-minded initiatives in the region, as similar prescriptions were doled out for countries' labor market ills. The role of international organizations is clearly important for understanding this policy diffusion, as well as some of the political difficulties surrounding implementation.[8]

International financial institutions shared a similar analysis of labor markets. The argument went as follows: "Rigid" labor legislation constrains job creation, encourages capital substitution for labor, and promotes the informal sector. Such employment constraints, together with centralized forms of collective bargaining and monopoly union representation, drive up wages and other labor costs associated with formal-sector workers past their "market price." This in turn distorts the labor market and encourages its segmentation into the "privileged" few that enjoy labor protection legislation and the majority, or at least the large minority, who lack protections and higher wages.[9] Since many

8. The role of international organizations in labor policy diffusion has not yet been studied systematically. Teichman (2004) reviews the role of the World Bank in market reforms in Mexico and Argentina, but does not specifically focus on labor policy.

9. See Cortázar, Lustig, and Sabot (1998, 195); Birdsall, Graham, and Sabot (1998, 5); Cox Edwards (1997, 130); Edwards and Lustig (1997, 20); Gill, Montenegro, and Döme-land (2002).

of those excluded from formal-sector work are women, young people, and the poorest workers, these distorted effects on the labor market contribute to widening inequality among different sectors of the population (Márquez and Pagés 1998; IADB 1998). Labor law reform became the way to address a range of problems, including unemployment, segmented labor markets, inequality, and even poverty.

This analysis has led to the following set of policy prescriptions and recommendations. In order to address restrictions on hiring and dismissals, changes have included limiting severance payments or converting these to deferred-compensation plans; permitting part-time and temporary employment contracts; lowering the amounts employers must pay in levies and contributions, sometimes requiring changes in the way social security is funded and administered; revising the definition of "just dismissal" to include economic distress of the firm; and instituting some form of unemployment insurance (Edwards and Lustig 1997; Cox Edwards 1997; Birdsall, Graham, and Sabot 1998; Lora and Pagés 1997; IADB 1998).

Why and when do Latin American governments adopt these policy prescriptions? Some analysts have noted that economic crises, especially sharp drops in GDP and increases in unemployment, have triggered labor reforms in the region (Lora 2000). We can assume that IFIs are most likely to proffer loans, conditioned on further structural and institutional reforms, during these periods of economic crisis. Given the consensus among IFIs that high labor regulation also causes unemployment, periods of increased unemployment may also lead to such recommendations. Even more important, domestic opposition to labor reform may be weaker during such periods. In short, recessions and unemployment may act as triggers for labor reform because support for reform may be stronger during such times, and hence the political costs of implementing reform are lower. Yet this may be true only for the first instance of reform. Unless reforms deliver promised results, opposition may become stronger and political costs of implementation higher in later rounds.

Governments must weigh the costs of failure to implement reforms, particularly when they are tied to IFI loans, against the domestic political costs of implementation. Conditionality tied to loans or trade benefits may explain why governments take on the substantial political risks associated with labor reform. The coercive aspects of conditionality provide the leverage governments need to overcome domestic resistance.

During the 1990s opposition to flexible labor reform grew. This was due in part to reformers' inability to show that the changes were having a positive impact on formal-sector employment creation (IADB 1998; OECD 1999; Márquez and Pagés 1998).[10] During the years in which fixed-term employment contracts became legal in Argentina (after 1991), unemployment reached its highest level (18.5 percent in 1995) and remained high (about 15 percent) for the rest of the decade. Brazil faced high unemployment rates despite the legalization of temporary and part-time work contracts in 1998. Other countries, most notably Spain, also experienced high unemployment despite their adoption of more flexible terms of contracting and dismissal (Sagardoy Bengoechea 1987). Critics claimed instead that flexible employment policies only led to increased job insecurity (Marshall 1995, 1996; Boyer 1987; Standing 1997; Blank and Freeman 1994). Indeed, the weak evidence linking flexibility policies to employment has led some analysts to suggest that the appeal of these policies was more political, in that they were used to discipline unions and their political allies (de la Garza and Bouzas 1998; Boyer 1987, 119). Supporters of flexible labor law reform counter that more time is needed to evaluate impacts and that reforms need to go further (Lora and Pagés 1997; Cox Edwards 1997).

FLEXIBILITY VS. RIGHTS?

In most formulations of labor flexibility, labor rights have taken a back seat to cost reduction as the driving rationale for reform. To the extent that worker rights have entered into the equation, they have often been cast in individual rather than collective terms, as in a worker's right to employment, which, ironically, is secured by easing employers' constraints on dismissals. Because this perspective ignored the power imbalance between workers and employers, and because it favored individual over collective rights, rights were divorced from the power

10. The OECD's *Employment Outlook* (1999) generated significant controversy with its conclusion that strong job protection laws restricting hiring and firing by employers had little or no effect on overall unemployment. The conclusion contradicted earlier reports by the OECD's economists, revealing a split between the organization's economists and its labor specialists. For an account of the controversy, see Taylor (1999).

to defend them. Neither strong unions nor a strong state, therefore, were seen as necessary counterweights to capital.

This individualistic view of rights also informed flexibility advocates' view of unions. Workers have a "right" to protection from the abusive practices of unions, which are often depicted as unrepresentative and undemocratic institutions (Nelson 1994). This view of unions provided the justification for policies advocating "right-to-work" and free association as an individual choice. Similarly, union gains were posited in zero-sum terms—the costs borne by informally employed or unemployed workers, women, and youth—rather than as potential vehicles for redistribution, with an overall positive effect on wages, working conditions, and labor standards (Elliott and Freeman 2003).[11] Despite evidence that union density (an important component of union strength) has declined dramatically in the region, flexibility advocates still saw unions as "unnaturally" strong.[12]

Nonetheless, since the mid-1990s labor rights have also garnered significant attention in the global economy. After the Singapore round of World Trade Organization (WTO) meetings in 1996, when developing countries succeeded in excluding labor rights from the province of the WTO, the ILO acquired greater importance in its role of overseeing countries' compliance with ILO conventions. In 1998 the ILO member countries adopted the Declaration on Fundamental Principles and Rights at Work. In conjunction with the declaration, the ILO instituted a reporting mechanism that requires annual government reports on how countries are complying with the core rights set out in the declaration, regardless of whether countries have ratified the corresponding conventions. The ILO also continues to respond to government invita-

---

11. Policies most likely to affect unions adversely include the decentralization of collective bargaining to the firm or enterprise level; recognition of several unions within a plant (plural or multiple unionism); forbidding the closed shop and encouraging the "right to work" (the prohibition of laws or contract clauses requiring workers to be members of a union, join the union, or pay union dues as a condition of employment); giving individual employment contracts priority over collective agreements; restricting the scope of topics that may be bargained in collective negotiations; expanding categories of employees that are excluded from unionization (such as "confidential" and supervisory personnel); permitting striker replacements; prohibiting solidarity strikes and boycotts; and expanding the definition of "essential services" with restrictions on strike and bargaining rights (Edwards and Lustig 1997, 20–21; Birdsall, Graham, and Sabot 1998).

12. Recognition of the positive role that unions may play in economic development has emerged relatively recently among IFIs, most notably in a World Bank report on unions and collective bargaining (Aidt and Tzanattos 2003).

tions to advise on labor law matters and on specific complaints filed
by aggrieved parties within countries or by actors outside the violating
countries.

Yet labor rights organizations such as the ILO are at a distinct disadvantage when compared with international financial institutions, which
can withhold financial assistance if market reforms or flexibility are not
implemented (Rittich 2003). Since the ILO operates via moral suasion
and technical assistance, it is only in limited cases that governments are
likely to heed its recommendations. One of these is the case of trade-
linked labor rights instruments, such as the U.S. Generalized System of
Preferences (GSP). Central American countries faced with the prospect
of lost GSP benefits resorted most often to the ILO for assistance with
reforming their labor laws (Frundt 1998; Compa and Vogt 2001; Murillo and Schrank 2005).[13]

The degree of influence that the ILO is able to wield may well depend
on the degree to which governments face economic pressures to bring
legislation into compliance with labor provisions of trade agreements.
The ILO has been criticized, however, for underestimating the role that
market pressures have in undermining core rights, and for being more
concerned with ratification of conventions than with compliance.
Nonetheless, the organization enjoys significant legitimacy in Latin
America and could become more influential, especially if neoliberalism
loses its cachet. For now, the tension between flexibility and rights advocacy remains, with the former continuing to define most policy and
legal reform in the region.

ASSESSING DIRECTIONS IN LABOR REFORM

The predominant policy orientation during the past two decades of
labor reform has been labor flexibility.[14] Yet in this period not all labor
reforms have moved in this direction. Some reforms have reinforced the
traditional protective orientation of labor law, while others have moved
in the direction of greater autonomy for unions and for the collective
bargaining process (Córdova 1996; Bronstein 1997; Cook 1998). This

13. The ILO has taken on more of a certifying role recently in the U.S.-Cambodia
textile agreement, but it is unclear whether this signals an expanded role in the future
(Polaski 2003).

14. Parts of this and the following sections draw on Cook (1998).

variability in labor reform outcomes, as well as the hybrid character of much national labor legislation, can be attributed to the fact that labor reform is a political process that reflects the struggles of social actors to exert their influence.

I begin this discussion of regional trends with several distinctions in labor law. First, it is important to distinguish between individual employment law and collective labor law when analyzing labor reforms. The differences between the two traditionally correspond to the different aims of Latin American governments. Consistent with the view that the state was to oversee industrial relations, mediate among the parties, and protect the weaker individual workers from employers, much employment law is highly detailed, regulated, and protective. The trend in collective labor law, on the other hand, is marked by a combination of efforts to secure control and incorporation, reflecting state efforts to control trade unions and also (in some cases) to secure an alliance between unions and the state.

As a result of these distinct aims, recent labor reform may also reflect different tendencies in each body of law. Reforms may flexibilize individual law but retain controls in collective labor law. Or they may extend protections in individual law while they liberalize collective labor relations. Despite distinct trends in each arena, the two areas of legislation are clearly related. Frequently the effect of flexibility in individual employment is to erode standards for collective agreements. Unions therefore have an interest in seeing that the erosion of individual employment protection is contained. Yet, under some circumstances, unions may be too weak to resist this erosion and may concentrate their resources instead on defending existing collective legislation.

A second important distinction must be made between labor legislation in the public and private sectors. In most Latin American countries, a separate statute governs public-sector employees. Although the tendency in recent reform rounds has been the liberalization of public-sector labor relations, such as granting rights to strike and to bargain in addition to organizing rights, important restrictions remain in place compared with private employees. This is especially true for public administration, where such constraints are typically stronger than for employees of state-owned enterprises. Generally, the public sector lags far behind the private sector in terms of flexibility. For this reason, it remains a target of reform for many Latin American governments. However, the public sector also tends to be resistant to reform, since in many countries it is highly politicized and organized.

A third distinction relates to what are considered labor rights. In recent years the literature on human rights has expanded to include economic and social rights. Minimum acceptable standards and rights have also evolved and even extend to the concept of a "living wage" in developing countries. Similarly, trade agreements range widely in what they include as labor rights: The GSP lists eight basic rights; the North American Agreement on Labor Cooperation (NAALC) cites twelve; the U.S.-Jordan and U.S.-Singapore trade agreements incorporate five. The ILO adopted four core rights in its 1998 Declaration on Fundamental Principles and Rights at Work.[15]

Whichever definition or list one adopts, it is important to note that not all labor protections are necessarily labor *rights*. This distinction is crucial, because some labor provisions defended by unions may not be related to labor rights at all and in fact may even restrict the rights of other workers. One example is established unions' efforts to prevent equal registration procedures for new unions. Moreover, some provisions that clearly involve individual freedom-of-association rights, as in workers' voluntary membership in unions, may undermine collective power and be opposed by unions. The promotion of labor rights may therefore have an ambivalent reception among its intended beneficiaries.

Another critical task in understanding the nature of labor reform in Latin America is to identify the terms that will be used to talk about changes. This is more difficult than it might appear, since there is no single accepted vocabulary for categorizing these changes, and reforms in a particular country may move in contradictory directions or produce ambiguous results. For example, the term "flexible" usually has a negative connotation for trade unionists, even though not all flexible reforms have negative consequences for workers; for instance, they may permit workers to upgrade skills and improve remuneration. Similarly, liberalization is often viewed positively, especially by those in the North favoring "pluralist" systems. Yet for many unions, liberalizing reforms

15. The core rights listed under the declaration are freedom of association and effective recognition of the right to collective bargaining; elimination of all forms of forced or compulsory labor; effective abolition of child labor; and elimination of discrimination in respect of employment and occupation.

that remove state favors or promote plural unionism may weaken unions in their encounters with employers.

Finally, although the term "rigidity" is commonly used to characterize protective worker legislation, I do not use the term in this book, for several reasons. The first is its ideological connotations—those who pursue labor flexibility label the target legislation "rigid" as a way to justify the campaign for its removal. In this way, legislation established to secure workers' rights, as well as legislation establishing minimum-wage laws, might be considered "rigid" or restrictive and costly for employers. Flexibility is thus cast as the sole public good, without regard for the social value of workers' rights and basic protections at work. Second, using the term rigidity to describe worker protections gives the false impression that employers cannot evade the legislation, which is simply not the case in most of Latin America.[16]

The terms I use throughout this book to characterize changes in labor law are *flexible, protective, liberal,* and *restrictive.* The first two terms may apply to both employment (individual) and collective labor law, while the latter two apply mostly to collective labor law. These terms are further explained below.

Flexibility as used here may refer to deregulation, understood as a lessening of regulation of the employment relationship, leaving it more open to negotiation between the parties; greater employer discretion and room for maneuver vis-à-vis employees; decreased legal protections and benefits for workers; or lower employer costs. Flexibility can be found in hiring (e.g., via fixed-term employment contracts, rather than formerly prevalent permanent contracts—technically of "indefinite" duration), and in dismissals (e.g., reductions in severance pay or other dismissal costs); in the determination of hours of work (greater flexibility in scheduling the workweek and overtime); in the definition of wages (e.g., converting from daily pay to hourly pay for work performed; minimal restrictions on wage setting); and in the special treatment of certain sectors, such as reducing legal obligations in small and medium enterprises, export-processing zones, and agriculture (Córdova 1996).

In collective labor relations, flexibility reforms may also apply. For instance, they can promote collective bargaining agreements that call

16. For a recent study examining the issue of enforcement of national laws in Mexico, Argentina, Brazil, and Chile, see Bensusán (2006). See also Camargo (1997) and Zapata (1997) for Brazil and Mexico, respectively.

for labor mobility and "functional flexibility"—the ability to redefine jobs and reassign workers—in addition to the inclusion of productivity clauses, incentive pay schemes, flexible work organization, and the like. This can also be seen as "internal" flexibility, and may not necessarily express itself in changes in labor law.[17] In Latin America much of this kind of flexibility has been introduced through collective agreements, often by means of strong employer pressure. De facto flexibility is also common because of low levels of enforcement of otherwise protective legislation (Córdova 1996, 323). Decentralization of collective bargaining away from industry-level agreements to enterprise-level agreements may also be considered a sign of flexibility, as would reform or elimination of laws that extend the terms and conditions of centrally bargained labor contracts to nonunionized enterprises in the industry or sector.

Protective legislation refers to legislation that embodies the philosophy that individual workers need state protection when facing employers. This philosophy guided the drafting of many countries' original labor legislation in the early twentieth century, and it persists today. Recent examples of this kind of legislation in the area of individual employment law include extending protection for female workers and children (e.g., maternity leave), shortening the workweek, restricting overtime hours, increasing benefits, making it more difficult to fire workers (mandating expanded notification time of dismissal, high severance payments, and/or reinstatement), indexing wages to inflation, and extending coverage of labor legislation to previously excluded categories of workers (e.g., domestic, rural).

In the area of collective labor relations, protective legislation is that which seeks to protect collective rights to organize, bargain, and strike, and generally to grant unions the best terms in which to exercise bargaining power. Such legislation would enable unions to form at industry and/or national levels and give unions ample freedom to strike, including in the public sector. It would eliminate determinations of "illegal" strikes and prevent striker replacements and lockouts. Protective collective legislation would also make union membership compulsory, discount dues automatically from paychecks, and prohibit the dismissal of union officers. In this sense, protective collective labor legislation may

17. See de la Garza Toledo (1997) for a discussion of flexibility in several Latin American countries. For firm-level and national case studies, see Wannöffel (1995); Dombois and Pries (1993); de la Garza (1993); Portella de Castro and Wachendorfer (1995); Köhler and Wannöffel (1993); and Pozas (1993).

be seen as interfering with individual worker "rights," such as the right of workers to refrain from joining a union.

Liberal reform refers to any reform that moves the system toward greater autonomy for the social actors involved in industrial relations. A key example of this type of reform is the relative withdrawal of the state from overseeing industrial relations. For example, liberalizing reform would remove state authority to intervene in union affairs. It would prevent the state from pronouncing on the legality or illegality of strikes or from otherwise intervening in strikes or in the collective bargaining process. Freedom of association would be guaranteed, including the right of individual workers to join or refrain from joining unions. Plural unionism would be permitted, even though representation rights might be restricted to the majority or most representative union. Liberal reform in collective labor relations may coincide with either flexibility or protective legislation in individual law. Liberalization may also be viewed as either unfavorable or favorable to workers and unions, depending on the circumstances.

As noted above, the common historical pattern in Latin America has been protection in individual employment law and restriction of collective labor relations. Restrictive legislation refers to legislation that calls for state involvement in overseeing and controlling such dimensions of collective labor relations as union registration, strikes, bargaining, dispute resolution, the internal activities of unions, and so forth. The mix of protections and restrictions found in most collective labor legislation reflects the "inducements and constraints" extended by the state to labor organizations in an effort both to secure their political support and to limit their potential to disrupt society (Collier and Collier 1979).

FORMS OF FLEXIBILITY

Flexibility takes many forms, making it difficult to cover all of its dimensions here.[18] Yet some schematic discussion of the arenas in which flexibility operates and of the mechanisms by which it is implemented is important for understanding the debates over labor reforms. Labor flexibility takes place in three main arenas: (1) internally, within the

18. For a good exploration of the concept of labor flexibility and its multiple meanings, see the articles in *Labour and Society* 12 (1), 1987, especially those by Boyer and by Meulders and Wilkins.

firm or workplace, in internal labor markets and in the organization of work and production; (2) externally, in labor law and institutions that affect external labor markets (hiring and dismissals) and other aspects of the employment relationship; and (3) through structural, contingent, or de facto conditions—for example, as a result of the informal economy, inflation, and noncompliance with labor regulations.

Internal flexibility, also known as functional flexibility, is implemented by employers through such innovations as work teams and quality circles that affect work organization and the production process, job mobility (e.g., between plants) and internal job rotation (within the firm), compact job classifications (broad-banding) and multiskilling, contingent compensation and merit-based promotion, variable scheduling of work, and so forth. Employers have implemented this kind of flexibility through collective bargaining agreements or unilaterally. These mechanisms of flexibility draw on alternative (primarily Japanese) production and work-process techniques. They are counterposed to the Fordist mass production processes of the early twentieth century, including the rigid job-control unionism of the post–New Deal period in American industrial relations, or the corporatist organization of industrial relations associated with import-substitution industrialization in countries like Mexico (Kochan, Katz, and McKersie 1994; de la Garza 1993). In Latin America this kind of internal flexibility has typically come into use regardless of broader legal and labor policy changes, and it often follows directives from transnational company headquarters.

Another arena in which flexible policies are implemented is through national laws and regulations. Laws and regulations that affect external labor markets (hiring and dismissals, labor supply, training) can affect external flexibility. Also known as employment or numerical flexibility, reforms in this area include measures that make it easier and less costly for employers to hire and lay off workers and that facilitate part-time and temporary employment. Reforms might limit severance payments to unjustly dismissed employees, lower or eliminate advance-notice requirements for dismissals, establish fixed-term employment contracts with lower payroll taxes or other special conditions, designate the economic circumstances of a firm just cause for dismissals, and so forth. In Latin America, national labor laws also typically regulate the length of the workday or workweek, overtime, and weekend and holiday pay.

Wage flexibility may operate in both external and internal dimensions. The external dimension refers to wage regulations, such as minimum wage, wage indexation, incomes policies, or other government action that may set limits on wage adjustments. Governments also set payroll taxes and other obligatory employer contributions (social security, housing, health) that affect the "social wage" paid to workers. Internal wage flexibility may be achieved via firm policies regarding productivity-linked wage increases or other forms of contingent or performance-based compensation that operate within the firm.

Finally, significant labor market or wage flexibility may exist despite the presence of detailed protective legislation and regulation.[19] For instance, a large informal sector may have the effect of placing downward pressure on wages and employment conditions, reducing labor costs for employers in the formal sector, and encouraging informal-sector traits (such as high job turnover) in the formal-sector employment relationship. High rates of inflation can also produce wage flexibility by lowering real wage costs. Weak legal enforcement and noncompliance with legislation may produce a de facto flexible labor market despite the existence of so-called rigid and extensive formal regulation. These factors have been present to some extent in most countries in the region.

In Latin America labor flexibility has taken a variety of forms. Functional or internal flexibility—flexible forms of work and production organization, including work teams, internal mobility, variable work schedules, and so forth—tend to operate in large transnational firms geared to export production, but are also present in domestic firms (de la Garza 1993; de la Garza and Bouzas 1998; Pozas 1993). Internal wage flexibility is achieved via incentive-pay schemes and productivity bonuses, among other measures. This type of flexibility is typically regulated through collective bargaining agreements in circumstances ranging from bilateral negotiation to coerced imposition of flexible terms in contracts. Aspects of functional flexibility also operate in a variety of smaller and medium-sized firms, as well as in export assembly plants (*maquiladoras*), yet these tend not to be as widely diffused as in the larger plants (García 1993, de la Garza 1999).[20] In some countries the

19. For a study showing this to be the case in Brazil, see Amadeo et al. (1995) and Camargo (1997), and, for Mexico, Giugale, Lafourcade, and Nguyen (2001).

20. See de la Garza Toledo (1997) and Munck (2004) on flexibility trends in Latin America, and Cook (1999) for a review of research dealing with functional flexibility in Latin America. For excellent empirical studies of flexibility in Mexico, see de la Garza and Bouzas (1998), and Zapata (1997).

existence of a significant degree of functional flexibility within firms lessens pressures for legal reforms that would increase flexibility in external labor markets. In Mexico, for instance, collective agreements exhibit a significant degree of functional flexibility, but there is relatively strong regulation regarding numerical or external flexibility (Bensusán 2000; de la Garza and Bouzas 1998).

Wage flexibility and other forms of de facto flexibility caused by economic conditions and noncompliance are also common in Latin America. Levels of informality are very high in some countries, especially Mexico, Peru, Bolivia, Guatemala, and Paraguay, where the informal sector makes up more than half of the economically active population. Although inflation rates came down in the 1990s, in the 1980s high inflation operated as an important adjustment mechanism for wages in the region. The minimum wage in most countries has lost its relevance as a guide for wage setting. In many countries, the real minimum wage was lower at the end of the 1990s than at the beginning of the 1980s (Márquez and Pagés 1998, 23). Noncompliance with labor legislation and ineffective enforcement by government authorities is a problem in many countries as well. While these factors may have lessened calls for labor law reform by employer groups in some countries because they produced de facto flexible conditions, they have bolstered others' arguments in favor of flexibility of regulations governing the formal labor market with the goal of increasing compliance and reducing informality.

Much of the debate over labor reform and labor flexibility in Latin America, as well as many of the policy prescriptions promoted by international financial institutions, revolve around changes in labor codes and labor regulation.[21] The key focus of the rest of this chapter is on reform of labor laws rather than on the unregulated practices used by employers within firms, or on the de facto flexibility produced by inflation, the informal sector, and weak legal enforcement, even though these dimensions may affect demands for reform.

---

21. There is a form of flexibility applied to production and the use of technology (technological-organizational flexibility), but here I focus on those forms of flexibility directed at the workforce, either through the regulation of labor markets or through other mechanisms employers use in relation to their employees. However, internal or functional flexibility is often linked to flexibility in the organization of production processes. For a positive evaluation of flexibility in production, see Piore and Sabel (1984) on the concept of flexible specialization.

TRENDS IN EMPLOYMENT (INDIVIDUAL) LAW REFORM

The following sections provide greater detail on both flexible and protective kinds of reforms in individual employment law implemented in the region. Those matters covered by individual employment law include the type of employment contract (apprenticeship, fixed-term, temporary, seasonal, and so forth); hours of work, including length of the workday and workweek, overtime pay, rest breaks, night work, paid holidays and vacation; and dismissals, including advance notification, unjustified and justified dismissals, severance pay, reinstatement, and so forth. The focus here is on those areas in which the greatest degree of change can be identified in the region during the 1990s: employment contracts, wages, and hours of work that reflect a trend toward greater flexibility; dismissal regulations that evince both a protective and a flexible thrust; and maternity leave, a hallmark of individual protectionism.

Employment Contracts

Flexibility in hiring and employment termination has received more attention in the region than have other forms of flexibility (Córdova 1996, 320). The measures adopted by several countries include multiple types of fixed-term individual employment contracts,[22] legalization of part-time work, extension of probationary periods in regular employment contracts, and the establishment of temporary employment agencies. For example, the Argentine National Employment Law passed in 1991 permitted a range of fixed-term "atypical" employment contracts ranging from six months to two years (this law was repealed in 1998). These contracts called for reduced payroll taxes and lower benefits, including pensions, social welfare, and family allowances (Murillo 1997; Oficina Internacional del Trabajo 1995; Bronstein 1997).

While Argentina was the most innovative in this area, other countries, including Peru, Chile, Colombia, and Ecuador, also developed a range of fixed-term contracts in an effort to increase flexibility (Bronstein 1997; Romaguera et al. 1995; Córdova 1996, 321). Several countries also developed special contracts for specific sectors, such as

---

22. These include temporary employment contracts, seasonal employment contracts, apprenticeship contracts, contracts with temporary enterprises, and student training contracts.

rural, domestic, and maquiladora workers, in which the benefits, wages, and conditions offered in these contracts are lower or more flexible than those provided to "normal" workers under the law.

Dismissals

Apart from the special terms provided by the "atypical" employment contracts described above, several countries have adopted changes in their laws regulating dismissals under regular, "indeterminate" employment contracts, which have long been the standard in the region. Most legislation addresses at least three categories of dismissal: dismissal without just cause; dismissal due to fault of the employee (just cause); and dismissal for economic or technological reasons of the firm (Oficina Internacional del Trabajo 1995, 112). The principle operating traditionally throughout most of the region is that of relative stability of employment. Workers dismissed without just cause are usually entitled to prior notification and owed severance pay by the employer. They may also choose to forego the severance payment and seek reinstatement. Despite the original intent of such legislation, which was to make dismissal more difficult, employers readily pay severance and workers accept severance pay rather than seek their reinstatement through the courts. This is because of the length of time it usually takes to go through the court system to seek reinstatement and the uncertain outcome, compared with the immediately available severance pay. In most countries, workers laid off for economic or technological reasons are also entitled to statutory severance pay.

The amount and determination of severance pay vary from country to country and typically depend on the seniority of the worker. In the 1990s Venezuela and Colombia, among other countries, increased the amount of severance pay owed to dismissed workers (Bronstein 1997). Venezuela also strengthened a number of other provisions relating to dismissals, including extending prior notice to three months and establishing double compensation plus wages during court procedures as well as double notice compensation (Marshall 1995). Chilean law, by contrast, grants considerable flexibility to the employer. Chilean law categorizes as dismissal for just cause that which occurs owing to the "needs of the company," including rationalization or modernization, reduction in productivity, changes in market or economic conditions, and the worker's deficient job or technical training.

The Brazilian system differs from those in the rest of the region. In Brazil dismissals were made easier under the military regime in 1966 with the installment of a capitalization fund, the Fundo de Garantia do Tempo de Serviço (FGTS). An employee dismissed without just cause may pull his or her money out of the fund, including interest, plus a percentage of the total fund as indemnization.[23] Similar individual capitalization funds for dismissals, as well as for retirement and pensions, have been established in Peru, Venezuela, Argentina, Chile, Colombia, and Bolivia. Only a few countries in the region have unemployment insurance systems. Most are relatively recent, and most have limited coverage (Marshall 1995, 17–18).[24]

Wages

Most countries fix a minimum wage (or several regional minimum wages), either via a tripartite arrangement or directly by the government. Many countries also fix a higher occupational minimum wage for various jobs. Laws may recognize a range of forms of compensation, such as piecework, commissions, prizes, bonuses, tips, and so forth (Oficina Internacional del Trabajo 1995, 109). Profit sharing is contemplated in the national legislation of Brazil, Chile, Colombia, Ecuador, Mexico, Peru, Venezuela, and the Dominican Republic (Córdova 1996, 314n2).

Flexibility in this area has come in efforts to define wages more narrowly so as to reduce the amounts paid to pensions and other benefits. In Colombia, for example, profit sharing, bonuses, and incentives were excluded from the scope of wages in the 1990 legislation. In Venezuela the definition of wages had been a divisive issue for years because it affected the calculation of the *prestaciones sociales* (social charges) paid by employers (Córdova 1996, 324; Ellner 1993, 214–16). Indeed, Venezuelan labor organizations agreed in tripartite negotiations in May

23. A change in the 1988 constitution increased the amount from 10 to 40 percent of the total in the worker's account that he or she may receive as indemnization to be paid by the employer (Amadeo et al. 1995). In 1988 this system was also made obligatory for all workers except those who had already obtained job tenure under the former system (more than ten years with a particular employer). Other circumstances in which workers may withdraw money from this fund include when purchasing a home, in case of illness, and upon retirement.

24. These include Argentina, Chile, Brazil, Venezuela, and Uruguay. Mexico does not have an unemployment insurance system.

1997 to a narrower definition of wages on which to calculate the prestaciones in exchange for an agreement by employers to increase wages.
Employers' failure to meet their part of the bargain led to a general
strike in August 1997—the first in eight years—and pressure by the
government on employers to meet their commitment.[25] In Argentina a
1991 decree stipulated that wage increases should be authorized only
when productivity increased. According to Efrén Córdova, "flexibility
is to be achieved here through the imposition of a rather rigid rule,
which may help to explain why this provision has never been fully applied" (1996, 325).

Hours of Work

Another area in which reforms have moved in a flexible direction is in
the scheduling of the hours of work and overtime. In some of the more
industrialized countries in the region, restrictions on the maximum
daily or weekly work hours have been lessened, so that the distribution
of hours worked is usually determined via collective bargaining (Oficina
Internacional del Trabajo 1995, 103). In Argentina, for example, the
National Employment Law permitted the parties in bargaining to use
averages over a period longer than a week to determine daily maxi-
mums. Peru and Chile also have flexibility in regulating the length of
the workweek. In one of Venezuela's flexible reforms in an otherwise
protective labor code, flexible scheduling was achieved by considering
work hours averaged out over a period of eight weeks, in which the
average number of hours per week could not exceed the legal maximum
of forty-four.

Colombian law permitted employers to spread the workweek more
flexibly across five days and to extend the regular eight-hour workday
to ten hours without overtime pay. It also allowed for continuous shift
work in certain cases, which would also limit overtime pay (Bronstein
1997; Córdova 1996, 324). Flexibility in the determination of work
hours has also been implemented in other countries, such as Brazil. In
some countries overtime pay has been increased, yet reforms affecting
the determination of hours of work tend to deprive workers of any
benefits of such increases.

Legal regulation of hours of work is different for the public sector in

---

25. *Latin American Weekly Report*, 5 August 1997, 371, http://www.latinnews.com.

most cases, and often for other special sectors, such as agricultural workers, as well. Although the standard throughout the region is the eight-hour day and forty-eight-hour week, Venezuela, Brazil, and more recently Chile have reduced the length of the workweek.

Extending Protection: Female Workers

Several countries have increased or extended protective legislation for individual workers. In some cases these reforms have been driven by the restoration of democracy and/or the sense that national legislation needed to be updated with regard to individual employment law. This is especially the case with one of the most common reforms undertaken in the region, the extension of protections for mothers. Chile provided for twelve weeks of leave and job tenure, leave for a sick child, rights for pregnant workers, daycare centers, and mandated feeding times for new mothers (Romaguera et al. 1995). Venezuela increased postnatal paid leaves of absence from six to twelve weeks and granted one year of tenure after childbirth, which was previously limited to the duration of pregnancy (Freije Rodríguez et al. 1995). In Brazil maternity leave was increased to 120 days and paternity leave was introduced. Colombian law improved maternity benefits and allowed female employees to transfer one week of their maternity leave to their husband or regular partner in the case of a birth of a child (Bronstein 1997). This extension of protection to women workers has been accompanied in some cases by nondiscrimination legislation, such as the removal of special treatment for female workers in cases of night work, increasingly recognized as discriminatory in effect.

TRENDS IN LABOR (COLLECTIVE) LAW REFORM

Among the issues that fall into this category are the formation and registration of unions, including who may unionize, unions' organizational structure, state intervention in internal union affairs, union security and union activities, job tenure for union officers; the levels, structure, and scope of collective bargaining, including who may bargain and extension of coverage; and regulations on strikes, including who may strike, kinds of strikes permitted, prerequisites and restrictions during strikes, and so forth.

Traditionally, collective labor relations in Latin America have been characterized by strong state regulation and control (Bronstein 1995). In reform rounds since the 1980s, there have been four identifiable, sometimes conflicting, trends in this area: (1) restoration of collective rights and protections; (2) change toward more autonomous (liberal/pluralist) collective relations, marked by a weakening of state intervention; (3) weakening of collective rights and protections; and (4) strengthening and updating of protective provisions favoring unions (though characterized by continued state intervention).

The first two patterns have typically been associated with democratic transitions. The first trend is characterized by the Argentine case, among others: Protections were restored during the 1980s where military regimes had severely weakened them. The second pattern toward more autonomous industrial relations is found in the Brazilian case. This was due in part to the strong role granted to the state in labor matters by the 1943 labor code and the anomalous situation this presented by the 1980s.

As countries that exhibited the first two patterns began to adopt market-oriented reforms, pressure to cut away labor protections followed. In both Argentina and Brazil governments tried, not always successfully, to restrict or reverse earlier collective laws and organizational protections. This effort was characterized by reforms aimed at decentralizing collective bargaining and weakening contract provisions in the Argentine case, and by restrictions on strikes in the public sector and in "essential services" in both Argentina and Brazil. In the Brazilian case these restrictions came despite the inclusion of broad support for the right to strike in the 1988 constitution (see Chapter 3).

Elsewhere in the region during the market reform era of the 1990s, the erosion of collective labor law protections was much more evident.[26] Peru and Chile best reflect the third tendency listed above: the weakening of collective rights and protections through changes in labor law. While the Chilean restrictions on collective provisions occurred during the Pinochet dictatorship in the 1970s and 1980s, the Peruvian government's gutting of collective labor rights took place under the "authori-

26. Uruguay deserves mention as a special case, since it lacks a labor code or extensive formal labor legislation. Instead, Uruguay opted to accept ILO conventions and recommendations regarding freedom of association and protection of the rights to organize, bargain collectively, and strike, to guide its practices on these issues. See Ermida Uriarte (2000).

tarian democracy" of President Alberto Fujimori in the 1990s (see Chapter 4).

The final pattern marks an anomaly in the context of market reforms. Even though governments began to adopt market-oriented economic reforms in these countries, labor laws reflected a largely protective labor-relations policy with a strong state role. The Venezuelan reforms are an example of this tendency, with the few labor reforms in the 1990s largely continuing the traditional, protective pattern. Central America also exhibits features of this pattern, since reform rounds in the 1990s have aimed to "update" legislation on unions, often under pressure from the GSP and ILO (Frundt 1998). While the Venezuelan case is best explained by unique political circumstances, and even the hesitant adoption of market reforms in the early 1990s (Burgess 2004), the Central American cases responded to trade-linked pressures to improve labor protections, and thus occurred in the context of market policies.

The tendency during democratic transitions was to strengthen collective labor rights, while during market reform periods in the 1990s it was to weaken, restrict, or ignore collective rights (with the noted exception of Central American countries). Nonetheless, with the exception of Peru, Ecuador, and Colombia, where changes in the labor code weakened collective protections, labor reforms in the 1990s did not succeed in addressing collective law as much as they did employment law. In Argentina and Brazil, for instance, reform initiatives aimed at collective laws were less successful. In some instances, however, presidents resorted to decrees to instate collective restrictions, such as constraints on the right to strike in so-called essential services.

Even in those countries where collective labor law was largely protective, little was done to address existing deficits in labor rights. For instance, in Mexico and Argentina legislation that strongly favored some labor organizations over others (thus curtailing freedom of association) went unchecked, despite complaints filed with the ILO by minority labor groups in both countries. In Brazil, changes to regulations on union structure and collective bargaining that would have liberalized both (and induced competition) were repeatedly set aside by democratic governments.

In countries where collective rights generally lacked protection, improvements were piecemeal and slow. In Chile, government efforts to address serious weaknesses in bargaining and the right to strike met with opposition by the conservative Congress. Despite improvements in 2001, gaps in protecting collective rights remain. In Central America, legal improvements to association and organizing rights have been undermined by the failure to enforce these protections.

In short, the dominant pattern in the region during the market reform period has been the weakening of employment protections traditionally present in the law, and at the same time failure to address deficits in the protection of collective labor rights. This assessment is somewhat at odds with other recent evaluations of labor reforms during the 1980s and 1990s. Lora (2000) and Lora and Pagés (1997), for example, assess reforms entirely in terms of their ability to make labor relations and markets more flexible and efficient. From their perspective, Latin American labor reform was found wanting since too few reforms had been implemented, and then only in piecemeal and gradual fashion.

In contrast, a study by the Latin American office of the ILO concluded that flexible reforms had been implemented in eleven of the seventeen countries it reviewed, making up approximately 70 percent of wage employment in the region. The study states that this conclusion "places in question the frequent assertions that labor reform in Latin America has been neither extensive nor deep and that, consequently, new and more intensive changes are needed" (Vega Ruíz 2000, 10).[27] Another comprehensive review of reforms in the region points to the tendency toward less state intervention and greater autonomy in collective labor relations, even though it acknowledges persistent problems in this area (Ciudad 2002, 76).

María Victoria Murillo (2005) presents a different view of the degree of labor rights erosion due to legal reform. Drawing on instances of legislative labor reform, she argues that employment laws were strengthened, not weakened, in countries where labor's party allies were in power, such as Argentina under Menem, Chile under Lagos, and Venezuela under Pérez. Argentina presents a more complicated case, however, since the Menem government implemented greater flexibility in employment laws throughout most of the 1990s, and a reversal of this legislation did not occur until 1998. Moreover, Argentina is typically cited as one of the two countries (the other is Peru), where significant flexibility reforms were passed in the 1990s (Ciudad 2002; Vega

27. My translation from the Spanish. Also cited in Ciudad (2002, 11).

Ruíz 2000). The Chilean case does reflect some improvements in employment protections, but placed in the larger context of a labor code defined by the dictatorship, the Chilean government did not go as far as it might have in extending labor rights.

Focusing on collective labor laws, Murillo and Schrank (2005) hold that labor rights protection has grown in much of the region since the mid-1980s, and that this has largely been due to the presence of transnational alliances in the case of Central America, and to national labor-governing party alliances in South America.[28] However, since they exclude decrees from consideration and look only at laws passed by the legislature, they tend to underrepresent the number and extent of flexibility reforms in both employment and labor law. This focus also overlooks the role of partisan governments in pushing through flexible reforms—often by decree—against labor's interests, or the degree to which labor has been able to block or alter more adverse reform proposals, despite partisan alliances. Looking only at laws passed ignores telling details about the broader political dynamics at play in labor law reform.

Distinct political and economic transition contexts are also collapsed in their study, so that the pro-rights reforms passed in the 1980s, during a period of democratic transition, are counted as improvements undertaken in the context of market reforms. I argue that pro-labor reforms were favored in democratic contexts regardless of the political party in power, and that the dominant tendency during the 1990s was to weaken or ignore collective legislation. Table 2.1 shows that during the economic reform period of the 1990s, protective legislation was passed in two countries, Argentina and Venezuela. Two other countries, Chile and Paraguay, also saw protective legislation early in the 1990s, but this was more a response to their late democratic transition contexts than to market reforms. Flexibility reforms, however, were passed in six out of eight countries implementing reforms, and in one of these (Argentina), the ruling party had a labor base.[29]

---

28. The authors include Central American countries in their overall assessment of labor rights in the region, whereas I treat Central America as a separate set of cases, given the region's unique set of circumstances, especially the use of GSP and these countries' heightened vulnerability to international influences.

29. Chile is excluded from this subset of countries passing flexible reform because the main flexibility legislation dates from the dictatorship during the 1970s–80s rather than the 1990s. Mexico, Bolivia, and Uruguay passed no reforms.

TABLE 2.1 Orientation of Major Labor Law Reforms, Regime Type, and Transition Contexts in Latin America, 1985–2004

Country	Tr Seq Rev	Democratic Transition		Economic Transition	
		Protective	Flexible	Protective	Flexible
Argentina		1988 (N)		1998, 2004 (Y)	1991, 1995 (Y) 2000 (N)
Bolivia					
Brazil		1988 (c) (N)			1995, 1998 (N)
Chile	X	1990–93, 2001 (Y)			1979–80 (N)
Colombia					1990 (N)
Ecuador					1991 (N)
Mexico	X				
Paraguay		1992 (c), 1993 (N)			
Peru					1991, 1992, 1995 (N)
Uruguay		1985 (Y)			
Venezuela				1990 (Y)	1997 (N)

Tr Seq Rev = transition sequence reversed (economic before democratic)
(N) = no labor party in power
(Y) = labor party in power
(c) = reform of constitution

If we consider Central American countries separately, we see that protective reforms are indeed concentrated in this region and promoted by GSP pressure, as Murillo and Schrank argue (Table 2.2). However, this focus on improvement in protective legislation overlooks the laws' persistent shortcomings in protecting labor rights. Moves in the *direction* of greater protection from a relatively weak baseline do not necessarily establish labor rights protections, a point that Frundt (1998) clearly establishes. In addition, several Central American governments (Nicaragua, Guatemala, Panama) passed laws or decrees that restricted

TABLE 2.2   Orientation of Major Labor Law Reforms in Central America
(1990s)

Country	Protective Reform	Flexible Reform
Costa Rica	1993	
El Salvador	1994	
Dominican Republic	1992	
Guatemala	1992	1995
Honduras		
Nicaragua		1990, 1996
Panama		1990, 1995, 1996

SOURCE: Frundt (1998).

labor rights, or that produced ambiguous consequences, given the mix
of liberal and restrictive reforms.

In this chapter I have referred only to changes in the law. When we
consider the erosion of protections linked to the impact of structural
reforms on the economy and labor market, the gap in labor rights protections appears even larger. For instance, structural reforms are partly
to blame for the sharp decline in union density in most countries of the
region. Declines in manufacturing, the most heavily unionized sector,
and increases in service-sector and informal employment have undermined unions, as have increases in unemployment and in short-term
employment. Since labor rights, especially collective rights to organize,
bargain, and strike, are most likely to be defended by trade unions, this
decline has a clear adverse impact on rights advocacy and protections.

The weakening of trade unions in the region and the lag, in many
countries, in altering national labor laws to bolster protection of collective rights, contrasts with a growing tendency to include labor rights
provisions in regional trade agreements. Freedom of association and the
right to organize and to bargain collectively are contemplated in
NAFTA's North American Agreement on Labor Cooperation (NAALC),
Mercosur's Declaration on Social and Labor Matters, and in similar
chapters in CARICOM, CAFTA, the U.S.-Chile agreement, and others.
The ILO's 1998 Declaration on Fundamental Principles and Rights at
Work has also had a more direct influence on recent labor rights provisions in trade agreements.

Nonetheless, few of these provisions have improved the enforcement
of collective rights protections or altered national legislation in ways
that strengthen labor rights. The result is a gap between international

attention to labor rights and national legislation, enforcement, and labor rights advocacy, which have had to contend with the counterpressures of competitiveness and flexibility. The ways in which international and national pressures, processes, and actors interact to shape labor law reform in each case is the subject of the following chapters.

Legacies of State Corporatism: Argentina and Brazil

Despite marked differences in founding labor legislation and labor-party relations, Brazil and Argentina exhibit important similarities in their labor law reform trajectories. By the critical democratic transition decade of the 1980s both countries had strong labor movements, which enabled them to obtain important favorable provisions in labor law. In the 1990s governments in both countries pursued labor flexibility, despite the prevalence of a labor-governing party alliance in one country and not in the other. Toward the end of that decade, labor movements in Brazil and Argentina were able to stall—and even to reverse—some flexibility reforms, particularly those affecting unions. This was possible because of organized labor's relative strength, its retention and use of political alliances, and the fact that each country's labor laws largely protected workers' collective rights, thus enabling unions to conserve key resources in mobilizing to block the most harmful reforms. By the mid-2000s, labor reform initiatives in both countries began to shift back toward a focus on labor rights and worker protection.

LEGACIES OF STATE CORPORATISM

Although labor legislation and the initial incorporation of labor can be defined as state corporatist in both Argentina and Brazil, the initial motivations behind the state's inclusion of labor were quite different in the two countries. Whereas, in Argentina, Juan Domingo Perón (first as labor secretary and vice president and later as president) used legislation to secure labor's political support, in Brazil demobilization and control were Getúlio Vargas's primary objectives in establishing the labor system under the Estado Novo (James 1988; Erickson 1977, 23; Collier 1982). This difference produced a comparatively weaker and more divided labor movement in Brazil than in Argentina, at least until the 1980s, and helps explain differences in the dynamics of labor reform in the two countries. At the same time, analogous features in the corporatist labor legislation of both countries accounted for the relatively strong presence of Brazilian and Argentine unions relative to the rest of the region, and likewise account for similar labor reform trajectories toward the end of the twentieth century.

Labor legislation in Argentina and Brazil allowed for high levels of state intervention and oversight. In both cases, laws regulating union structure and representation restricted interunion competition and new entrants. In Argentina, the Law of Professional Associations from the Peronist era established requirements for union registration and distinguished between registration and state recognition. The latter gave unions the "legal personality" (*personería gremial*) to negotiate contracts, launch strikes, and collect dues (Ranis 1995). The law also established one union per area of economic activity (James 1988, 10). In Brazil the Consolidação das Leis do Trabalho, or CLT,[1] established the principle of *unicidade,* the formation of one *sindicato* per professional category and geographic zone.[2] Here, too, official recognition enabled

---

1. The CLT was promulgated by Getúlio Vargas in 1943 and represented the systematization of the body of labor legislation written since 1930.

2. I use the term "sindicato" rather than "union" in reference to Brazil, given its specific meaning in the Brazilian legal context. Employers are also organized into sindicatos in Brazil. Unless noted otherwise, reference to sindicatos here means worker sindicatos.

sindicatos to undertake a range of activities denied to unrecognized organizations, including bringing cases before the labor courts (Erickson 1977, 23, 39). While unicidade restricted competition, however, it also fragmented unions by limiting their scope of representation.

This structuring of labor organization was accompanied by important subsidies to unions in the areas of bargaining and financing. In Argentina the 1953 law on collective bargaining established industry-wide contracts, obliged employers to bargain with the recognized union, and extended bargaining terms to all workers in the industry regardless of whether they were unionized (James 1988, 10). Later, control of vast health insurance funds was transferred to the unions, enabling them to set up health and other services for their members from worker and employer contributions. These *obras sociales* became an important source of revenue for unions, rivaling income from dues (McGuire 1997, 225). This package of legislation enabled the Argentine labor movement to become one of the most powerful in Latin America. More significant, this legal framework helped labor to sustain that strength even as antilabor regimes came to power.

In Brazil labor laws also provided workers' organizations with key subsidies. Collective agreements were between worker and employer sindicatos in a particular territory and professional category, and their terms extended to the entire sector regardless of union membership. Sindicatos were subsidized through the involuntary deduction of one day's pay per year for all organizable workers, regardless of union membership. Referred to as the union tax or *imposto sindical,* these funds could be used to finance nonpolitical activities of the unions, especially the operation of social services such as schools, placement services, and medical assistance (Erickson 1977, 36–37). Although union membership was voluntary, many workers joined sindicatos in order to gain access to the social services they provided.

Argentine labor's political party ties also contributed to its influence and political strength. With Perón, and in alliance with the Laborist and later the Justicialist Party, union leaders were able to participate in Congress and government and as candidates in local and national elections. Indeed, the strength of Peronist unions overshadowed that of the party for much of its existence during the twentieth century, and the party often took up unionist demands (McGuire 1997). During periods of dictatorship, the labor movement's strong Peronist identity was a factor in its and the party's survival. By the 1990s, when the Peronist president began to implement market reforms, union influence in the party had declined dramatically (Levitsky 2003). Nonetheless, unions remained largely Peronist, and that allegiance and the influence it conferred would be reflected in government policies after the 2001–2 crisis, especially as regards labor reform.

In Brazil labor organizations were weaker and more divided than in Argentina for much of the twentieth century. Nonetheless, the organizational resources and financial subsidies labor gained through the law provided a source of protection for workers' organizations. And despite their demobilizing tendencies, these corporatist features failed to suppress labor militancy in the 1970s and 1980s.[3] Worker dissatisfaction in Brazil in the 1960s and 1970s led to an increasing number of strikes during the military dictatorship, culminating in the formation of the left-oriented Partido dos Trabalhadores (PT) in 1979 and the Central Unica dos Trabalhadores (CUT) in 1983 (Keck 1992). Even as democracy in Brazil enabled the growth and consolidation of a militant, independent labor movement, the corporatist provisions of the CLT and the Brazilian constitution remained in place.

The labor movement's involvement in the creation of a labor party was possible in part because of the long-standing weakness of political parties and of party identities in Brazil (Mainwaring 1997). Unlike Argentina, in Brazil no party emerged to successfully represent labor's interests during the state's incorporation of labor in the 1930s and 1940s. Labor was therefore politically autonomous and available for representation by a class-based party (Collier 1982). However, this alliance between the CUT and the Workers' Party in the 1980s and 1990s did not necessarily give labor greater influence in governments of the time. Even as the PT won the presidency in 2003, it was forced to seek alliances with more conservative parties in Congress.

This legacy of state corporatism proved important for the labor reform debates of the 1980s and 1990s in both countries. Despite some differences in reform dynamics, due mainly to the greater fragmentation of unions in Brazil, the overall trajectories and outcomes of labor reform were similar. As we shall see, in both cases key corporatist provisions—including those that established monopolies of representation and guarded against competition, provided important financial subsid-

---

3. See the interesting discussion by French (2001) on the diverse interpretations of the CLT and its impact on workers' ability to organize autonomously.

ies and union control of service provision, and extended collective bargaining terms to all workers in a sector regardless of membership—protected workers' collective interests even as the political and economic environment turned unfavorable. Most unions therefore defended these provisions during reform rounds in the 1990s, leading to a greater degree of change in individual labor law than in collective legislation. The sequence of transitions is another factor that helps to explain similarities in the way unions in both countries confronted the issue of labor reform.

THE SEQUENCE OF TRANSITIONS: DEMOCRACY BEFORE MARKET REFORM

In both Argentina and Brazil, labor played an important role in the protests calling for an end to the dictatorship.[4] In neither country, however, did labor-based parties come to power in the transition. In Argentina the Radical Party won the elections and Raul Alfonsín became president. The Peronists, with whom the trade unions were still closely allied, occupied the opposition. In Brazil Vice President José Sarney from the centrist Partido do Movimento Democrático Brasileiro (PMDB) became president after the death of president-elect Tancredo Neves. The largest labor central, the CUT, supported the opposition PT.

Despite the lack of a strong labor link to the governing party, both of these moderate "first-round" democratic governments came to implement important pro-labor reforms. In Argentina the Alfonsín government eventually restored all of the prerogatives the unions had enjoyed in the Peronist era. In Brazil the Sarney government promoted significant changes in the role of the state and in the autonomy of unions and bargaining that were eventually incorporated in the new constitution of 1988. In both countries, moreover, pro-labor reforms were implemented during economic crises and government efforts to carry out structural adjustment plans.

Argentina

While both governments were obliged to address the economic crisis as a priority, equally important was the restoration of civil rights and

4. Parts of this discussion draw on Cook (2002).

democracy, at least to the extent that these had existed in each country prior to the military coups. The Argentine government, for instance, went further than any of its neighbors in punishing the former military rulers for their human rights violations and set a tone that helped to restore the value of human, civil, and political rights in Argentina (Hunter 1998, 302).

Despite Alfonsín's relatively quick action on human rights and other political reforms, however, his administration was slower to restore the labor movement's former rights and prerogatives. The trade unions were the backbone of the main opposition to the government, the Peronists. There was therefore little incentive to return all of the provisions that had helped to make the unions so strong in previous decades. The military government had effectively weakened the trade unions by removing many of their rights and privileges, including their key sources of funding (Drake 1996; Pozzi 1988). The Alfonsín government tried to take advantage of this situation by designing reforms that would further weaken the entrenched Peronist union leadership (McGuire 1997, 191). The goal was to undermine the political opposition and to eliminate the Peronist trade unions as a possible threat to democracy.[5]

Among the first government measures were the return of the assets of the Confederación General del Trabajo (CGT) and restoration of the right of trade unions to participate in politics. Both measures were consistent with the return of basic rights characteristic of the period. But the Alfonsín administration also attempted several reforms that met with strong union opposition. The government tried to revise the Law of Professional Associations in order to increase minority (i.e., non-Peronist) representation in union secretariats. The CGT worked with Partido Justicialista (PJ) deputies to stop the reform bill in Congress, and a weaker version of the bill passed later in 1984 (Buchanan 1995, 137; McGuire 1997, 192).[6] A second package of reforms aimed to decentralize collective bargaining, and included a proposal on strikes that

5. The relationship sustained between some union leaders and the military junta during the dictatorship fed this view of the Peronist unions as being hostile to democracy (Drake 1996; Munck 1998, 155).

6. The new union elections regime allowed for a majority of Peronist leaders but it also permitted the triumph of a number of opposition lists (Etchemendy 1995). For more on modifications to the Law of Professional Associations under Alfonsín, see Ranis (1995, 46–47).

would narrow the definition of a legal strike, outlaw political strikes, and prohibit strikes during the life of a collective contract. The struggle over this proposal continued in Congress until 1988, when it was dropped in a final negotiation with the labor movement (Buchanan 1995, 139–40).

The lack of clear business support for Alfonsín's labor reform proposals weakened the government's hand. Much of the business sector was critical of the government's attempts to address the economic crisis. Business was divided: Some sectors had benefited from protective tariffs and would suffer with liberalization. Nor was business solidly behind the Radical Party. Some sectors of business were skeptical of democratic government entirely; others were Peronists. Moreover, Alfonsín was not considered a business-friendly president, as evidenced by some of his economic policies and his concessions to the CGT (Acuña 1994).

The government initially adopted a tripartite approach to addressing the economic crisis, in keeping with the more inclusionary politics characteristic of the transition. The administration brought in labor along with business in consultation over measures such as wage and price freezes. But these efforts at concertation were short-lived. The inability to bargain over wages and the failure to hold the business sector to its obligation to control prices generated tension within the tripartite arrangement. The government's economic stabilization plan spurred a further drop in real wages and produced private-sector layoffs and even irregular wage payments (Ranis 1995, 63). Tripartism failed as both business and labor pursued short-term "survivalist" options (Buchanan 1995, 152).

The climate of economic instability was further fueled by thirteen general strikes, spearheaded by the combative faction of the CGT. The CGT was divided at this time between this more militant group and a more conciliatory faction (the "15") that collaborated closely with the administration near the end of Alfonsín's term.[7] Although the government attempted to exploit divisions within the labor movement, the strategy backfired as Peronists advanced in the 1987 elections and labor pursued a strategy of legislative activity through its party allies.

In the context of the transition to democracy, political stability and the consolidation of democracy were issues of paramount concern, gov-

7. Two other factions (the "25" and the "62"), although quite different from each other programmatically, preferred to work through the PJ in Congress (McGuire 1997, 204). This enabled an important sector of labor to play a role as part of the political party opposition, which gave labor another source of influence in legislation and in elections.

erning most policy decisions. In a 1993 interview with James McGuire, former president Raul Alfonsín revealed the forces at play in his decision to reach out to a sector of the labor movement by appointing one of its leaders labor minister in 1987: "I had too many conflicts. We put up not just with 14 [sic] general strikes but also with thousands of strikes. It was too conflictive a situation. Also, the situation with the armed forces was getting increasingly tense. So, I wanted to calm social conflict a bit, to have the support of all the workers. . . . I did things I wouldn't have done had it not been for the fear of instability, and I didn't do things I would [otherwise] have done, because I had the obligation to consolidate democracy" (McGuire 1997, 202–3).

The CGT eventually succeeded not only in defeating the labor reforms it viewed as antithetical to its interests but also in extracting from the government and Congress most of the key prerogatives that had been removed during the military dictatorship. These included the law on collective bargaining, which restored bargaining by sectors, the law of professional associations, which meant that the national craft union structure could prevail, and the law on social welfare funds, which returned control of the funds to the unions. In addition, all restrictions on strikes as originally proposed by the government were dropped as part of this legislative package.

The results of the 1987–88 period of labor reforms led former labor minister Hugo Barrionuevo to remark that the unions had gotten back the entire apparatus (*"Se les devolvió el aparato intacto"*) of favorable laws and union prerogatives (Etchemendy 1995). In particular, the CGT's core organizational interests, including its control over social welfare funds, the monopoly structure of one union per industry, sectoral collective bargaining, and the right to strike had been maintained or restored (Ranis 1995, 48–49).

Brazil

Like his Argentine counterpart, President José Sarney of Brazil also inherited a worsening economic crisis in 1985, characterized by rising inflation. In February 1986 his government implemented the Plano Cruzado, a heterodox stabilization package aimed at reducing inflation and stabilizing the economy. Also like the Argentine government, Sarney tried to promote bipartite and tripartite social dialogue and concertation on economic and social policy during the crisis. But, as in

Argentina, these efforts were short-lived. The CUT boycotted tripartite talks when the government refused to suspend foreign debt payments.[8] Labor's commitment to tripartism was also weakened by its mistrust of the business sector's role.

Continued high inflation, real wage decline, and the government's failure to mitigate the effects of austerity contributed to tensions between labor and the state. But the government's labor policy also encouraged greater separation. Labor Minister Almir Pazzianotto issued a directive ordering ministry officials not to meddle in internal union affairs and to refrain from using their powers of intervention during strikes (Keck 1989). This relaxation on strikes led to an initial upsurge in strike activity in 1985–87 (Payne 1995, 226). The government reportedly tolerated the strikes as an escape valve during economic crisis, and as part of an effort to promote "negotiated settlements as the foundation of new democratic labor relations" (Buchanan 1995, 192).

In this context of greater political liberalization, the CUT soon resorted to more confrontational tactics. It abandoned its participation in tripartite forums and "reverted to a basic defensive struggle to preserve real wages and employment" (Buchanan 1995, 186). The confrontational strategy was evident in the increase in strikes and slowdowns. But the CUT also adopted a partisan strategy of exerting political pressure through its alliance with the PT, especially in order to influence the debate over labor law reform (Buchanan 1995, 189, 194). Like the Argentine CGT, the CUT turned away from the consultative mechanisms proffered by government to more traditional militant tactics *and* toward a political strategy of working with its party allies in the opposition.

In 1986 Brazilians turned their attention to writing a new constitution, and a constituent assembly was formed. Among the many provisions to be addressed were those affecting labor. The Sarney government took the lead by originating most of the major reform proposals in order to "democratize labor-capital relations in Brazil, mod-

---

8. One tripartite experience the labor movement viewed in hindsight as positive was the National Forum on Collective Contracts and Labor Relations, which proposed the need for a transition to a more participatory and transparent model of labor relations that included freedom of association, union representation in the workplace, and the conversion of the Labor Ministry into an agency that would stimulate collective bargaining between employers and workers. The political weakness of the transition government and the inflationary crisis, however, took these issues off the agenda (Portella de Castro 2001, 51–52).

ernize relations of production, and put an end to the corporatist structure of the CLT" (cited in Buchanan 1995, 182). Although there was considerable opposition and delay in the constituent assembly, the final version of the constitutional reforms contained many provisions favorable to workers. Yet the tenor of these labor provisions was more liberal than populist. In part this was due to the government's original draft, which had set out to reduce state intervention in labor relations and to make capital-labor relations more autonomous. Labor's influence was seen in the constituent assembly through the presence of former sindicato leaders and others with a labor orientation (L. M. Rodrigues, cited in R. Smith 1995, 4). Nonetheless, many corporatist elements of the constitution remained unchanged because of disagreements between the CUT and the Confederação Geral dos Trabalhadores (CGT) and their party allies over whether to end unicidade, the imposto sindical, and other corporatist provisions (Buchanan 1989; Gacek 1994, 102–3; Córdova 1989, 262).

The business sector also played an important role in the constituent assembly, which it saw as dominated by the left (Weyland 1998). Although business was opposed to several of the reform proposals, it was also divided. However, business was able to defeat the proposals it viewed as most threatening, and watered down a number of others (Kingstone 1999, 53). The reform proposal that most concerned the business sector was a job security measure that would have provided guarantees against arbitrary dismissal (Payne 1995, 229). Other pro-labor provisions had already been implemented in practice, and business therefore did not act strongly to oppose them. Since the mid-1980s, for instance, the government had already promoted greater bargaining autonomy as well as a more open environment for strikes.

Among the most significant changes introduced in the constitution were the role of the state in labor relations and the right to strike. The new constitution removed the state from registering unions, intervening in internal union affairs, or deciding in collective conflicts (R. Smith 1995). These reforms altered the formal corporatist landscape of labor relations that had prevailed since the 1940s.[9] Other changes recognized the strike as a social right for all, eliminated the concept of the illegal strike, and removed restrictions on strikes for public-sector workers.

---

9. See Erickson (1977) for a comprehensive analysis of the corporatist features of Brazilian labor relations.

Additional strong protective measures included extending the right to organize to workers in public administration, establishing job security for union leaders and candidates for union office, and permitting retired union members to vote and run for office. With regard to employment and working conditions, the reforms established an increase in the fine that the employer paid to the worker in cases of "unjustified" dismissal, a reduction in the maximum workweek from forty-eight to forty-four hours, an increase in minimum overtime pay from 20 to 50 percent, and a reduction in the maximum length of a continuous work shift from eight to six hours, along with other measures (Amadeo et al. 1995, 37–38). A provision calling for profit sharing was added to the constitution. Another change, which remained unimplemented, provided for workers in firms with more than two hundred employees to elect a workers' council to negotiate with the employer, but the council could not engage in collective bargaining.

While there were significant changes in some of the corporatist provisions of the constitution, others remained intact despite government efforts to alter them. These included the structure of union organization, which continued to be based on one union per economic activity per territorial unit (the system of unicidade sindical); the union tax (imposto sindical), which every worker paid regardless of union membership in order to finance the unions' nonpolitical activities; and the labor court system, which, through its *poder normativo,* could make laws as well as apply them.[10] These, along with state intervention, were the mainstays of corporatist labor relations in Brazil. Substantial reform of these provisions threatened sindicato interests. While key actors acknowledged that these features would someday need to change, most advocated for their gradual withering away rather than for their abrupt termination.

The debate over the imposto sindical reflected the advantages that some sectors obtained from the corporatist provisions of labor law. Widely regarded as a system enabling state control, the imposto sindical was administered through the government and strictly monitored as to its use for nonpolitical activities, i.e., social programs. The fact that all workers paid a day's wages for this tax regardless of their membership in a union guaranteed the sindicatos a strong subsidy (Keck 1989).

10. For a more complete description of these features, see Erickson (1977), R. Smith (1995), Gacek (1994), Buchanan (1989), and Córdova (1989).

While the CUT supported the elimination of the union tax precisely because of the aspects of state control as well as its tendency to make sindicato leaders complacent, centrals such as the CGT wanted to retain the tax because they feared that its removal would threaten their sindicatos' financial viability. These labor organizations were joined by employer sindicatos who also benefited from the tax, as well as other sectors of business that feared the loss of state control over unions that the lifting of the tax implied (Buchanan 1995, 181–83).

The new constitution produced in 1988 was therefore an ambiguous and hybrid document where labor relations were concerned (Córdova 1989; Cardoso 1999). While it eliminated one of the key features of the corporatist system, state intervention, it left others, such as the system of unicidade, the imposto, and the labor courts. Yet without a strong oversight role for the state, a fair amount of flexibility in union formation and collective bargaining could emerge in practice (R. Smith 1995). Despite delays in passing implementing legislation for the new constitutional provisions and the subsequent passage of more restrictive laws and decrees, the Sarney government's labor reforms proved relatively favorable for the labor movement.[11]

Summary

In the context of democratic transition, labor in both Brazil and Argentina gained or recovered important labor rights and organizational resources. This was so even though in both cases centrist parties without a labor base dominated the government. The principal labor organizations, the CGT in Argentina and the CUT in Brazil, were closely allied with opposition parties that had a presence in the legislature. In both countries the governments tried to establish tripartite mechanisms for addressing economic and social policies. But the severity of the economic crisis, labor's mistrust of tripartism, and the growing weakness of the executive vis-à-vis the legislature and the opposition led the key

11. Some of these more restrictive measures could be seen in one of the first laws written to implement Article 9 of the constitution regarding the right to strike. In general, the new strike laws permitted significant freedoms for workers exercising this right (Amadeo et al. 1995, 41; R. Smith 1995). But the 1989 strike law introduced the new designation of "abuse of the right to strike" and gave the courts power to rule on the propriety of the strike. Delays also occurred with some of the more controversial constitutional provisions, such as the profit-sharing provision and the establishment of workers' councils in firms with more than two hundred employees.

labor groups in both countries to pursue a more confrontational sectoral strategy through engagement in strikes, together with a political strategy of working with legislative party allies in order to defeat unfavorable labor reforms and press their own interests.

In neither case did the government initially incorporate labor's agenda in its list of reforms, but neither did the government pursue business's interests exclusively. On the contrary, both administrations had their own conceptions of the kinds of changes needed to democratize labor relations and increase the autonomy of the bargaining process. In the broader context of democratization after transition from military rule, the focus was on institutional change in labor relations over labor market flexibility, which, although also on the agenda, was a secondary concern.

Yet neither government counted on labor's strong support (or on business's strong opposition) in issuing these labor reforms. Instead, the administrations frequently faced opposition by the labor movement and its party allies. In Argentina reforms aimed at "democratizing" the labor movement were seen as a threat to the Peronist union leadership, while the government's claims to support collective bargaining were undermined by its anti-inflation policy and restrictions on wage bargaining. Labor resistance rendered the government incapable of breaking the Peronists' power over the labor movement. Indeed, labor and its allies proved strong enough to secure the return of all of the unions' key prerogatives and sources of power. In Brazil many of the Sarney government's liberalizing reforms coincided with the CUT's own reform agenda, although there was no explicit alliance between them. Yet in the case of other key changes in the corporatist framework, the government bowed to interests of other labor and employer sindicatos.

ECONOMIC TRANSITION AND LABOR LAW REFORM

The 1990s brought a different set of challenges to governments and labor in Argentina and Brazil. The year 1989 in particular, when "second-round" democratic presidents took office in Argentina and Brazil, signaled a departure from the primary tasks of democratic consolidation during the 1980s. This period began a shift in which both countries began to pursue economic and structural reforms aimed at opening their economies and reducing the role of the state consistent with neoliberal economic reforms implemented elsewhere. Argentina's president, Carlos Saúl Menem, was more successful initially at pushing through these reforms, thanks in large part to the political circumstances of his coming to power and his base in the Peronist party. In Brazil, Fernando Collor's impeachment in 1992 followed by transition president Itamar Franco stalled the implementation of economic and structural reform. A more concerted effort to pursue economic reforms did not gain momentum until the presidency of Fernando Henrique Cardoso in 1994. Both Menem and Cardoso, in 1994 and 1999, respectively, were reelected to second terms on the strength of their economic policies.

Despite these broad similarities, there were numerous differences between the two regimes. Whereas neither government had a labor base during the initial transition to democratic rule, after 1989 the Argentine government was headed by the Justicialista (Peronist) Party, which maintained its strong labor constituency. In Brazil, by contrast, Collor had narrowly defeated the PT's (and the CUT's) candidate, Luis Inácio Lula da Silva, a former leader of the metalworkers' union. This electoral outcome was repeated when Fernando Henrique Cardoso defeated Lula in 1994. As a result, Brazil's largest labor organization, the CUT, opposed both the Collor and Cardoso governments from the beginning, whereas Menem initially enjoyed support for his economic reforms from organized labor (Ranis 1995).

Both governments, however, set out to implement flexible labor market reforms that threatened the interests of organized labor. The labor movements' relative difficulties in blocking these reforms reflected the changes in political climate, wherein the task of restoring democracy had given way to that of saving the economy. The implementation of such free-market policies as privatization and trade liberalization had the effect, in turn, of further weakening trade unions. The result was a generally more hostile environment for labor, and one in which its strategic options were more limited.

Argentina: The First Menem Administration (1989–1994)

Among the first accords President Menem extracted from the legislature were the Law of Economic Emergency and the Law of Reform of the State. Both laws enabled Menem to undertake a broad range of economic and institutional reforms such as trade liberalization, privatization, and monetary and fiscal reforms. Menem immediately set about privatizing a number of state-owned enterprises in areas such as tele-communications, the postal service, and railroads. His economic reforms earned him the support of a private sector and middle class that were not historically Peronist, thus broadening his reform coalition. At the same time, Menem retained the loyalty of the Peronist party and the CGT, even though some factions within both were critical of the government's neoliberal orientation. Nonetheless, most analysts saw Menem's ability to bring about economic reforms with relatively little public opposition as due in part to his alliance with labor through the party (Ranis 1995, 214–15; McGuire 1997, 235).

Another factor in Menem's success in passing economic reforms was his ability to centralize executive authority in order to wield significant discretionary power. This concentration of authority was evident in his handling of the Supreme Court, his ability to convince the legislature to grant him the authority to execute decrees of "urgent necessity," and his willingness to use the veto and partial veto against legislative initiatives to an extent not seen before.[12]

The Menem government also turned its attention to labor reform, and in the process it resorted to the use of decrees as well as legislation. In some instances decrees were issued only after it became clear that proposed legislation would not pass Congress (McGuire 1995, 224). Indeed, most labor initiatives sent to Congress prior to 1994, including a comprehensive reform package issued by Labor Minister Enrique Rodríguez in 1993, were not sanctioned because of labor opposition (Etchemendy and Palermo 1997). In contrast, Peronist deputies supported passage of a number of economic initiatives, including the Convertibility Law,[13] the Law of Economic Emergency, the Law of Reform of the State, as well as several pieces of legislation dealing with privatization (Etchemendy 1995, 146).

12. Between 1853 and 1989 Argentine governments issued twenty-five decrees of urgent necessity; from 1989 to August 1994 Menem issued 336 decrees! In the case of the Supreme Court, Menem was able to increase the number of justices from five to nine and to pack the court with his own appointees, thereby gaining control over the judicial branch. In 1990 the court upheld the president's authority to pass decrees deemed of urgent necessity (Jones 1997, 283–86, 288, 298).

13. The Convertibility Law passed in 1991 required the central bank to acquire an additional dollar in gold or foreign currency for every peso added to the monetary base. The convertibility plan devised by economy minister Domingo Cavallo fixed the Argentine peso at a ratio of 1:1 to the U.S. dollar (Acuña 1994, 46–47).

Included in the array of labor reforms implemented by decree in this period were one decree that restricted strikes in essential services and others that tied wage hikes to productivity increases and permitted greater decentralization of bargaining (from industry-level to branch- and firm-level). Menem also made use of his delegated authority through the Law of Economic Emergency to revise wage clauses in public-sector collective bargaining agreements (Etchemendy 1995, 138). Decrees affecting the unions' welfare funds and programs (obras sociales) were issued but not implemented because of labor opposition (McGuire 1995, 226).[14]

Among the pieces of labor legislation sanctioned by Congress before 1994 were Law 24028, which altered the definition of occupational accidents and reduced the amount employers were obligated to pay; Law 24185, which regulated collective agreements for state employees; and Law 24241, which changed the retirement and pension system by establishing a capitalization fund.

The most comprehensive piece of legislation was the National Employment Act, passed by Congress in 1991 after two years of discussion and debate. This act (Law 24013) established a broad range of temporary employment contracts for new categories of workers. The temporary contracts permitted employers to hire and dismiss workers at greatly reduced cost (severance pay did not apply if the employee worked to term), including greatly diminished employer taxes and contributions to such payroll items as social security, social welfare, and so forth. In an effort to address skyrocketing unemployment rates, the law created special terms for the hiring of women, war veterans, persons over the age of forty, and the disabled. There were also incentives for hiring young people under the age of twenty-four, who made up a large proportion of the unemployed. The new law also facilitated the hiring of apprentices and included a training component and a modest unemployment insurance program. Contracts covered under this legislation had a number of restrictions that diminished their use by employers.[15]

14. Obras sociales were established to provide health services for union members and their families. They were financed through union member and employer contributions and constituted a major source of revenue for the unions, surpassing income from dues (McGuire 1995, 224). In addition to health, the obras sociales expanded to include such services as tourism, recreation, libraries, life insurance, and funeral services.

15. Although the 1991 Employment Act represented the greater flexibility of employment contracts, labor allies in Congress succeeded in constricting its broad applicability. Among the restrictions were the provision that unions had to consent to employers' use of

Relief from some of these restrictions was offered to small businesses (those employing fewer than forty employees) in a subsequent reform that added two additional types of employment contract to the four initially contemplated in the 1991 law (Oficina Internacional del Trabajo 1995, 99).

Despite these restrictions, the 1991 Employment Act represented the flexibilization of individual employment contracts, a change the government saw as necessary to combat growing levels of unregistered employment and unemployment, which reached 18.6 percent in 1995. These were tolerated by the CGT in part because of the alliance that the leadership maintained with Menem and because labor had managed to take some key labor topics off the agenda (Etchemendy and Palermo 1997, 31).

The measures that finally succeeded in riling the trade unionists were Menem's decrees in 1991 and 1993 affecting the obras sociales. These decrees threatened a core organizational interest of the unions, namely, their ability to manage the funds and social welfare programs that provided them with revenue and services for their membership.[16] The CGT resisted the decrees by threatening to call a general strike in response to two of them. This led the government to withdraw one decree and to ameliorate the effects of the other by supplementing the obras sociales with funding to compensate for a fall in employer contributions produced by the decree (Murillo 1997, 84). In a third instance, the unions refused to cooperate in turning over the lists of beneficiaries vital to implementation of the decree, which led to its postponement.

Dissatisfaction with Menem's economic and labor policies and the labor leadership's support for the government divided the CGT on several occasions throughout the decade. Between 1989 and 1992 the CGT split into two factions, one more conciliatory (CGT-Azopardo) and the other more combative (CGT-San Martín). A pragmatic third current led by leaders of powerful unions shifted between conciliatory and combative positions (McGuire 1995, 233). The CGT reunited in 1992 when the

---

the new contracts in collective agreements, and a limitation on the number of workers who could be hired under temporary employment contracts.

16. One decree made the tax board rather than the obra social the initial recipient of payments by workers and employees. The threat of a general strike led the government to withdraw the bill writing this into law (McGuire 1997, 226, 231). A second decree (decree 9/93) abolished compulsory affiliation with the obra social of one's union, enabling free competition among health insurance plans (Ranis 1995, xvii–xix). A third decree (decree 2609/93) reduced employer contributions to the funds.

government presented legislation to Congress that posed a threat to the obras sociales. The same year, however, a small group of more militant unions broke away from the CGT to form the Central de los Trabajadores Argentinos (CTA). In 1994 a dissident current within the CGT, the Movimiento de Trabajadores Argentinos (MTA), formed in protest when the CGT cancelled a general strike in exchange for government funds directed to the obras sociales. The CTA and MTA would later participate together in national protests and general strikes in 1994 and 1995.

The largely pro-Menem conciliatory stance of the CGT generated increasing controversy as wage increases, which were tied to productivity by law, became increasingly rare; as temporary work contracts increased job instability; as unemployment continued to grow; and as other measures such as constraints on strikes in essential services and low compensation caps for workplace accidents took effect. Moreover, some unions had "bought into" privatization through stock purchases or by joining boards of enterprises, inviting criticism from those opposed to neoliberal reforms (Murillo 1997; Levitsky and Way 1998).

Yet on some issues the CGT's resistance to reform was particularly strong. This led to significant compromises of government initiatives. What emerged was a trade-off between *individual* flexibilization through such reforms as the 1991 National Employment Act, and the preservation of *collective* resources, evident in the CGT's resistance to reform of obras sociales through the use of the general strike.

This largely defensive strategy emerged as the product of two distinct but related political dynamics. The first concerned the limited room for response by a labor movement under attack in a hostile economic environment. Industrial restructuring, privatization, fiscal austerity, wage controls, and high unemployment were all profoundly threatening to organized labor. The Menem administration clearly saw labor flexibility as a component of economic reform. In this context the CGT leadership saved what it could by concentrating on preserving institutional and legal arrangements that conserved organizational—financial, representational—resources, even if this meant ceding on areas of individual employment protection.

The second dynamic in play was that an important sector of the CGT leadership sought to maintain its privileged relationship with the Menem administration by going along with some of the reforms in the belief that labor would conserve political access and influence down the road. Both dynamics help us understand the conciliatory response of labor in the face of economic and labor reform—up to a point. That point came when crucial resources involving organizational preservation and power were threatened.

In the wake of threats of a general strike over Menem's decrees, and in light of the upcoming presidential elections in which Menem sought re-election, the government adopted a different tack in labor policy. Spearheaded by Labor Minister Armando Caro Figueroa, employer and labor groups met to talk about reforms in the areas of employment, collective bargaining, training, occupational health and safety, work accidents, employee participation, and other topics. The result was the "Framework Agreement for Employment, Productivity, and Social Equity" (Acuerdo Marco) signed by the parties in July 1994.

Drawing on the Acuerdo Marco, the government submitted a number of initiatives to Congress, which were passed in late 1994 and 1995. However, the degree of flexibilization ultimately promoted by the reforms led to strong criticism of the CGT's conciliatory position during the Acuerdo Marco talks. Carlos Tomada, who had been a legal advisor and negotiator for the CGT during the talks, said that their side underestimated the employers' resolve to push these broad agreements toward flexibilizing and cost-lowering initiatives. At the time, he noted, the CGT saw the Acuerdo Marco initiative as an opportunity to reestablish social dialogue and to recover labor's position as a key actor (*protagonismo*) in policymaking. The resulting compromises reflected what was possible under the circumstances: "*la reforma posible.*"[17] The unintended result, however, was an advantage for the coalition of employer organizations and government officials who wanted to further flexibilize Argentine labor law and who then proceeded to press for more reforms.[18]

The Second Menem Administration (1995–1999)

The beginning of Menem's second term was marred by an unexpected turn of events. Mexico's sharp devaluation of the peso in December

17. Carlos Tomada, labor lawyer and professor of labor relations at the Universidad de Buenos Aires, interview by author, 5 November 1999, Buenos Aires, Argentina. (Tomada became Néstor Kirchner's labor minister in 2003).

18. Among the new laws passed in this period were one that created more flexible terms for employment contracts for small and medium-sized businesses (Law 24467); one that regulated part-time, "atypical," and apprenticeship contracts; and a controversial initiative that dramatically reduced employer liability in occupational accidents.

1994 had sparked a global financial crisis that affected "emerging markets" around the world, including Argentina, whose capital account deficit and other macroeconomic indicators looked similar to Mexico's. Investment in Argentina slowed, sparking further concerns about the Argentine economy.

Unemployment in Argentina grew at an alarming rate, peaking at 18.6 percent in 1995 (McGuire 1997, 222). This gave rise to an extended debate about the sources of unemployment and possible remedies. Some argued for further labor market reform, even though unemployment continued to rise after earlier flexibility measures had been adopted. These included the temporary contracts made possible by the 1991 National Employment Act, a growing number of flexibility clauses in collective agreements, and the de facto decentralization of collective bargaining through a growing number of plant-level contracts, as well as an increase in informal or unregistered employment (*trabajo en negro*) (Murillo 1997, 80; Etchemendy 1995, 141).

The economic and employment context increased tensions between labor and government. In 1996 the government agreed to implement a package of economic adjustment measures recommended by the IMF. It also proposed labor reforms that coincided with an IMF memorandum urging labor law reform in Argentina.[19] The adjustment package and proposed labor reforms spurred the labor movement to action, and in August and September the unions engaged in mobilizations, work stoppages, and strikes, backed by both opposition parties. Menem downplayed the significance of the mobilizations and announced plans to flexibilize labor legislation further in a "second reform of the state" needed to produce economic growth.[20]

---

19. Among the IMF proposals were the substitution of the system of severance pay with an individual capitalization fund similar to those that had been established elsewhere in Latin America, and removal of the provision concerning "ultraactividad" (*Latin American Regional Report: Southern Cone*, 17 October 1996, http://www.latinnews.com). The latter referred to the stipulation in the Argentine law on collective contracts that the terms of a contract would remain in force upon the contract's expiration if no new agreement had been negotiated. Some collective agreements had not been substantially renegotiated since 1975 because of labor's fear that earlier victories in bargaining would be rolled back. Other IMF interests included the decentralization of collective bargaining and extending the length of the probationary period for new hires from one month to six months.

20. Among the reforms Menem said were needed were the decentralization of bargaining, more flexible working hours and holiday arrangements, cuts in severance pay, and reduction of the "13th month" bonus (*Latin American Regional Report: Southern Cone*, 17 October 1996, 2, http://www.latinnews.com).

Menem followed through with more labor decrees. In October 1996 he issued a decree calling for deregulation of the obras sociales and for employees' "free choice" among plans. The measure, which had been successfully blocked before, angered labor and succeeded in unifying the CGT. Menem also issued decrees terminating "*ultraactividad*" and decentralizing collective bargaining.[21] In contrast to the government's earlier flexibilization policies, which largely affected individual contracts, these reforms threatened core organizational interests such as union control over social welfare funds, contract terms in branch-level agreements, and the level at which collective agreements would be negotiated.

Labor's mobilization against the economic and labor reforms occurred in a relatively favorable political climate. Unemployment and economic crisis had provoked widespread discontent. Menem's overuse of decrees was beginning to wear on the population. And opposition parties were willing to support labor mobilizations and capitalize on the dissatisfaction with the government in view of the legislative elections coming up the following year.

In this context the CGT spearheaded a third general strike on 26 December 1996, announcing, "If there are more decrees, there will be more strikes."[22] In response to the CGT's legal challenge to Menem's decrees, the court ruled that the decrees concerning collective bargaining were unconstitutional, given that only recognized unions (those with *personería gremial*) could be charged with the task of negotiating collective agreements. Menem immediately threatened to impeach the judge who had issued the decision and appeal to the Supreme Court, but after a similar finding against two other decrees by a second judge, he backed off.[23]

After this failed round of efforts to impose labor reform by decree, Menem offered to work with the CGT on a new labor reform package. The government spent early 1997 working on a draft reform bill with the CGT and in "consultation" with business groups. But rejection of the draft reform bill by business as well as by the MTA and CTA and some PJ deputies in Congress led the administration to postpone labor reform until after the legislative elections in October 1997.

21. See earlier note for a definition of ultraactividad.
22. *Latin American Weekly Report*, 7 January 1997, http://www.latinnews.com.
23. Ibid., 14 January 1997.

In the elections, a center-left alliance formed by the Frente País Solidario (FREPASO) and Unión Cívica Radical (UCR) won a majority in the lower house of Congress. The labor law reform bill was taken up again. It went through several rounds of revisions in discussions with the CGT and business representatives, passed the Senate in May 1998, and then moved to the lower house. There it faced considerable opposition from the FREPASO-UCR majority. Menem also encountered difficulty in mobilizing members of his own party in support of the reform. Meanwhile, the dissident labor groups MTA and CTA held rallies outside Congress every Wednesday, when the lower house met in session, to protest the reform bill.[24] Supporters of Menem's proposal attempted to call a vote on the labor bill on three separate occasions, but they could never secure a quorum. The reform package finally passed on 3 September 1998, after Menem personally pressured the president of the Union Industrial Argentina, also a deputy, to appear on the floor for the vote.

The labor reform that passed in September 1998 (Law 25013) was a mix of changes to several laws affecting both individual and collective labor relations. While some measures did address the lowering of employer costs, the most notable thing about the law was how it reaffirmed the CGT's chief organizational interests and how much it seemed to disregard IMF recommendations. Employers dubbed the law the *contrareforma* (counterreform). Virtually all of the atypical contracts that had been set up earlier under the National Employment Act in 1991 were rescinded in this 1998 law. The unions had long opposed such contracts as *contratos basura*, "garbage contracts" that did little to combat unemployment and instead encouraged more job insecurity. The trade-off for retracting these temporary contracts, however, was to lower severance payments for new workers hired under indefinite employment contracts. The law also reduced the probation period for new employees to one month, which differed from the IMF recommendation that the probation period be extended to six months.[25] In the collective area, Law 25013 reaffirmed ultraactividad and centralized collective bargaining.[26] The CGT regarded this as a victory, given the long-standing pres-

24. Héctor Recalde, legal advisor to MTA, interview by author, 1 November 1999, Buenos Aires.
25. The probation period could be extended to 180 days through collective bargaining.
26. Collective contracts that expired would maintain their terms until the negotiation of a new contract rather than revert to basic labor law, and the responsibility for bargaining would reside with the industry or branch-level union.

sure from the IMF and employers as well as from government to change these very provisions.

Why the turnaround on labor reform at the end of Menem's term? First, the electoral calendar clearly colored the government's decision to negotiate the labor reform package with the CGT. The success of the FREPASO-UCR alliance in the 1997 legislative elections signaled trouble for the Peronists in the 1999 presidential elections. Menem's rapprochement with the CGT can best be understood in this light. Second, the labor movement had become more combative in Menem's second term, carrying out a total of three general strikes in response to the president's labor decrees and economic reforms. The emergence of more militant labor formations both outside and inside the CGT (the CTA and MTA) also established the CGT leadership as a more desirable negotiating partner for the 1998 labor reform. Finally, the government had pledged to the IMF that it would issue a labor reform bill before the end of the year. The only way to comply with this deadline was to collaborate with the CGT, even though this produced an outcome that fell well short of IMF expectations.

For most of the decade, however, the Menem government had implemented a number of flexibility-inducing labor reforms despite its alliance with the CGT (see Table 3.1). Yet even in an unfavorable economic transition context, the labor movement still managed to resist or shape those reforms that would most affect the CGT unions' core interests, their financial and organizational resources. These included the deregulation of obras sociales, from which unions derived financial resources, but also the further decentralization of bargaining and the lapse of contract terms upon a contract's expiration, or the end of ultraactividad. The CGT accomplished this by resorting to traditional militant tactics such as strikes and by working with PJ deputies in Congress, much as it had during the democratic transition period. But these methods were less effective in an environment where government commitment to reform was high and international pressure, particularly from the IMF, was strong. Against this pressure, flexibility was able to advance in the area of individual legislation, especially in hiring and dismissals, while labor concentrated its defense on collective legislation.

Brazil: The First Cardoso Administration (1995–1999)

The success of the Real Plan and Cardoso's election to the presidency marked the beginning of a more concerted neoliberal policy period in

TABLE 3.1   Selected Labor Reform Legislation Under President Menem, Argentina (1989–1998)

Law	Content	Orientation
Decree 2184/90 (October 1990)	Limited right to strike in essential services	Restrictive[1]
Decree 1334/91 (June 1991)	Linked wage increases to rise in productivity	Restrictive
Decree 2284/91 (November 1991)	Facilitated decentralized bargaining	Flexible[2]
Law 24013-Ley Nacional de Empleo (December 1991)	Set short-term employment contracts; set cap on severance pay	Flexible
Law 24028 (December 1991)	Set restrictions on qualifying events for occupational accidents	Flexible/restrictive
Law 24185 (December 1992)	Regulated collective agreements in national public administration	Protective
Decree 9/93 (January 1993)	Allowed workers to choose obra social	Flexible
Decree 470/93 (replaced 1334/91) (March 1993)	Introduced new criteria for govt. approval of collective agreements; established "articulated" bargaining	Restrictive/flexible
Law 24241 (October 1993)	Set capitalization fund as option in retirement and pensions	Flexible
Decree 2609/93 (December 1993)	Reduced employer contribution to obras sociales/social security (later modified)	Flexible[3]
Law 24465 (March 1995)	Created part-time, apprentice, and probation contracts	Flexible
Law 24467 (May 1995)	Mandated special contract terms and lower costs for small and medium-sized enterprises	Flexible
Law 24522 (July 1995)	Set special contracts for firms in economic emergency	Flexible
Law 24557 (September 1995)	Shifted workers' compensation liability from employer to social security in occupational accidents	Flexible
Decree 292/95 (September 1995)	Lowered employer contributions to obras sociales	Flexible
Law 24635 (April 1996)	Made conciliation obligatory before appeal to labor courts	Indeterminate[4]

Law	Content	Orientation
Decree 1141/96 (October 1996)	Gave workers option to switch obra social	Flexible
Law 25013 (September 1998)	Reformed contracts, severance, bargaining (see Table 3.3)	Mixed: protective with some flexibility

1. *Restrictive* refers to measures that place limits on collective bargaining rights, strikes, and worker organization, or that otherwise restrict protections and rights to which workers are entitled by international standards (e.g., reductions in health and safety protection, workers' compensation, etc.).

2. *Flexible* refers to measures that lower employer costs, ease their ability to dismiss workers, or correspond to recommendations of IFIs in collective labor relations (see Chapter 2).

3. The Menem government compensated obra social funds for loss due to employer reduction in contributions after the CGT threatened to strike.

4. Unions typically regard obligatory conciliation as unfavorable and court decisions as favorable to workers, even though the latter are often delayed.

Brazil (Haggard and Kaufman 1995, 199). Like Menem, Cardoso enjoyed a number of advantages not shared by his predecessors. In particular, the severity of the economic crisis in 1994 provided Cardoso with a window of opportunity for pushing further on economic and state reform (Mainwaring 1997, 104).

The recession of the early 1990s had already hurt wages and employment, particularly in manufacturing. Although Cardoso's stabilization policies helped real wages by bringing down inflation, his efforts to broaden privatization of state-owned enterprises and to further liberalize trade (programs that had been initiated by Collor) led to more layoffs and disruption for workers. Trade opening especially affected the auto and textile sectors, leading to a sharp reduction in employment. The decline of employment in manufacturing as well as in banking and the civil service, which were traditionally highly unionized sectors, reduced union membership levels. High levels of unemployment and an increase in temporary and informal-sector work also reduced union influence. Unions went on the defensive, shifting their focus from wage increases to job security (Bureau of National Affairs 1996). Unemployment soon became a central issue in national politics and remained on the agenda into the 1998 presidential elections.

The political context was also unfavorable for labor. The relationship between the union centrals and the Cardoso administration was tense from the beginning, especially in the case of the CUT, which had backed the PT candidate in the elections. Cardoso also indicated early on that he was willing to take a hard line with the unions. This was made clear in May 1995, when Cardoso sent in the military to break a strike by Petrobrás oil workers.[27]

Congress was also unsympathetic to labor's concerns. Among the first actions Congress undertook concerning labor was to denounce Brazil's ratification of ILO Convention 158 on termination of employment.[28] The rationale for such a move was to make labor markets more flexible by removing restrictions on dismissals; numerous court cases filed by unions charging unjustified dismissals under the convention were a leading incentive for the action. The denunciation angered the CUT and remained a sore point in its relations with the government for years after (von Bülow 1998).

The Cardoso government matched its economic policies with labor reforms intended to lower costs and to make employment and labor relations more flexible. Rather than introduce a comprehensive reform, the government issued incremental regulatory changes in a way that was described by labor advocates as *comendo pelas bordas* (nibbling around the edges) of Brazilian labor law. Cardoso resorted to the use of "provisional measures" and legislative decrees to pass several labor provisions during 1995–96.[29] In theory, such measures should only have been used in emergency situations, or cases of "relevance and urgency" (Mainwaring 1997, 62–63). But, like his counterpart in Argentina, Cardoso resorted to such measures to overcome potential opposition in Congress. The government argued that introducing piecemeal reforms was the only way to pass legislation through Congress, and that provisional measures were necessary in cases that required

---

27. *Latin American Regional Report: Southern Cone*, 8 June 1995 and 13 July 1995, http://www.latinnews.com.

28. The Termination of Employment Convention (No. 158) obliges ratifying states to establish the grounds upon which a worker can be terminated from employment. Employment may not be terminated by the employer unless there is a valid reason connected with the capacity or conduct of the worker or based on the operational requirements of the undertaking. See http://www.ilo.org/public/english/standards/norm/whatare/stndards/empl.htm.

29. Article 62 of the 1988 constitution allowed presidents to use these provisional measures, which had the force of law for thirty days without congressional approval. The constitution calls for such measures to be rejected if not approved by Congress within the thirty days. Presidents have regularly reissued these decrees after they have expired, and in practice they remain in effect unless rejected by Congress. Provisional measures have been used widely to legislate key provisions of the Real Plan and of Collor's economic plan, and Sarney relied heavily on them during his term. They have also been applied to labor policy.

emergency action linked to economic matters, such as the de-indexation of wages.[30]

Most provisional measures issued on labor matters were restrictive on collective activities and flexible in employment relations. One provisional measure called for substituting unions with "representative commissions" in profit-sharing negotiations, a measure that was later successfully challenged in court (von Bülow 1998).[31] Two other provisional measures ended wage indexation, which had been in place since the military dictatorship. One decree limited the right to strike for federal employees. A bill was introduced granting the labor ministry authority to levy strike fines in the case of "abusive" strikes. And, although not a government initiative, a cooperatives law put forward by a PT deputy to help landless peasants was being used by employers to create "false cooperatives," vitiating the employment relationship and thereby enabling employers to avoid their legal obligations.

One development that undermined opposition to labor reforms was the willingness of the CUT's main rival, Força Sindical (FS), to accept many flexible provisions in its collective agreements. FS's more flexible contracts were seen as a forerunner of the broader kinds of changes the government and employers wanted to see implemented in a labor reform (von Bülow 1998). FS's actions undermined the CUT's position and curried favor with the Cardoso administration. Indeed, FS's allies in Congress were instrumental in backing labor reform initiatives in this period (Cardoso 2000).

In early 1996 the labor minister, Paulo Paiva, introduced in Congress a labor law package that addressed short-term employment, flexible workdays, and flexible compensation. The government proposals would establish fixed-term employment contracts, reduce employer contributions to the FGTS, establish an "hours bank," in which workers would be compensated with time off rather than pay in cases of over-

30. Paulo Paiva, vice president, Inter-American Development Bank and former minister of labor of Brazil (January 1995–March 1998), interview by author, 22 March 2000, Washington, D.C.

31. The expanded use of profit sharing effectively decentralized bargaining since profits were determined at the firm level, whereas collective agreements in Brazil traditionally and legally took place at the level of the sindicato. A provisional measure on profit sharing regulated this constitutional right, but in a way that labor criticized, by making profit sharing a "faculty," not an "obligation," of employers, and by limiting workers' right to financial information about the firm, among other things (Freitas 2000).

time, and enable employers and workers to negotiate flexible work schedules. The measures, intended to address unemployment and meet employer demands for greater flexibility, were controversial and moved slowly through Congress (Bensusán and von Bülow 1997, 205).[32] In January 1998 final approval for the legislation came from the Senate, after passing in the lower house.[33]

With the exception of the "hours bank" proposal, which the CUT-affiliated metalworkers' union in Sao Bernardo supported, the CUT and CGT remained opposed to the labor reforms, arguing that they would erode the rights of all workers. FS, by contrast, had pursued similar provisions in its earlier collective agreements and thus supported the proposals that would legalize its efforts. Some employer organizations also resisted the temporary contracts measure because the reduction in employer contributions (a feature of the short-term contracts) meant fewer revenues accruing to employer federations that managed professional training and social assistance programs financed by the payroll taxes (Sistema "S").[34]

The Cardoso government also revisited the question of constitutional reform in 1998, focusing on those provisions that had remained untouched in the constitutional convention. The government introduced a constitutional amendment addressing the elimination of the union tax, reform of Article 8 dealing with unicidade, and the removal of the labor courts' "normative power."[35] Included in the proposal was a measure that would limit sindicatos' representation to cover only unionized

---

32. Neither did the measures improve unemployment rates or the precarious nature of employment. The percentage of self-employed workers and workers without a formal contract jumped from 48.9 percent in 1996 to almost 60 percent by the end of the decade (Portella de Castro 2001, 55).

33. While aimed at generating greater flexibility, the package of labor legislation contained a number of restrictions. Temporary employment contracts would be legal, but they were restricted to a maximum of 20 percent of the workforce in firms employing more than 200 workers, 35 percent for medium-sized firms (between 50 and 199 workers), and up to 50 percent for smaller firms (fewer than 50 employees) (von Bülow 1998). The precise allocation of temporary contracts would be determined through bargaining with the sindicato in the case of medium-sized and large firms. Moreover, only new jobs would be subject to temporary contracts, and then only in firms that increased the overall number of employees in a given period. According to the labor minister, these constraints were needed to ensure that the temporary contracts would be used to increase employment and not to substitute temporary for "indefinite" workers, and to curtail a dramatic reduction in revenue from payroll contributions. Paiva, interview.

34. Paiva, interview.

35. The labor courts' "normative power" (poder normativo) refers to their ability to make laws rather than simply apply them (Amadeo et al. 1995, 43–44).

workers rather than the entire professional category. Labor opposed the absence of mechanisms to determine which union would have bargaining rights in the event that more than one union claimed them, as well as the restrictions on representation to members only (Portella de Castro 2001, 57–58). Moreover, the CUT and other labor organizations were wary of reforming these parts of the constitution, given the context of economic instability provoked by the Asian financial crisis, growing unemployment, and increasing flexibilization. Because of divisions within government as well as the opposition of labor and employer sindicatos, changes to these core features of the Brazilian corporatist system were shelved in 2000.[36]

Despite earlier speculation that no further labor reforms would be introduced in 1998 because of the upcoming elections, two factors helped to change the environment for reform: high unemployment, made worse by the financial instability caused by the Asian crisis and speculation about an upcoming devaluation, and the presidential elections. In April 1998 unemployment in Brazil and particularly in São Paulo, the largest industrial center of the country, hit a high of 13 percent. Cardoso was concerned about re-election in October, and public worries over unemployment had lowered his standing in the polls. His chief rival again would be Lula, who was capitalizing on this public dissatisfaction. Cardoso appointed a new labor minister and charged him with devising solutions to unemployment that would have a strong short-term impact in time for the elections.

Under pressure from the Cardoso administration and just before the 1998 elections, Congress approved a provisional measure aimed at easing unemployment. Among the items included in this "package against unemployment" were a provision permitting part-time contracts of up to twenty-five hours a week and a measure permitting temporary suspensions of employees of up to six months. During this period workers would participate in training programs and receive benefits equal to unemployment insurance. At the end of the period, employers could rehire these workers or dismiss them. The controversial measure was meant to facilitate dismissals for employers during the economic recession, while at the same time providing some protection and training for the employee. A third provision modified the earlier measure regarding

36. An exception was Senate approval for a controversial constitutional amendment ending job stability for public servants in March 1998.

the hours bank and extended the period during which comp time could be used from four months to one year. This was to allow for greater flexibility in scheduling and deploying the workforce, but many observers felt that it would end overtime pay altogether (von Bülow 1998).

By the end of Cardoso's first term, the government had implemented two separate flexibility packages in addition to a number of provisional measures that constrained collective activities. Efforts to remove the final vestiges of the corporatist system remained unsuccessful.[37] Labor reforms targeted greater flexibility in employment and working conditions without further liberalization of the corporatist system or a deeper democratization of industrial relations in Brazil. As in Argentina, high unemployment and the electoral cycle were the key factors motivating the substance and timing of labor reform packages.

The Second Cardoso Administration (1999–2003)

In October 1998 Fernando Henrique Cardoso won re-election easily, handing Lula his third defeat at the polls. Cardoso's new labor minister, Francisco Dornelles, continued to speak of the need to further flexibilize Brazilian labor laws and to amend the constitution in the areas of union organization, the union tax, and the system of labor justice. The backdrop was concern about the economy in the wake of the Asian financial crisis. The government devalued the *real* in January 1999 and the IMF set aside US$41.5 billion in reserves, which it doled out in installments and which was contingent upon lowering federal expenses through pension and tax reform. Unemployment continued unabated, particularly in the state of São Paulo.

The Cardoso government turned its attention again to the constitutional amendment proposal it had introduced in Congress in 1998. The four constitutional changes the government wanted to target were elimination of the union tax; an end to unicidade and the establishment of "union pluralism"; the elimination of tripartite representation and poder normativo in the labor courts; and flexibilization of working conditions listed under Article 7, including wages, work shifts, and length of the workday. The amendment to end the tripartite structure of the

---

37. A 1997 constitutional amendment to abolish the union tax and regulate contributions to confederations remained stalled in Congress (von Bülow 2000).

courts (*juiz classista*) was the only one of these initiatives to pass.[38] An amendment that would have restricted the normative power of the labor courts remained stalled in Congress. Another amendment to change the system of unicidade also met with such opposition that the government did not push it. Similarly, there was still considerable resistance to eliminating the union tax.[39] The government's proposal for a constitutional reform of Article 7, which would have allowed the "negotiated to supercede the legislated" by permitting parties in bargaining to agree to exceptions to standards on working conditions listed in the constitution, caused such a negative reaction that it was withdrawn.

Instead of pushing the most controversial items (the imposto, unicidade, and poder normativo), the government proceeded quickly in two additional areas. The administration chose to target the backlog of cases in the courts. It called for the creation of a layer of labor courts to deal with *pequenas causas,* cases involving sums of less than forty times the minimum wage. A second measure, related to the first one, established "prior conciliation commissions" in the workplace. Grievances would have to pass through the commission, made up of employer and employee representatives, before going to the court system. This was to be another means of lowering the caseload of the courts but also of encouraging direct negotiations between employers and employees. PT deputies were divided in their support for this measure. Some were concerned about the lack of a union role in the commission while others argued that this was an opportunity to obtain representation of workers at the workplace, for years a CUT demand.[40] Both of these reforms, as well as the reform terminating the juiz classista system, went into effect in January 2000 (see Table 3.2, for a list of reforms under Cardoso).

Toward the end of Cardoso's second term, the government revived the proposal to enable parties to negotiate exceptions to legislated standards. The focus was now on a reform of the CLT rather than the constitution, which would make its passage through Congress relatively

---

38. In this case the CUT supported the measure and the PT played a key role in its passage in Congress. Parties closer to the Cardoso administration continued to defend the old legislation; the appointments to juiz classista were coveted for their high salaries and were an important means of state cooptation of sindicatos (von Bülow 2000).

39. Ives Gandra da Silva Martins Filho, special advisor to the president in juridical affairs, interview by author, 27 August 1999, Brasília, Brazil.

40. The argument against the measure was that without union involvement employers might be able to manipulate workers on the commission. The law allowed unions only to oversee the selection of workers' representatives to the committee (von Bülow 2000).

TABLE 3.2   Selected Labor Legislation and Reform Initiatives Under President Cardoso, Brazil (1994–2002)

Law	Content	Orientation
MP[1] 1053/95	Prohibited wage indexation clauses in contracts	Flexible
MP 1070/95	Made court decisions immediately applicable to collective conflicts before appeal[2]	Flexible
Decree 2100 (12/96)	Denounced ILO Convention 158	Flexible
Law-project 1802/96	Enabled tribunals to fine unions engaged in "abusive" strikes	Stalled
Law 9468/97	Allowed voluntary retirement of federal employees	Flexible
Constitutional amendment 20/98[3]	Expanded social security reform by adopting complementary pension system, including individual capitalization	Flexible
Law 9601/98 (January 1998)	Set fixed-term contracts with union negotiation, imposed caps on percentage of workforce; set up "hours bank" that permitted flexible scheduling with "time off"	Flexible
PEC[4] 623/98 (1998)	Proposed to amend constitution regarding union tax, unicidade, and labor courts' normative power	Withdrawn
MP 1709-4/98 (November 1998)	Allowed part-time employment contracts;[5] extended "hours-bank" term to one year	Flexible
MP 1726/98 (November 1998)	Allowed temporary suspension of employment contract	Flexible[6]
Law 9957 (January 2000)	Set separate procedures for low-cost cases before labor courts (rito sumaríssimo)	Flexible[7]

Law	Content	Orientation
Law 9958 (January 2000)	Set commissions for individual conflict resolution (*comissões de conciliacão prévia*)	Flexible[8]
Project to amend CLT	Allowed "negotiated" to supersede "legislated"	Passed lower house December 2001, stalled in Senate

Sources: Portella de Castro (2001); U.S. Department of Labor, ILAB, *Foreign Labor Trends Report* (Brazil 2002), at http://www.ilo.org/dyn/natlex; von Bülow (1998, 2000); Freitas (2000). The legislation can be found in ILO-NATLEX, at http://www.ilo.org/dyn/natlex/natlex_browse.home; and Senado Federal do Brasil, at http://www.senado.gov.br/sf/.

1. *Medida provisória* (provisional measure). See text for explanation.

2. This changed previous law, which permitted conditions to stand until appealed to supreme labor court.

3. Regulated by complementary laws 108 and 109, passed in 1998.

4. PEC stands for "project to amend the constitution" in Portuguese.

5. No consultation with union necessary for part-time contract use. Allowed temporary suspension of part-time contracts.

6. Allowed for worker education or training during suspension of contract.

7. Administrative measure aimed at moving smaller cases more quickly through labor justice system (favorable to workers).

8. Aimed to make resolution of individual grievances more agile. It was seen by unions as potentially favorable, as it allows commissions to involve several unions or firms and therefore provides a basis for transcending the confines of the legal union structure (Portella de Castro 2001, 56).

easier. The lower house passed the measure in December 2001. In response, the CUT began to plan a general strike for March 2002, when the bill would reach the Senate. However, the reform bill remained stalled in the Senate through the remainder of Cardoso's term.

What impact did the Cardoso labor reforms have? The measures to expedite procedures in the labor justice system did appear to help, although complaints about delays and the backlog of cases persisted. The initiatives aimed at reducing unemployment proved less successful. Legislation easing the hiring of temporary workers reportedly created relatively few jobs (41,377 in the first four years), while employers and workers resorted infrequently to laws permitting flex-time via the hours bank and training for laid-off workers. These limited results revived the debate about the causes of unemployment, the Cardoso government placing the blame on union resistance to these policies, and trade unionists claiming that the labor market in Brazil was already flexible and that such reforms would thus not produce employment gains (U.S. Department of State, 2003b, 12).

In both Argentina and Brazil the divisive character of labor law reform was evident in the methods employed by the Menem and Cardoso administrations: decrees, provisional measures, and hardball tactics vis-à-vis Congress. The labor-party alliance in Argentina gave labor some influence over the outcome of the final labor law packages passed before the 1999 presidential elections. In Brazil, however, there was no labor-state alliance between the largest central, the CUT, and the government parties (although FS tried to play the role of ally). Yet more extensive collective reforms, especially those that would affect financial resources and sindicato organizational structure, were not altered despite the government's intentions. Most worker sindicatos resisted reforms that would affect their core organizational resources through elimination of the union tax and unicidade.

The advantages of the corporatist system were widely diffused in Brazil, extending to the labor courts as well as to employer sindicatos. Opposition to reforms of collective provisions of the constitution, therefore, came from multiple sectors: labor unions, employer sindicatos, Congress, and the courts. The CUT itself remained divided on many proposed reforms. In the past, the CUT had publicly shared the government's goal of eliminating corporatist provisions from the constitution. But in the new, more hostile economic environment of the late 1990s, labor was less inclined to support such changes, especially without institutional guarantees for sindicatos during a transition period (Crivelli 1998). Increasing trends toward outsourcing, subcontracting, and industry relocation, as well as persistent high unemployment, threatened the bargaining power of unions and commanded labor's attention more immediately than changes in the labor code.[41]

TOWARD LABOR RIGHTS AND PROTECTION IN THE 2000S

Although both the Argentine and Brazilian labor movements were able to resist further flexibilization attempts by their governments, the cases diverged when Fernando de la Rúa came to office in 2000. The new

41. Marcelo Sereno, national secretary of organization, CUT, interview by author, 24 August 1999, São Paulo, Brazil.

Alianza government of de la Rúa tackled labor law reform early in the administration. It capitalized on its strong mandate after the elections to push through labor reform quickly and set the tone for its dealings with labor for the rest of its term. The government drafted a labor reform bill that again addressed those provisions the Menem government was unable to change. These were also the key concerns of the IMF: ultraactividad, level of bargaining, and an extended probationary period.[42]

The reform project split the CGT. While some CGT leaders, led by Rodolfo Daer, called off a scheduled strike on the eve of 24 February 2000, after an eleventh-hour agreement with the government, the secretary general-elect of the CGT, Hugo Moyano, went forward with a rally that drew more than twenty thousand people to downtown Buenos Aires and vowed to continue to fight the reform bill. Meanwhile, the bill passed the lower house of Congress, where the PJ voted against it as a bloc, even though on individual parts of the bill party deputies were split. The bill then went to the Senate, where the PJ majority threatened to amend it.

Caught off guard and internally divided, the CGT was in a weak position in this round of reform. The de la Rúa government took advantage of the CGT's low prestige and lack of readiness to launch a strong public relations attack on the unions. The government wanted to demonstrate that it would not bow to union pressure (Warn 2000). It also bet on other politicians' interests in working with the new government in gaining support for the reform bill. Many PJ governors, intent on maintaining good relations with the federal government, publicly backed the bill. The reform was also intended to demonstrate to the IMF the new government's ability to meet its commitments. The government reached several agreements with the IMF in this period, and both the IMF and the World Bank praised de la Rúa's labor and economic reforms. Although the labor reform was presented as a series of measures intended to combat unemployment and unregistered employment, it also reflected an effort to further erode the national union leadership's political influence.[43]

42. A key concern of the unions was the decentralization of collective bargaining, whereby employers could determine the level of bargaining (regional, enterprise) and in case of dispute the issue would go to mediation or arbitration.

43. The de la Rúa government also addressed some issues of concern to the ILO. Decree No. 843/2000, for example, permitted strikes in essential services and called for an inde-

The Senate finally passed the government's reform bill in April 2000, but victory came at great political cost.[44] The CGT had waged four general strikes against the reform. Violent protests left one person dead at the hands of police and dozens wounded. In June 2000 journalists reported that senators were bribed in exchange for their support of the measure. In October 2000 the vice president, from the government's coalition partner FREPASO, resigned in protest over the cabinet promotion of the labor minister (who had been implicated in the bribery scandal), thus creating a political crisis.

The allegations—later confirmed—of bribery in the Senate gave the law's opponents greater leverage. Members of Congress moved to suspend the labor law in light of the bribery allegations. Meanwhile, 2001 saw deterioration into greater economic and political instability, culminating with de la Rúa's resignation in December 2001 (Epstein and Pion-Berlin 2006).

While Interim President Alberto Rodríguez Saá vowed to repeal de la Rúa's labor reform, the next interim president, Eduardo Duhalde, also from the PJ, was more interested in rescuing some of its positive aspects, and motions to draw up a new proposal began in Congress (Rodríguez Yebra 2002). The Peronists again obtained the majority in both houses of Congress, further aiding labor's quest. However, a sector of the Peronist bloc in Congress presented a proposal that not only would rescind the reform law but would also restore provisions from earlier laws, namely ultraactividad and a return to centralized collective bargaining. Both of these were controversial points and ones not supported by the Duhalde government, which threatened to veto the bill if it passed.[45]

---

pendent commission (instead of the government) to determine which minimum services to offer in the event of a strike. Decree No. 757/2001 allowed for "merely registered" unions to defend and represent the interests of their members and changed the tax status of such unions to the same status enjoyed by nonprofit organizations. This went to the issue of recognition by the government (personería gremial), which granted certain privileges to "recognized" unions over those with registration only. See ILO-CEACR (2001).

44. The bill passed the Senate by a vote of 121 to 84. Newspapers reported that proceedings in the Senate clearly revealed that prior agreement had been reached, thus facilitating a positive vote. Among the apparent agreements was the government's commitment to dedicate more funds to a job creation program, the Planes Trabajar, a measure that passed unanimously minutes before the labor reform bill was introduced. La Nación, 9 December 2000, Página Política, available at http://www.lanacion.com.ar/oo/o9/12/p.17.htm.

45. Gustavo Ybarra, "Vuelve al Senado la reforma laboral," La Nación, 13 March 2002, available at http://www.lanacion.com.ar/o2/o3/13/dp_380510.asp.

By early 2004 the new government of Néstor Kirchner (who assumed office in May 2003) announced that it was ready to present a draft labor bill that would replace Law 25250, now known as the *ley de sobornos,* or "law of the bribes."[46] The bill reduced the probationary period to no more than three months, restored the traditional severance pay formula for dismissals, restored ultraactividad, and established "articulated" bargaining, in which sectoral agreements (*por actividad*) would establish the floor upon which regional, local, or firm-level agreements would be based (see Table 3.3). More important, all three labor centrals (the two CGTs and the CTA) and the UIA, the key employer group, were in agreement on the draft proposal.[47] In a sharp reversal of previous government positions, Labor Minister Carlos Tomada stated that the new bill "seeks to establish job stability, which improves workers' prospects for consumption, as well as the competitiveness and productivity of employers."[48] The new law, he said, "is protective, but balanced and respectful of the constitution and of the general principles of the ILO in the areas of employment law, labor law, and labor administration" (Tomada 2004).[49] Tomada insisted that it was not the task of labor law to create jobs; rather, it was up to economic policy to generate employment.[50] The new law was passed by the Senate in February 2004 by a vote of 66 to 1, and sent on to the lower house, where representa-

46. In December 2003 former Senate clerk Mario Pontaquarto admitted to receiving from a state intelligence agency, under the direction of a close friend of de la Rúa's, US$5 million, which he was to distribute to senators in exchange for their votes for the labor reform bill in April 2000. This admission reopened the criminal case. See "Argentina: Bribery Scandal Prompts Senate Reform," *Brazil Report,* 27 January 2004, http://www.latin news.com.

47. "Ya se definió la reforma laboral y hay acuerdo sindical," *La Voz del Interior* online, Córdoba, Argentina, 25 January 2004, available at http://www.lavozdelinterior .com/; "Sancionó diputados la ley laboral del gobierno," *La Nación Line,* 3 March 2004, available at http://www.lanacion.com.ar/04/03/03/dp_578108.asp.

48. *La Nación Line,* 11 February 2004, available at http://www.lanacion.com.ar/04/ 02/11/dp_572249.asp. In addition to addressing the issues of probation, severance, and collective bargaining, the draft bill restored the concept of ultraactividad and sought to strengthen the enforcement capability of the labor ministry as well as to improve the process of labor registration.

49. According to Labor Minister Carlos Tomada, the new law was guided by two main criteria: to offer solutions that would assist in generating decent work, that is, quality work realized under conditions of freedom, equality, security and human dignity, and, second, to promote legal formulas that would stimulate collective bargaining, norms that favored the worker, and the solution of conflicts via agreement (Tomada 2004).

50. *La Voz del Interior* online, Córdoba, Argentina, 16 February 2004; available at http://www.lavozdelinterior.com.ar.

TABLE 3.3   Comparison of Argentine Labor Law Reforms Under Presidents
Menem (1998), De la Rúa (2000), and Kirchner (2004)

Provisions	Menem Law 25013 (1998)	De la Rúa Law 25250 (2000)	Kirchner Law 25877 (2004)
Probation period	Reduced from three months to one month, with extension to six months possible via collective agreement (Art. 3)	Three months; can be extended to six months via collective agreement. For small and medium-sized enterprises, 6 months with possible extension to 12 months (Art. 1)	Three-month maximum, without severance but with fifteen-day advance notice (if no advance notice given, fifteen-day severance to be granted) (Arts. 2, 3)
Severance[1]	One-twelfth of remuneration over last year or period of time over ten days for hires after October 1998 (Art. 7)	Same	One month's wages per year worked or period of time greater than three months (Art. 3)
Collective Bargaining			
Contract expiration-ultra-actividad	Two-year period for renegotiation upon petition of either party for contracts after 1988 (Art. 12)	Mandatory renegotiation of all expired agreements. Labor Ministry may intervene if no agreement (Art. 8)	Ultraactividad restored. No renegotiation required (Art. 13)
Bargaining level/scope	Bargaining carried out by higher-level union[2] (Art. 14)	Priority granted to agreement at most decentralized level (Arts. 22, 24, 25)	"Articulated" bargaining with level to be determined by parties (Art. 23); agreement most favorable to employee prevails (Art. 24b)

Provisions	Menem Law 25013 (1998)	De la Rúa Law 25250 (2000)	Kirchner Law 25877 (2004)
Right to strike: essential services[3]	NA	NA	In case of conflict, minimum services to be maintained for essential services (garbage and hospital services, water, gas, electricity, and air traffic control) (Art. 24)
Employment incentives	NA (short-term and atypical contracts from 1991 and 1995 laws annulled)	One-third reduction in social security contributions for employers who increase workforce on "indefinite" contracts (Art 2)[4] For small and medium-sized enterprises, government wage subsidy for new hires that include unemployed males over forty-five years old and female heads of household and that increase net total of workers under indefinite contract (Art. 3)	For small and medium-sized enterprises of up to eighty employees, a reduction of 33% of payroll taxes for each new employee hired, until end of 2004. 50% reduction for hires from Jefes y Jefas de Hogar program (Art. 6)

1. For cases of dismissal by the employer without just cause. Prior severance set at one month's salary per year worked. After 1998, new hires face lower severance.

2. Bargaining may be delegated to decentralized level by higher-level union association.

3. Essential services were regulated by a 1990 decree. Later decrees under de la Rúa modified the regulations in response to ILO criticism regarding excessive restrictions on the right to strike. The new law scales back the occupational categories to which essential services legislation applies.

4. The 50 percent reduction in social security contributions applies when new employees are males over forty-five years old, female heads of household, or youths up to twenty-four years old (Art. 2, Law 25250).

tives approved it 215 to 23 and rescinded the "law of the bribes" on 2 March 2004.[51]

Certain features of the Argentine situation under Kirchner appeared similar to those under Menem, at least on the surface: The president was from labor's party, thus giving labor greater access and leverage than it faced under the opposition government of de la Rúa. But while Menem pursued flexibility despite his labor allies, Kirchner aimed to reverse elements of an illegitimate reform passed under a discredited government. This difference was crucial. The depth of the Argentine economic crisis in 2001–2 and the strong public reaction against IMF policies altered the political balance in Argentina. Employer groups and neoliberal reformers, powerful political forces in the 1990s, lost clout. Meanwhile, the CGT retained its ability to mobilize and pressure, not only shaping the political changes that followed but also demonstrating its ability to stabilize a political and social situation on the verge of collapse. The crisis galvanized the labor opposition, enabling the centrals to work together and enhancing their influence. The discrediting of the neoliberal model in Argentina and Kirchner's strong popular support and pro-labor sympathies enabled the labor movement to regain the upper hand on labor reform.

In Brazil, Lula's electoral victory in 2002 ushered in a PT president for the first time. Early on, Lula set out to address the need for broad reform of Brazil's system of labor relations. Where the Cardoso government encountered strong opposition to its efforts to reform the labor provisions in the constitution, Lula's government—with the president's strong labor credentials—was able to overcome initial resistance to some of the same reforms. This was not only a matter of Lula's own origins, however, but, more broadly, of his administration's approach to the entire problem of reform.

Lula called for a national consultation on labor law reform and promised that reform would be "discussed, not imposed." The focus of the Lula government was on removing the vestiges of the Vargas era in collective labor law through tripartite dialogue and consensus. The first priority was to reach consensus on changes in collective law (*reforma sindical*) in the areas of union organization, collective bargaining, and

---

51. "El Senado aprobó en general la ley laboral," *La Nación Line*, 24 February 2004, http://www.lanacion.com.ar.

strikes, in order to later address reforms in employment law (*reforma trabalhista*) (Zylberstajn 2005, 591).[52]

The new government formed the Conselho de Desenvolvimento Econômico e Social (CDES), made up of "civil society representatives," which compiled a report with recommendations for reform in mid-2003. Among the points of consensus were the need for an end to the "obligatory union contribution" (the union tax); adoption of union autonomy and freedom; and the adoption of regional, state, and municipal collective agreements, among other things. In July 2003 the government created the National Labor Forum (Fórum Nacional do Trabalho, or FNT)—with representation from labor, employer groups, and government—whose charge it was to arrive at a set of agreements for collective labor reform on which new legislation could be based.

The results of the FNT's deliberations were presented to the government in April 2004. The government then used the FNT agreements to develop its proposals for a constitutional amendment and a new law on collective labor relations, which it submitted to the Congress in March 2005.[53] Since the parties in the FNT could not reach agreement on some points, the government adopted the union proposals on several of these issues before submitting the final text to Congress (Zylberstajn 2005, 592). The main collective reform provisions are summarized in Table 3.4.

In principle, the proposed reforms reflected compromise between established interests, yet the balance was tipped in favor of labor unions and especially labor centrals. For instance, the proposed changes in the area of collective bargaining would allow unions to determine the level of bargaining, opening the way to possible bargaining at national, branch, and sectoral levels. Centrals would also be able to represent unions in collective bargaining, which they were unable to do under the existing system. The parties in higher-level agreements could establish a "floor" with nonnegotiable clauses at lower bargaining levels. The "negotiated contribution" that would eventually replace the imposto sindical would guarantee a percentage of revenues to federations, con-

52. This second area would cover health and safety, education and training, microenterprises and cooperatives, employment standards, and labor system organization.

53. Both proposals would have to go to the lower house and Senate, requiring at least nine months after their introduction before approval (*Correio Sindical Mercosul* 4 [169], 21 October–10 November 2004.) For greater detail on the reform proposals, see Fórum Nacional do Trabalho (2005).

TABLE 3.4   Selected Collective Labor Reform Proposals in Brazil (2005):
Comparison with Existing Laws

Issue	Existing	Reform Proposal
Collective bargaining	No guaranteed right of collective bargaining inside the workplace. Bargaining typically covers economic category in one or more municípios.	Unions may choose to bargain at any level. Articulation among levels possible.
Strikes/ essential services	Strike law allows labor judges to declare illegality of strike or to require service employees to work during strike.	Concept of illegal strikes abolished. Protection for essential services maintained.
Sindicato structure/representation (unicidade)	One sindicato per category per geographical unit (município).	Only representative unions may exist. Representation may be *demonstrated* (at least 20% union members) or *derived* from federation, confederation, or central. Exclusivity an option for existing unions.
Union contribution	Unions financed by annual tax of one day's wages per worker.	Replaces union contribution and other fees with single compulsory negotiated contribution for entire category.
Workplace union organization	No legal recognition of workers' right to organize at enterprise level.	Employee representation in the workplace by elections organized by union in companies with thirty or more employees.

SOURCES: "Brasil: concluído debate de reforma sindical," *Correio Sindical Mercosul* 4 (169) (21 October–10 November 2004): 1–2; Zylberstajn (2005); Ministério do Trabalho e Emprego (2005).

federations, and centrals. The combined effect of these reforms would be a strengthening of economic, organizational, and political power for higher-order labor organizations (Zylberstajn 2005, 603).

The mainstays of corporatist labor legislation—and the most controversial areas for reform—were addressed in the proposal. While the abolition of poder normativo was agreed to relatively quickly, changes to the imposto sindical and to unicidade required important compromises that later led critics to accuse the government of failing to break fully with these corporatist provisions. The union tax and voluntary fees to higher-level organizations such as federations and centrals would be phased out over time, to be replaced eventually by a single, compulsory "negotiated contribution" for the entire category.

The reform of the sindicato structure reflected an especially interesting compromise between the exclusive representation of the unicidade system and greater freedom of association. The proposal would establish the categories of "demonstrated" and "derived" representation for unions; only "representative" unions could represent workers in a given jurisdiction. Unions could achieve representative status by showing that at least 20 percent of the workers in their area of representation were union members. Otherwise, unions could "derive" representative status by borrowing from federations, confederations, or centrals with "spare" representation. The reform proposal would allow the registration of more than one union in a given jurisdiction, provided the unions met the criteria for representation laid out by the new law. Existing unions could still opt for exclusive representation within a designated time period after the promulgation of the new law, provided they met certain criteria, including proving that they were representative.[54] Maintaining the principle of exclusive representation was the compromise solution in order to gain consensus on moving the system toward "more dynamic representation" of union members (Ministério do Trabalho e Emprego 2005, 24).

The reform would also establish workplace-level representation for workers, meeting a long-standing demand of unions. The proposal called for workplace representation in companies with more than thirty employees, to be determined via elections organized by the union. In

---

54. The município would also be maintained as the smallest unit of representation for unions, although they were no longer restricted to this and could organize as intermunicipal, state, regional, and even national unions.

the FNT, employer groups resisted union involvement in elections and no agreement was reached. Unions would also be authorized to file complaints against a company in the labor courts in name of an individual worker or category of workers, and they would be guaranteed the right of recourse to the labor courts in cases where companies failed to comply with the law or provisions of the collective bargaining agreement (Zylberstajn 2005, 603–5). These provisions of "procedural replacement" and other legal guarantees would strengthen unions' role in overseeing employers' compliance with individual or collective workers' legal or contractual rights.

Despite the lengthy process of consensus building in the FNT, many parties were critical of the proposed labor reform. Most employer organizations did not support the procedural replacement and workplace representation provisions, which they had rejected in the FNT. Some labor unions and federations also rejected the proposal, especially the sections on union representation (Zylberstajn 2005, 606). Others criticized the reform proposal for not making a sharper break with the corporatist features of the old legislation. The labor reform proposal did not represent either Lula's or the CUT's "dream" project. Yet it was the *reforma posible* given the involvement of actors with vested interests in the system.[55]

By mid-2005 it was clear that the labor reform proposals would not advance through Congress, not only because of disunity over the reform but also because of the electoral calendar. Elections for federal Congress, the Senate, state legislative assemblies, governors, and the president were all slated for 2006. Moreover, by 2005 a series of corruption scandals had hit the PT leadership and the Lula government, derailing any plans for reform and throwing Lula's re-election prospects into jeopardy. Nonetheless, the fact that some consensus had been forged around the key areas requiring change meant that the proposals were likely to become an important reference point in future reform efforts.

Under Lula's government, the reform process represented a significant effort to address both the need for systemic change and the concerns of key actors in a context of negotiation and consensus. As such, it differed sharply from labor reform under Cardoso. The emphasis on tripartism and consensus marked a departure from the previous govern-

---

55. Presentation by Hélio Zylberstajn to the Fifth Regional American Congress of Industrial Relations, Santiago, Chile, 26–28 July 2005.

ment's policy of issuing decrees and provisional measures. The attention paid to phasing in many of the changes while providing institutional guarantees to sindicatos was instrumental in securing union support. The goal of fortifying union organization in order to strengthen collective bargaining overall also stood in sharp contrast to the experience of other governments (FNT 2004, 1). While inconclusive, these important steps toward comprehensive labor reform led Brazil to join Argentina in reversing the policy trend of the 1990s away from a predominant focus on flexibility to one on new or restored protections and expanded rights.[56]

CONCLUSION: CORPORATIST LEGACIES, SEQUENCING, AND REFORM OUTCOMES

Argentina and Brazil share similar trajectories and outcomes in their labor law reforms during the 1980s–1990s and into the early 2000s. In both countries democratic transitions produced an expansion of protections and labor rights, and in both countries neoliberal governments implemented measures to establish greater flexibility in the 1990s. In both cases, moreover, government attempts to target collective legislation were more limited and less successful than reform of individual legislation. Support for more labor-friendly reforms emerged in both countries under left-leaning governments in the early 2000s.

What accounts for these similar trajectories and outcomes? I have argued that the shared legacy of state corporatism and the sequence of transitions were important factors. Corporatist legislation contributed to building strong union organization by limiting competition, creating monopolies of representation, and providing financial security. Although the military removed labor's rights and privileges, Argentina's unions were able to restore organizational resources and legal protections under the favorable conditions of the democratic transition. In Brazil corporatist labor legislation remained in place during the dictatorship. Democracy gave unions the opportunity to influence labor pro-

---

56. In Argentina the discourse focused on recovering "decent work," while in Brazil employers and unions alike praised the reform process's compliance with ILO Convention 144 on tripartite consultation. *La Nación Line*, 11 February 2004, available at http://www.lanacion.com.ar/04/02/11/dp_572249.asp; and *Jornal do Comércio* (São Paulo), 9 August 2003, A-17.

visions in the new constitution. In both instances the collective rights and protections secured during democratic transition were largely retained in the neoliberal period, despite government efforts to weaken them.

The Argentine government's threats to collective legislation forced unions to accept greater flexibility in employment law. Early in the decade labor's alliance with the government party also facilitated labor concessions, yet by the mid-1990s opposition to flexibility had grown. In Brazil corporatist legal protections affected not just worker unions but employers and labor judges as well. Opposition to reform was more widely diffused, and may have compensated for the weaker position of Brazilian unions compared to Argentina. In Argentina, labor's party ties ultimately proved important for labor's ability to reverse the reforms of the earlier Menem years and the de la Rúa presidency. Yet state corporatism produced no labor-party alliance in Brazil, a difference with Argentina that appears to have mattered relatively little in accounting for similar reform trajectories and outcomes during the 1990s.

Brazil and Argentina illustrate the importance of strong unions in defending collective rights and protections. But more important, perhaps, these cases suggest that the organizational resources and collective rights established in national labor laws can provide a beachhead from which labor unions could weather political and economic storms. When the storms passed and more favorable governments came to power in the 2000s, unions in both countries were in a better position to shape the terms of labor reform. This, too, was part of the state corporatist legacy.

Legacies of Radical Regimes: Chile and Peru

Chile and Peru are rarely thought of as similar countries. Chilean economic performance has typically surpassed that of Peru, and Chile has generally been stronger on a range of socioeconomic indicators. Chile's military experience in the 1970s and 1980s was far harsher than Peru's revolutionary-nationalist military regime from 1968 to 1980. Yet the outcomes for labor reform in each country, and the experiences that produced them, are remarkably similar.

In both Chile and Peru flexibility was introduced and collective rights were curtailed during authoritarian regimes. In both cases this occurred as part of a backlash against an earlier period of radical pro-worker policies. While the radicalism was not always intentional, especially in the case of the Peruvian military, both regimes were "radical" in the polarizing effects of their labor policies, especially those that threatened property rights, and in the surge in labor organization that their policies engendered. In both cases, moreover, labor reforms took place in the context of extensive market-oriented economic change. In the 2000s, both countries moved to moderate the "extreme flexibility" of their labor laws.

LEGACIES OF RADICAL REGIMES

Although recent developments in Peru and Chile show parallels, their initial periods of labor incorporation reveal sharp differences. In Peru the Confederación de Trabajadores Peruanos (CTP) developed close ties with the Alianza Popular Revolucionaria Americana (APRA), the party founded by Víctor Raúl Haya de la Torre in 1924. In contrast, the political incorporation of the Chilean labor movement occurred via the state, and labor legislation was a key component in structuring the state-labor relationship.[1] The use of labor law to establish state regulation and control over unions was less important in Peru than in Chile. Peruvian labor law was "a collection of scattered measures dictated by oligarchical regimes to favor the arbitrary action of the employers" (Angell 1979, 10). This was due in part to the fact that the Peruvian labor movement remained relatively weak and did not pose a threat to government or employers until the 1970s (Angell 1979, 1). In Chile the labor movement developed strong ties with the anarcho-syndicalists and Socialist and Communist parties early in the twentieth century. The drafting of labor legislation was therefore explicitly geared toward securing employer and state control over a radicalized labor movement (Angell 1972, 58). Labor laws were passed in Congress at the insistence of the military and further developed into a labor code in 1931 under the government of Colonel Carlos Ibáñez (1927–31).

Throughout the middle decades of the twentieth century, Peruvian labor's fortunes rose and fell with APRA's relationship with power. APRA's initial alliance with the government of President José Luis Bustamante y Rivero (1945–48) provided labor with a favorable environment for organizational and wage gains. Union recognition reached unprecedented levels, and real manufacturing wages in 1947 were 67 percent above 1944 levels. Worker representatives belonging to APRA and the

---

1. Collier and Collier (1991) list Peru as a case of party incorporation and Chile as a case of state incorporation of labor.

Communist Party found their way to Congress, and for a brief period several members of Bustamante's cabinet were from APRA (Collier and Collier 1991, 324–25). This period was followed by a military coup, whereupon General Manuel Odría outlawed the Aprista CTP.[2]

APRA's ability to lead a popular mobilization posed a profound threat to elites, and the armed forces tried to circumscribe its activities throughout much of this period. An electoral ban on APRA prevented its leader, Haya de la Torre, from running for the presidency, forcing the party to seek electoral alliances. Since APRA was the only mass party in Peruvian politics, its political support was usually critical. Under the government of Manuel Prado y Ugarteche (1956–62), an alliance with APRA produced another increase in unionization and advances in labor legislation, leading to a "far higher level of legal inducements for the labor movement" (Collier and Collier 1991, 480). Another sharp increase in union recognition followed, as APRA forged an alliance with the government of President Fernando Belaúnde Terry (1963–68). However, APRA's increasingly opportunistic tactics and abandonment of social reform alienated many workers, and new actors emerged to play a role in politics. By the time of the 1968 military coup, the CTP had lost support, and the Communist-supported Confederación General de Trabajadores del Perú (CGTP) emerged as an important force.

In his analysis of the politics behind the development of Chile's legal industrial relations system, James O. Morris describes the 1924 labor laws as a "historical accident," the product of a small group of intellectuals and the military. Seven separate labor laws that were passed in 1924 grew out of two very different reform projects in the Congress, one linked to the Conservative Party and the other to the Liberal Alliance (Morris 1966, 35). The laws reflected the inconsistency of these opposing projects, which nevertheless agreed on the need to exert control over the labor movement. Concerned with the "social question," military officers pressed President Alessandri to pass the laws in 1924. Not until Colonel Carlos Ibáñez took power in a military dictatorship (1927–31), however, were the laws incorporated into a more elaborate industrial relations framework through the 1931 labor code. Even then, implementation was slow and enforcement sporadic; it was only when

2. President Bustamante had already outlawed APRA in 1948, after a failed insurrection in a bid by APRA to oust Bustamante and secure new elections (Collier and Collier 1991, 329).

the Popular Front government was established in 1936 that unions were able to gain advantage from the laws.

Labor itself was not consulted during the elaboration of the labor code and remained ambivalent toward it. Unions were divided over whether to reject the code or accept it and use it for their own ends. The majority of unions decided that government protection might enable the labor movement to extend its influence into new areas, and were drawn to the code's profit-sharing provisions (Morris 1966; Angell 1972, 58).

The labor code created a "highly paternalistic and authoritarian system of government-worker relations" (Loveman 1979, 249). It greatly restricted the economic power of unions and regulated their internal structure and activities. The unintended result, however, was a labor movement that sought alliances with political parties so as to exert political influence, and one in which the gap between union leaders, who lacked special privileges or financial advantages, and rank-and-file members was small (Angell 1972, 59, 61, 65). This helped to create a democratic and politicized labor movement, albeit one that was also structurally weak and fragmented.[3]

The 1931 labor code served as the foundation for Chilean industrial relations for the next four decades, including the Allende presidency of 1970–73 (Loveman 1979, 249). There was also an important continuity between the more restrictive aspects of the 1931 code and the Labor Plan under the Pinochet dictatorship. Parts of the 1931 labor code deliberately reinforced limits on union influence. For instance, the code contained no sanctions against employers for violating labor laws, and it gave employers extensive authority to interfere in union affairs (Angell 1972, 77). Unions were unable to set aside funds for strike purposes, and union leaders were required to work full-time in the plant or workplace and could not receive additional compensation beyond their regular wages for carrying out union duties. Union organization was confined to a single plant, and the blue-collar (*obrero*) and white-collar (*empleado*) employees had to form separate unions.[4] Public-sector

3. From 1948 to 1957 the Law for the Defense of Democracy aimed to purge Communists from the trade unions and gave employers an additional tool with which to undermine labor unions (Angell 1972, 59).

4. Empleado unions were eligible for higher minimum wage and social security advantages, and skilled workers often sought to upgrade to empleado status (Angell 1972, 67). This obrero-empleado distinction was dropped with the Pinochet-era Labor Plan, but the plant union designation remained.

unions were not legally recognized, although in practice the law was ignored (Angell 1972, 68). Collective bargaining was also limited to the plant level and the agreement applied only to signatories, but workers in all firms could bargain regardless of union status. Regulations on strikes were so complicated that in fact many strikes were technically illegal (Compa 1973).

Labor Under the Allende Government in Chile

The victory of the Unidad Popular in September 1970 presented the Chilean labor movement with a tremendous opportunity. Unidad Popular's pro-labor platform promised to broaden the political space for labor to an extent unknown previously. Although a divided Congress hindered the passage of a new labor code, the Allende government used executive decrees, pro-labor policies, and permissive government attitudes to establish a supportive environment for labor. Under the Unidad Popular, labor was able to expand its organization, increase collective bargaining, and engage in strikes without fear of government repression. Notwithstanding constraints in the labor code, a worker-friendly government made union gains possible both within and outside the confines of the law.

Despite the Allende government's favorable orientation toward labor, new tensions and contradictions emerged. The first concerned the labor movement's relationship with the Unidad Popular regime. The Chilean labor movement had been among the most autonomous and independent of the state in all of Latin America, a product of its close alliance with Marxist parties in the early twentieth century (Bergquist 1986). The alliance with the Unidad Popular threatened labor's autonomy and independence, as the Central Unitaria de Trabajadores (CUT) became increasingly integrated into the regime (Zapata 1976). The government, too, faced its own contradiction. Although the Allende government wanted to reward its strong labor base by supporting wage increases, the economic success of the regime also depended on wage constraints (Compa 1973). These tensions manifested themselves in the government's ambivalent position toward labor actions.

Upon Allende's inauguration in November 1970, the administration entered into an agreement with the CUT to promote a number of pro-labor policies and reforms, including legal recognition of the CUT, an obligatory dues system, worker participation in management, legal reforms of collective provisions, and a range of monetary improvements (Zapata 1976, 87). An executive decree issued the same month established tripartite commissions empowered to fix minimum wages and conditions for an entire industry by a majority vote, thereby making it possible to circumvent the decentralized bargaining restrictions that had prevailed up until then and enabling the CUT to engage in bargaining at the national federation level (Compa 1973, 33; Zapata 1976, 88).[5]

Under Allende there were also dramatic increases in union organization, collective bargaining agreements, and strikes. Two hundred-eighteen new nonagricultural unions formed in 1970, followed by another seven hundred new unions in 1971. Most of these were organized by the higher-status empleado, or white-collar, workers. The number of bargaining agreements increased; these covered production issues as well as wages and working conditions. The number of strikes grew dramatically, especially in the absence of government intervention and repression. Given the highly regimented nature of the legal code governing strikes, most strikes fell outside the law; as many as 90 percent of the strikes carried out in 1971–72 were illegal (Compa 1973, 37–38).

Many of the strikes centered on workplace occupations, an action linked in turn to perhaps the most important—and controversial—policy innovation of the Allende regime. This was the creation of "social property," by way of nationalization, of some of the largest manufacturing enterprises. While Chilean law had long granted the government authority to "intervene" in private companies or to requisition them under certain conditions,[6] Allende used this authority to turn seized properties into areas of social property based on worker participation. Workers also were entitled to participate on the boards of directors of the publicly owned property sector. Moreover, workers formed production councils to discuss production improvements with management. According to Francisco Zapata, at its peak worker participation

5. The president was empowered to create tripartite commissions under a 1968 law passed during the Frei government. Allende provided the implementing legislation to establish the commissions (Compa 1973, 30).

6. Under the law the government could legally take over struck companies where the strike threatened national security or the welfare of the population. The government was also permitted to take over companies guilty of economic malfeasance. Traditionally, the government returned such properties to their private owners, but the Allende government retained many of these for the creation of the *área social* (Compa 1973, 39).

involved more than two hundred thousand workers in the publicly owned sector of the economy, mainly in textiles, mining, energy, steel, and transportation (Zapata 1976, 89).

As problems with the economy grew and political opposition to the Allende regime mounted, the labor movement also became divided in its support for the Unidad Popular government. The government's repressive response to a strike at El Teniente copper mine underscored its differential treatment of strikes carried out by obreros versus empleados (Zapata 1976, 91–92). Truck drivers engaged in some of the most crippling economic acts of sabotage against the regime. Certainly the prospects of a looming Chilean socialism—reflected in part by extensiveness of the social-property sector—were profoundly threatening to the capitalist class. The Chilean experiment in worker participation and socialism "via the legal way" came to a violent close on 11 September 1973.

Labor Policy Under the "Revolutionary" Military Regime in Peru

A military coup on 3 October 1968 ushered in a "revolutionary" and nationalist regime that implemented a range of pro-worker measures. Claiming to enact a "revolution from above," the military regime led by General Juan Velasco Alvarado aimed to preempt popular insurgency through structural reforms, redistributive policies, and incorporation into state-controlled organizations (Stephens 1983, 57). Although the regime's efforts to garner broad popular support failed, its pro-labor policies helped to expand the organizational strength of workers. As in Chile, the military's policies provoked a conservative backlash on the part of foreign investors, the U.S. government, and the Peruvian business sector. These pressures forced the regime to take a more repressive turn in 1975, when General Morales Bermúdez became head of the junta. At no point, however, did the level of repression reach that practiced by Pinochet in Chile or the Argentine military during the same period. Support for leftist parties grew significantly, and the strengthened labor movement was able to play an important role in bringing the Peruvian military regime to an end in 1980.

The mobilization of labor under the Velasco regime was in part the product of divisions within the regime itself. While some members of the junta saw the need to weaken organized labor to eliminate class struggle, others saw in worker mobilization the opportunity to move the regime further to the left (Stephens 1983, 65). The latter position was buttressed initially by the fact that the "left wing" of the military government oversaw the creation of an agency in July 1971, SINAMOS, whose task it was to encourage popular mobilization under state tutelage.[7] The regime recognized the Communist-linked Confederación General de Trabajadores del Perú (CGTP) and the Christian Democrat Confederación Nacional de Trabajadores (CNT), with the goal of creating counterweights to the Confederación de Trabajadores del Perú (CTP), a confederation linked to APRA, which remained the military's bitter enemy. The recognition of the CGTP and CNT and the encouragement of union organization led to a near doubling in the number of unions between 1966 and 1976, an accomplishment that rivals that of Chile's under the Unidad Popular (Stephens 1983, 61). State sponsorship of a new labor confederation, the Central de Trabajadores de la Revolución Peruana (CTRP), in 1972 only served to strengthen support for existing party-linked organizations, since workers found the CTRP's no-strike policy and less militant stance less appealing.

In the window of opportunity prior to the creation of the CTRP, key departments of the military government encouraged union organization and favorable wage settlements in workers' dealings with employers (Stephens 1983, 74). While this open-door policy led the CGTP to temper its criticism of the regime, the number and militancy of independent leftist unions grew (Stephens 1983, 70). This was one of the many unintended consequences of regime policies that aimed to control mobilization and preempt class conflict.

The early policies of the Peruvian "revolutionary" military regime must be understood in the context of the military officers' broader analysis of Peruvian society. In their view, the weaknesses of Peru's economy and political system were due to the intransigence of the Peruvian oligarchy and the stark inequalities of a divisive class system. Continuing down that path meant certain popular insurgency and a victory by Marxist parties. The Peruvian military therefore set out to restructure society through redistributive reforms in the agrarian and industrial sectors.

In this regard, one of the most significant policy initiatives of the Velasco government was the creation of the Industrial Communities (Comunidad Industrial, or CI). The goal of the CI was to encourage

7. SINAMOS stood for Sistema Nacional de Apoyo a la Movilización Social (National System to Support Social Mobilization).

worker participation in the ownership, management, and profits of firms. The idea was that workers would identify as co-owners of enterprises and end their militancy, eventually making unions superfluous and helping to build the harmonious society at the heart of the military's blueprint for social change (Stephens 1983, 66).

The similarities with the Chilean *área social* are remarkable. Under the CI plan, every firm of at least six employees and 1 million *soles* gross annual income was required to give 25 percent of before-tax net annual profits to the employees. Ten percent of this would be in the form of cash payments to individual workers and the rest would go to the CI via newly issued shares or shares purchased from shareholders. In addition, the law required representation of the CI on the company's board of directors, beginning with one representative and increasing in direct proportion to the CI's share of ownership, up to 50 percent of the enterprise (Stephens 1983, 66). Although unions were legally barred from participating in the CI, many of them played a major role, and unionization increased as a result of this forum for worker participation and claim making (Stephens 1983, 69). By the end of 1974 the CI sector had expanded to include 5.9 percent of the active labor force (about 199,070 workers) and contributed 20.8 percent to the GNP. It also accounted for 13 percent of the capital of the sector, and participation in profits accounted for 4.8 percent of workers' earnings (Angell 1979, 33).

As with the Unidad Popular government's social property laws, the industrial communities in Peru elicited strong negative reaction from the private sector. The CI directly attacked existing property rights by threatening long-range ownership of enterprises and by putting workers on boards of directors. Employers regarded such policies as an "intolerable infringement on their prerogatives" (Stephens 1983, 68). Employers circumvented CI regulations by reducing their declaration of profits and making key decisions outside board meetings. Workers occupied bankrupt enterprises to demand incorporation into the social property sector, recalling the factory takeovers of Allende's Chile and raising concerns among the more conservative government officials (Angell 1979, 35). According to Alan Angell, "overall the employers used the existence of the CI to attack the government, and the unions used the CI as an instrument for confronting the employers" (1979, 33). As an experiment in class harmony, the CI was a failure. These unintended consequences, together with employer pressure, led the government to make important changes in the CI law in 1976.

In an attempt to halt massive firings of workers by employers protesting the CI law, the government issued a decree-law (D.L. 18471) in November 1970 (Stephens 1983, 69). The new law, known as the job stability law (*ley de estabilidad en el empleo* or *ley de estabilidad laboral*), increased legal sanctions against the dismissal of employees beyond the three-month probation period.[8] Dismissals were subject to just cause, which was defined as either serious misconduct (for individuals) or *force majeure* (for collective dismissals), which required government authorization. Workers fired in violation of the law would be entitled to either reinstatement with back pay or severance pay amounting to three months' wages. Employer reaction to this law was extremely negative, even though it applied to only about 15 percent of the workforce and evasion was high (Angell 1979, 12).[9] The law transferred employers' power to discipline their workforce to the state by specifying the grounds for dismissal, granting the legal system the authority to evaluate employers' justifications, and even setting out a category of "faults by the employer" (Balbi 1997, 136).

In addition to the mounting opposition of the business sector, the military government faced increasing economic problems, generated in part by lack of investment and by natural disasters, including a devastating earthquake in 1970. The Morales Bermúdez government was forced to adopt economic austerity policies and agree to a stabilization plan with the IMF. By 1979 real wages had fallen to 62 percent of their 1973 levels (Stephens 1983, 77). At the same time, the military lacked support among the very sectors it had tried to help, workers and peasants. Unions continued to mobilize against the regime, and did so in alliance with shantytown organizations. According to Carmen Rosa Balbi, the 1970s produced "a vigorous, class-conscious, and combative labor movement" (1997, 140). The country saw massive national strikes in 1977–78, including Peru's first general strike, in July 1977.

8. The official name of D.L. 18471 was "Causales de despedida de los trabajadores sometidos al régimen de actividad privada." See http://www.congreso.gob.pe/ntley/Imagenes/Leyes/18471.pdf.

9. Angell points out that the new law would not apply to half the workforce, which was underemployed or unemployed, or to the 19 percent of workers who were self-employed, or to public-sector employees or special categories of workers, such as construction workers (1979, 12).

The government turned to repression. It declared a state of emergency for the entire country in 1976, which made labor leaders subject to arrest. The government declared strikes illegal and authorized the massive firing of striking workers (Stephens 1983, 60). Indeed, the transfer of power to Morales Bermúdez in 1975 marked a turning point in which political forces on the right were increasingly able to assert influence over policymaking (Durand 1997, 159).

One indication of this in the area of labor policy was a decree issued in March 1978 (D.L. 22126) that, while increasing severance for unjust dismissals to twelve months' wages for workers employed more than three years, also made it relatively cheaper to dismiss workers employed for fewer than three years.[10] The new law opened the door to dismissals, and employers were able to use it to control dissidents and generate greater job insecurity.

By 1978 the government was trying to extricate itself from power. The 1978 Constituent Assembly election gave the combined leftist parties more than 33 percent of the popular vote. The Assembly drew up a new constitution in 1979, which contained a detailed list of economic, social, and cultural rights, including a provision that recognized "the right to job security."[11]

Despite the growing influence of the left, elections in 1980 brought back former president Fernando Belaúnde Terry of the moderate Alianza Popular. Belaúnde kicked off a decade that saw the disintegration of organized labor as a powerful social, economic, and political force. Labor fragmentation increased with the return of democracy and political competition, and high levels of unemployment, real wage decline, and heightened battles with employers further weakened the unions (Stephens 1983, 78).

The economic crisis deepened during the government of Alan García (1985–90) of the APRA party. While one sector of the labor movement reacted by adopting a moderate strategy that focused on job preservation, more militant union leadership pursued a strategy of intensifying strikes and conflict with employers. From 1980 to 1992 the CGTP carried out twelve national strikes, yet by 1992 real wages remained at

10. In this case, a ninety-day advance notice was required for dismissal. Under D.L. 22126 workers employed for fewer than three years who did not receive a ninety-day advance notice of dismissal were entitled to ninety days' wages as compensation.

11. Article 48 of the 1979 constitution also stated, "The worker may only be fired for just cause."

one-third of their 1979 levels (Balbi 1997, 141). The strategy's lack of results further eroded unions' legitimacy. Although the García government restored job stability in 1986, a simultaneous emergency employment program enabled many employers to circumvent the new strictures (Saavedra 1999, 6).[12] By 1990, then, labor unions had been weakened both economically and politically. Moreover, employers pressed hard for flexibility in labor law as the economic recession grew worse.

MARKET AND LABOR REFORM UNDER ANTILABOR REGIMES

Although the Pinochet dictatorship in Chile and the Fujimori government in Peru had different origins—Fujimori was elected while Pinochet seized power via a bloody coup—both regimes proceeded to implement market-oriented economic policies, and both curtailed labor rights and actively undermined trade unions. The constraints on labor rights in each country were among the most severe in the region. In Chile the attack on labor rights and protections was a response to the labor radicalism of the Allende period. In Peru, Fujimori reversed the pro-worker legislation passed under the military at a time of mobilization by labor and the left. The backlash against previous legislation establishing job security was especially evident in the labor reforms of the 1990s.

Chile became one of the first countries in the region to implement market-oriented economic reforms. Beginning with the Plan of Economic Recovery or "shock plan" in 1975, the Pinochet dictatorship used orthodox monetary policies to reduce inflation and the fiscal deficit (Vergara 1985, 74). The government also began to privatize state-owned enterprises and to liberalize trade through a dramatic reduction of its tariff rates, which boosted the volume of both imports and exports (Corbo 1985, 114–15; de la Cuadra and Hachette 1991, 218–19, 233–35). Despite two major recessions, in 1974–75 and 1982–85, the Chilean economy sustained high rates of economic growth and in the late 1980s and 1990s was held out as a model of what market reforms could accomplish.

12. Law 24514 of June 1986 restored severance for workers dismissed without just cause to three months if employed for less than one year, to six months if employed between one and three years, and to twelve months if employed more than three years. The Programa Ocupacional de Emergencia (PROEM), in place from 1986 to 1989, allowed employers to hire without paying benefits or following job security requirements.

This growth had a dark side, however. Not only did it occur under a harsh political regime that persecuted trade unionists, but the effects of deep recession and economic restructuring affected workers negatively. Unemployment expanded with each recession. Between 1973 and 1975 unemployment grew from 5 to 15 percent. In 1982 unemployment reached nearly 20 percent, and between 1980 and 1982 the average duration of unemployment doubled from five to ten months.[13] As economic recovery resumed, the composition of employment changed, so that wage employment fell from 65 to 48 percent, owing to the downsizing of the public sector and the drop in industrial employment (Martínez and Díaz 1996, 102–3). The informal sector also expanded, especially after new, more flexible labor laws were put in place in 1979 (Martínez and Díaz 1996, 114–15). Changes in the labor laws also created more precarious employment conditions, which in turn further undermined workers' bargaining power and organization.

Labor Reform Under the Pinochet Dictatorship

In Chile the protective policies of the Allende regime gave way to widespread repression with the 1973 coup of Augusto Pinochet. Pinochet's military dictatorship (1973–90) decreed the suspension of rights and carried out the killing, torture, exile, and disappearance of trade unionists.[14] Eventually, however, the dictatorship established a new labor relations regime that restored union organization and bargaining, although with significant restrictions. This came in response to increased labor conflict on the part of a more unified labor movement, and to the threat of a boycott of Chilean goods orchestrated by the Organización Regional Interamericana de Trabajadores (ORIT) in 1978 in solidarity with Chilean workers (Barrera and Valenzuela 1986, 232).

The new labor laws, known as the Labor Plan and laid out by decree

13. International Labor Office, Bureau of Labor Statistics, LABORSTA, *Labour Statistics,* http://laborsta.ilo.org. High unemployment in this period led the dictatorship to create an emergency employment program, which at its peak generated as many as half a million jobs (Martínez and Díaz 1996, 115).

14. Early antiunion measures taken by the dictatorship included suspending the presentation of union demands (and hence collective bargaining), preventing union officers from leaving work to attend to union affairs, allowing employers to dismiss workers who had led illegal strikes, suspending all agreements concerning wages and benefits, and prohibiting union meetings except for administrative or information purposes, which required advance notification of the police (Barrera and Valenzuela 1986, 236).

in 1979, set out many of the labor provisions that would continue to operate under postauthoritarian governments (Barrera 1998, 138; Barrera and Valenzuela 1986, 253–60).[15] The laws contained serious constraints on collective bargaining, strikes, and the right to organize, and they gave employers broad discretion in managing their employees.

In the area of union organization, the Labor Plan eliminated the distinction between industrial, professional, and agricultural unions, and set out four types of unions: enterprise-level; interenterprise, joining workers from no fewer than three different enterprises; unions of independent workers; and construction unions.[16] Only enterprise unions could engage in collective bargaining; the rest had to limit themselves to education and mutual assistance activities. The new law established the possibility of union pluralism: Only 10 percent of the workers (a minimum of twenty-five) in an enterprise were required to form a union, and multiple unions could form in a workplace. Workplaces of fewer than twenty-five employees needed only eight workers to form a union. Union membership was to be voluntary. In agriculture, union organization was further fragmented, bargaining was restricted to the specific agricultural holding, and apprentices and seasonal workers were not allowed to join unions (Ruíz-Tagle 1985, 46–48, 153–54).

In collective bargaining the dictatorship imposed several important changes. Bargaining was limited to the plant level and to wage adjustments and work conditions only, not issues such as promotion, use of technology, or pace of production. Negotiations could not extend to any matters pertaining to the organization, direction, or administration of the firm. Coverage extended only to those employees engaged in bargaining, and workers hired in the two-year period after a negotiation were not entitled to its benefits until renewal of the agreement. Multienterprise bargaining was strictly prohibited. Public-sector employees and workers in firms with more than 50 percent public ownership could not bargain (Ruíz-Tagle 1985, 50–51). "Bargaining groups," separate from unions, could also form for the purpose of talking to employers, but they had no other function and had to be disbanded after the "agreements" were signed. For this purpose a separate category of *convenio* was devised, which gave employees no bargaining or strike rights. Em-

15. These decrees were later codified in the 1987 labor code.
16. Public-sector workers were able to form unions under the same terms as the private sector, in contrast to earlier legislation that prohibited union organization (Ruíz-Tagle 1985, 47n5).

ployers would simply present an offer that workers could accept or not. In fact these groups were often set up by employers to compete directly with unions (Haagh 2002).

The new strike laws technically permitted strikes, but employees who wished to strike encountered so many restrictions that it was virtually impossible to do so. Employers were allowed to hire striker replacements from the first day of the strike, and strikes had a time limit of sixty days, after which employers could dismiss striking workers. After thirty days on strike any worker could return to work without penalty. Moreover, at any point in the strike, 10 percent of the workers could vote to censure the bargaining commission, consider any offer made by the employer, or move to arbitration. Employers could also enforce a total or partial lockout if the strike affected more than half the workforce. In this case, the work contract would be suspended and employers would be absolved from paying wages or benefits. Finally, many sectors (e.g., public employees, "strategic enterprises," agricultural workers during harvest season) were excluded from the right to strike (Ruíz-Tagle 1985, 52).

Several additional laws passed in 1981 modified earlier legislation regulating employment contracts and dismissals, compensation, and work schedules, among other things. Short-term employment contracts were extended from six months to two years and could be renewed only once. Employees could be dismissed without possibility of reinstatement and their maximum severance was one month's pay per year of service, but the value of that severance was frozen at 1979 levels. Employers no longer needed to inform the government in the event of collective dismissals. Regarding compensation, the legal minimum wage for youth under twenty-one years of age and workers over age sixty-five was eliminated, leaving people in this category to negotiate their pay with their employers. Profit sharing, formerly a right protected by law, was now subject to negotiation on an individual or collective basis. Another change involved the length of the workday, which went from eight hours to twelve, limiting overtime pay (Ruíz-Tagle 1985, 61–71). One of the most devastating impacts was felt with law 18134, passed in June 1982, which eliminated automatic wage adjustments for inflation, along with the guarantee that bargaining began from the base of the wages and benefits of the expiring contract (Barrera and Valenzuela 1986, 258).

In 1986 the AFL-CIO petitioned the U.S. trade representative to review worker rights in Chile under the U.S. Generalized System of Preferences (GSP). The petition not only provided a test of the new GSP mechanism, since this was the first worker rights review, it also coincided with increasing efforts among private groups, especially human rights organizations, to sanction the Chilean dictatorship. The Pinochet government made slight modifications but did little to address the rights violations that had become entrenched under the Labor Plan. The U.S. government withdrew trade benefits from Chile in 1988 and did not reinstate them until 1991, after the democratic government was installed (Frundt 1998, 94–95).

The combined effect of the Labor Plan was to weaken workers' organizations. Under the guise of giving workers individual choice, collective rights were undermined. The unionization rate dropped dramatically, falling from 30 percent to 7.9 percent between 1973 and 1989 (Barrett 2001, 577). Collective bargaining was severely hindered, and strikes were made virtually impossible to carry out. Nonetheless, the legislation reactivated rank-and-file participation in local unions and unified labor against the plan's provisions.[17] The Chilean labor movement would emerge to play an important role in opposition to the regime throughout the 1980s (Barrera and Valenzuela 1986, 232).

Labor Reform Under the "Authoritarian Democracy" of Alberto Fujimori

The two presidential terms of Alberto Fujimori (1990–95 and 1995–2000), a political newcomer, revolutionized Peru in a way different from that of the 1968–80 military regime. Fujimori inherited a severe economic crisis and proceeded to implement the market reforms and stabilization policies denominated "Fujishok" soon after taking office. Along with structural economic reforms, Fujimori introduced a range of labor decrees and policies that further weakened organized labor and elicited criticism from the ILO's Committee on Freedom of Association for labor rights violations. Although Fujimori's was technically a democratic election, his rule by decree, attacks on democratic institutions, efforts to increase the power of the armed forces, and reliance on intelligence services clearly demonstrated the authoritarian leanings of his

17. Some of the new legislation resembled provisions of the 1931 labor code, especially with regard to plant-level bargaining, leadership selection, and state oversight (Barrera and Valenzuela 1986, 255).

presidency (Cameron and Mauceri 1997, 224). In April 1992 Fujimori closed down Congress and declared a state of emergency on the pretext of combatting terrorism by the Shining Path guerrilla movement, which had reached heightened levels. While many Peruvians supported the drastic measures, they also entailed a significant curtailment of rights reminiscent of nonelected governments.

Fujimori's economic policies yielded results. His early price stabilization policies reduced inflation from 139 percent in 1991 to just 15 percent in 1994. Fujimori also pursued structural reforms such as privatization and trade and financial liberalization, and he reduced the fiscal deficit. Economic growth resumed between 1993 and 1995. In 1994 Peru's GDP growth rate of 12.5 percent was the highest in the world! Fujimori looked to Chile as a model of economic reform and growth (Wise 1997, 102). Not only did Peru's economic reforms resemble Chile's, but Fujimori's authoritarianism also earned him the nickname "Chinochet" (Cameron and Mauceri 1997, 221–22).

Despite his authoritarian politics, Fujimori garnered broad popular support, especially during his first administration, for his ability to turn the economy around and for his "toughness" in dealing with terrorists, whose attacks on the capital had increased in the late 1980s. This support for Fujimori increased the gap between rank-and-file workers and the union leadership, who roundly condemned Fujimori's *autogolpe* in 1992.

In addition to his market reforms, Fujimori implemented a range of decrees that substantially altered labor relations and further eroded union bargaining power (see Table 4.1). Fujimori successfully appealed directly to the people rather than to organized interests (other than the military). Few Peruvians protested the draconian labor decrees that would harm the discredited unions. Three months after taking office, the government issued Supreme Decree 077-90-TR, which allowed employers to hire temporary workers without providing justification (Balbi 1997, 138). The decree also eased up on dismissal restrictions, allowing employers to dismiss up to 4 percent of the workforce annually without justification. Workers could now be fired for such "grave offenses" as disloyalty or "lack of diligence." The results were an immediate increase in the number of temporary workers, which in turn created divisions between the core of stable workers and the new, often younger, temporary employees (Balbi 1997, 147–48).

In 1991 the Fujimori administration issued a package of decrees

TABLE 4.1   Selected Labor Legislation in Peru Under Fujimori (1990–2000)

Law	Content	Orientation
D.L. 728 (November 1991) Law of Employment Promotion	Implemented short-term contracts, youth contracts, flexible scheduling; ended job security (in post-1991 contracts), broadened cause for dismissal, facilitated collective dismissals; promoted subcontracting for temporary services, weakened severance protections, ended union officer protection (*fuero sindical*).	Flexible
D.L. 25593 (July 1992) Law of Collective Relations	Established union pluralism, promoted decentralized collective bargaining, favored small unions and stronger government oversight of union registration and intervention in union activities, increased strike restrictions.	Liberal/Restrictive
Law 25897 (July 1993)	Established private pension system.	Flexible
Law 26513 (July 1995)	Set longer time periods for short-term contracts; replaced absolute labor security with "adequate protection against arbitrary dismissal."	Flexible
D.L. 871 (November 1996)	Raised severance from one month's to 1.5 months' wages per year of service, to a maximum of twelve months' wages.	Protective

SOURCES: Balbi (1997), Campana (1999), Saavedra (1999), Parodi (2000).

known as the Law of Employment Promotion (Ley de Fomento de Empleo, D.L. 728), which established a range of new, short-term employment contract categories, eased collective dismissals, further eroded the principle of job stability, and weakened severance laws. Nine types of short-term employment contract were established; employees could be hired under these terms for periods of three years (expanded to five years in 1995). Subcontracting contracts were also created, in which the firm contracting with a cooperative or temporary service firm was exempt from paying benefits. Youth contracts for students or people between sixteen and twenty-five years of age, which provided for minimum benefits only, could be used for up to 40 percent of a firm's workforce. In the case of dismissals, just cause was broadened to include the employee's behavior and "productive incapacity" (Chacaltana and García 2001, 14). Collective dismissals were made easier by introducing the "economic cause" provision in the law, and dismissal protections for union leaders, known as the *fuero sindical,* were eliminated. Severance was also weakened.[18] No severance applied in the first year of employment, rendering the three-month probationary period moot (Saavedra 1999, 6).

Given that the 1979 constitution incorporated the principle of job stability as an economic right, D.L. 728 applied only to employees hired after 1991. Therefore, two dismissal regimes existed until 1995, when Law 26513 finally established a single regime for pre-1991 and post-1991 hires, substituting job stability with "relative job stability" (Saavedra 1999, 6–7). Law 26513 was possible because of the new constitution drawn up in 1993, which replaced the principle of job security with that of "adequate protection against arbitrary dismissal."[19] The 1993 constitution also curtailed most of the social rights that had been inserted in 1979 (Balbi 1997, 144). As in other countries, the constitution did include a list of basic conditions, among them the forty-eight-hour workweek, a weekly day of rest, annual vacation, and prohibition of workplace discrimination, rights frequently violated in practice (U.S. Department of State 2002b).

Some of the most extensive changes targeted collective laws. These were organized under the Ley de Relaciones Colectivas de Trabajo (D.L. 25593) in July 1992, in the wake of Fujimori's autocoup. In general, this law made collective bargaining and strikes far more complicated, greatly increased state control over union formation and activities, and further fragmented unions by allowing union pluralism, i.e., enabling more than one union to form at the level of the firm. According to Balbi, the effect of the law was to greatly weaken the state's role in protecting the rights of individual workers, while strengthening its ability to intervene in unions, strikes, and collective bargaining (1997, 139).

18. In 1991 severance was set at three months' wages for workers who had served between one and three years on the job, and one month's additional wages for each year worked, up to a maximum of twelve months (Saavedra 1999, 7).

19. Article 27, Constitución Política del Perú of 1993, available at http://tc.gob.pe/legconperu/constitucion.html.

Several of the changes had especially dire consequences for union bargaining power and collective labor rights. The right to organize was not effectively promoted by the law and scant protection was given to the exercise of union activities (Campana 1999, 29). Union pluralism reduced the unions' bargaining power dramatically (Saavedra 1999, 10). While unions were permitted to form at various levels, from the firm to economic sector, regulations favored small unions, those where only twenty workers were needed to form a union, compared with a hundred at more aggregated levels of organization. Government control over union registration and its ability to intervene in union activities were also strengthened (Campana 1999, 29).

A liberal regime operated in collective bargaining, where different levels of bargaining were recognized in the law. However, regulations became more complex as collective bargaining reached more aggregated levels, so that the law in fact encouraged the most decentralized level of bargaining (at the level of the firm). For example, branch-level bargaining required that all parties agree to bargain at this level, that the union represent the majority of workers, and that the union be present in the majority of the firms in that sector. Critics noted that this liberalization of collective relations presented strong disadvantages to unions, which were forced to deal with much stronger employer counterparts with far fewer protections than before. While the "autonomy" of the actors theoretically increased, it was autonomy among unequal parties and thus detrimental to the exercise of collective rights (Campana 1999, 31).

The right to strike was also restricted relative to earlier legislation. Strikes could be waged only after a secret-ballot election involving an absolute majority of workers, including nonunion workers, and the election had to be witnessed by a notary or a judge. Even with the secret ballot, workers were hesitant to participate, as the names of all workers present at these meetings were submitted to management (U.S. Department of State 2002b). Other restrictions included the prohibition of solidarity strikes and other forms of work stoppage; suspension of contract and remuneration until the end of the strike; limiting the use of the strike as the "final solution" in bargaining rather than as a tool to force bargaining; and broadening the services denominated "essential," in which workers were not permitted to strike (Campana 1999, 33). During strikes employers also frequently hired temporary employees through subcontracting firms authorized by the Labor Ministry (Parodi 2000, 156).

Among other changes in this period, Peru converted to a private pension system in July 1993. Individual capitalization accounts were managed by private firms, called Administradores de Fondos de Pensiones (AFPs). In 1995 the contribution was increased from 9 percent (split 6-3 between employer and worker) to 11 percent borne entirely by the employee (Saavedra 1999, 10–11). New profit-sharing laws shifted the bulk of the profit to the individual workers rather than to a community fund. In 1997 an additional reform set a limit of eight months' wages for each worker to receive from profit sharing, with the remainder to be sent to the National Fund for Training and Employment. In practice only the mining sector ever had sufficient money left over to contribute to this fund.

The impact of these reforms was dramatic. While the labor market became more flexible and competitive, there was a change in the composition of employment (Chacaltana and García 2001, 32). The percentage of employees with permanent contracts fell from 40 in 1991 to 24 by the end of the 1990s. At the same time, the percentage of workers without a contract increased from 34 in 1991 to 45 in 1999. Informal employment grew from 47.5 percent in 1991 to 54 percent in 1999. Job turnover expanded, so that the average length of time a worker spent on one job fell from seventy months in 1991 to forty months in 1999 (Chacaltana and García 2001, 17). Despite employment growth in the early 1990s, the quality of employment was low.

Unionization rates dropped from 33 percent in 1991 to 6.2 percent in 2000 (as a percentage of workers that had unions or union committees in their workplace) (Chacaltana and García 2001, 14).[20] The decentralization of bargaining had greatly limited the political influence of the unions. Strikes were also reduced: The number of man hours lost in strikes fell from 38.3 million in 1988 to 8.9 million in 1991 and to 0.3 million in 1998 (Saavedra 1999, 10). Collective relations inside the firm were divisive, and high turnover had negative consequences for training and productivity (Chacaltana and García 2001, 32).

Under Fujimori the Ministry of Labor became practically inoperative, as the government refused to give it the necessary resources. Labor

20. Data are for metropolitan Lima. Also see Saavedra and Torero (2002, 11–13) on unionization decline, especially after passage of the Law on Collective Relations.

Ministry staff was reduced to less than one-quarter of what it had been at the beginning of the decade (Chacaltana and García 2001, 14). A government proposal to fold the Labor Ministry into the Ministry of Development and Promotion, though never carried out, provided further indication of the scant importance granted to the functions of this ministry. As a result, there was little enforcement of those legal protections for workers that did exist.

The Peruvian labor reforms under Fujimori did generate strong criticism from several quarters. The CGTP called several strikes, with little success. Striking teachers held out for three months. In 1991 a front of public unions, including mining, oil, and electricity, formed to demand the repeal of legislation ending wage indexation, among other things. Yet labor's struggles had limited effect in this period, and many rank-and-file workers did not support union leaders in this fight.

Criticism from outside the country had greater, if limited, success. The ILO Committee on Freedom of Association reviewed twenty-nine cases from Peru between 1990 and 1999. In particular, the ILO criticized various aspects of the 1992 Law of Collective Relations and the Law of Employment Promotion for their violations of ILO Conventions 87 and 98 (Campana 1999, 152–55). The ILO also condemned the climate of violence in which antiunion dismissals, repression of demonstrations, and even the assassination of trade unionists all took place.[21]

The AFL-CIO also weighed in on the Peruvian labor laws by filing a GSP petition. Its first claim, filed in 1992, was rejected by the U.S. trade representative's office. A subsequent petition, filed in June 1993 with the Coordinadora de Centrales Sindicales del Perú, was accepted by the U.S. trade representative (USTR). The petition was accepted on the grounds that Peruvian laws ran counter to ILO conventions. However, the USTR determined that there was not enough concrete evidence regarding actual rights violations, and that Peru was "taking steps" to improve conditions. The problem was that the Peruvian unions were unable to supply sufficient detailed information to supplement the petition because of their unfamiliarity with the process and lack of preparation. The Fujimori government also countered effectively by claiming that the decrees it had passed were not really enforced, so that workers were not actually suffering their consequences (Frundt 1998, 97)!

---

21. The complaints submitted to the ILO's Committee on Freedom of Association in the 1990s are discussed in detail in Campana (1999).

Despite these disappointing results, the administration did feel international pressure to improve its record on labor rights and responded by incorporating ILO Convention 1, on hours of work, into national legislation. It also established workers' right to be compensated in cases of unjust dismissal (though it did not set up the insurance scheme as required in ILO Convention 44). In 1995 the Peruvian government promised to reform its collective legislation to reduce the number of workers required to form a union from one hundred to fifty in the cases of suprafirm organization (Frundt 1998, 97). In 1994–96 Congress took up the debate over labor law reform, and a number of initiatives were presented, including a government proposal and several others from the opposition. The labor commission of Congress also asked the ILO to review and comment on the proposals (Campana 1999, 55). Between January and March 1997 an effort was made to combine the government's initiative with one developed by an opposition congressman with assistance from a labor NGO, Centro de Asesoría Laboral del Perú (CEDAL). The opposition proposal was the only one that adhered to ILO conventions. Still, the move to reform Peru's labor laws remained stalemated in Congress at the end of Fujimori's second term (Campana 1999, 52–53, 55).

DEMOCRATIC TRANSITION AND LABOR REFORM IN CHILE

Unlike Argentina or Brazil, neoliberal economic reforms were already in place in Chile long before its transition to democracy began (Drake 1996; Barrera 1998). Chile's democratic transition began in 1988, when a national referendum was held on whether to continue Pinochet's rule. The victory of the "no" vote in that plebiscite led to democratic elections in 1989. Patricio Aylwin, from a broad center-left coalition of parties (Concertación de Partidos por la Democracia), became president. Yet unlike the Argentine military, which left power ignominiously in the midst of an economic crisis and after the loss of the Falkland Islands War, General Pinochet and his military cabinet held substantial sway over the terms of the transition. These terms included amnesty for military officers for crimes carried out during their rule, the continuation of Pinochet as commander-in-chief of the army, and the designation of Pinochet-appointed "senators for life" in the new Congress. Another condition was that the neoliberal economic model established in Chile would continue. These conditions signaled a strong continuity between military and civilian regimes (Hunter 1998, 304; Silva 1998, 236–37).

Labor reform was on the agenda of the three democratic administrations that governed Chile after 1990, but not until 2001 was the government able to implement reforms that expanded the collective rights of Chilean workers, and even then the results were modest. Among labor's early demands were the extension of bargaining rights to all workers, repeal of the legality of bargaining groups, and more consultation about flexible work arrangements within firms (Haagh 2002, 93; Frank 2002). Still, for ideological as well as economic reasons, resistance to more protective labor reform was strong among employers and opposition politicians (Silva 1998, 238–40; Haagh 2002). Employers especially resisted reforms calling for an end to striker replacements and the expansion of collective bargaining rights. This effective resistance derived from the strong political clout employers enjoyed during the transition and their far better bargaining position vis-à-vis workers and trade unions. Business's biggest bargaining chip was economic stability. This was critical for establishing the legitimacy of the new democratic government with those in the best position to challenge it: business, landowners, the military, and the political right (Epstein 1993, 59).

The parties of the Concertación, ranging from Christian Democrats to Socialists, consequently saw business groups as potentially threatening to democratic stability and chose to appease them in the economic and labor arena.[22] According to Patrick Barrett, the center-left gave greater priority to "maintaining the regime's economic model and gaining the confidence of business" (2001, 565). Louise Haagh (2002) notes that political elites sacrificed the opportunity to significantly expand collective labor rights in order to ensure business support for the new democratic regime. The successful consolidation of market-oriented economic reforms during the dictatorship produced a political coalition—which included employer organizations, government politicians, and members of Congress—that was strongly committed to maintaining these policies under democracy.

Labor entered the democratic transition greatly weakened by the political and economic circumstances of the dictatorship. The "binomial"

22. For an especially insightful discussion of this part of the transition, see Barrett (2001, 578–82).

electoral system and the composition of the Congress, where designated senators had veto power over constitutional changes, added to a hostile environment for labor reform.[23] Moreover, during the first eight years of democratic government, right-wing opposition parties dominated the Senate. Yet labor's dependence on political parties that were now in government also presented disadvantages. Because of its alliance with the Concertación, labor showed restraint in the early years of the transition. However, politicians in the ruling coalition were also divided on whether to pursue labor law reform (Frank 2004, 99).[24] Unlike labor in Argentina or Mexico, then, Chilean unions sought an expansion of collective rights rather than the defense of rights or resources already provided in the labor code. This was to be a far more difficult task, even in the new democratic context.

The Government of Patricio Aylwin (1990–1994)

The government of Patricio Aylwin, a Christian Democrat, implemented some modest changes to expand worker protections and extend union freedoms. Although the government initially claimed that it would do more, strong employer opposition and the Concertación's concerns with appeasing the business sector during the transition limited its reach.

An early framework accord, or Acuerdo Marco, signed by the government, the CUT, and the Confederación de la Producción y del Comercio (CPC), included agreements confirming property rights and the central role of free enterprise, the market, and the open economy, among other things. It also stated that an accord on labor reform would be sought. Yet even this agreement to discuss labor reform was strongly resisted by business leadership (Barrett 2001, 583). The business community's hostility toward labor ran deep. This was especially true for

23. The binomial electoral law enabled minority parties or coalitions to obtain 50 percent of the seats with only 34 percent of the vote through the creation of two-member electoral districts, which had the effect of overrepresenting the right. Nine of the Senate's forty-seven members were to be "designated," according to the 1980 constitution, in the following manner: two by the executive, four by the National Security Council, and three by the Supreme Court (all nine were originally designated by the outgoing Pinochet government) (Barrett 2001, 579n33).

24. These divisions came to light under the Lagos government (2000–2006), when the importance of opposition senators declined and the Concertación came to hold the majority in both houses of Congress (Frank 2004, 99).

La Sociedad de Fomento Fabril (SOFOFA), the most powerful member of the CPC. Business groups feared that engaging in dialogue with the CUT would open the door to bargaining beyond the firm, and they were committed to retaining the regime of labor flexibility, which they credited with the economic growth of the 1980s (Barrett 2001, 584).

In pushing ahead on labor reform talks, the government negotiated separately with the CPC and the CUT but favored the former. Government officials began to view elements of Pinochet's Labor Plan more positively, seeing in them the basis for a competitive and dynamic economy. Employers' core issues were clear: They strongly opposed any change that would interfere with "the power to determine the destiny of their firms" (Barrett 2001, 585–87). Employers were willing to expend considerable time and resources in limiting the labor reforms, an indication of how important a threat these were to their notion of property rights. Ultimately the Aylwin government scaled back its own proposal for labor reform, negotiated with the right, and pressured its own congressional members to vote in favor (Haagh 2002, 98–99). One sign that the government was not as committed to stronger protections for labor was its introduction of the reform projects in the Senate, which was dominated by the conservative opposition (Barrett 2001, 585–87).

In the end several laws were passed between 1990 and 1993, as well as a labor code in early 1994 that incorporated these laws.[25] However, the new legislation did little to respond to unions' concerns and did not fully protect workers' rights (Pier 1998). Although there were some improvements, the important constraints on bargaining and strike rights remained unaffected. The scope of bargaining was not expanded to include nonwage issues in the plant, the issue of bargaining groups was not addressed, and bargaining coverage was not extended. Although multiemployer bargaining was permitted for the first time, it required the agreement of employers, a condition that was rarely met. Collective bargaining was not possible among public employees and in enterprises with more than 50 percent state ownership, nor were unions other than plant-level unions allowed to bargain collectively, which included workers in strategic sectors such as construction, agriculture, and ports (only about 10 percent of the Chilean labor force was covered

---

25. The labor laws were Law 19010 (Labor Contract Termination and Employment Stability, 1990), Law 19049 (Labor Centrals, 1991), Law 19069 (Union Organizations and Collective Bargaining, 1991), and Law 19250 (Individual Employment Contracts, 1993).

by a collective bargaining agreement.) Some workers were allowed to sign convenios with employers on wages and conditions, but these did not allow bargaining over the terms or grant the right to strike (Frank 2004, 118n29). Moreover, employers often used the convenio process to undercut collective bargaining with the union (Barrett 2001, 567, 571).

Modifications in strike law were minimal. Employers could replace strikers on the first day of the strike if their final offer contained terms identical to the last contract and wage adjustment to at least inflation. Even though the sixty-day limit was lifted in the new law, in order to be classified as legal strikes had to conform to strict procedures and only applied to the limited percentage of workers who had a legal right to bargain collectively (Barrett 2001, 567). Employers' legal ability to replace striking workers also effectively voided this right. Minimal reforms that made employers wait a prescribed period before replacing striking workers did not fundamentally alter this fact. Moreover, the scope of bargaining was restricted by law to wage adjustments and could not extend to any other matters that pertained to the "organization, direction and administration of the firm." The right to strike remained severely curtailed in Chile. Indeed, union leaders claimed that strikes became even more difficult in democracy than they were under Pinochet (Haagh 2002, 104).

Improvements in the new law included less state control over union finances (but other forms of state direction continued); an increase in the cap on severance pay from five to eleven months' wages; an increased fine for unjust dismissals (but employers could dismiss under clauses that did not permit severance); and a requirement that employers provide written justification for dismissal (although employers could claim as cause the necessities of the firm or changes in market conditions) (Haagh 2002, 100). Nonetheless, these changes had no real effect on employers' freedom to dismiss workers, since worker appeals in cases of unjust dismissals were a "practical impossibility" (Barrett 2001, 566–67).

These changes had a minimal impact on workers' bargaining power or trade union rights (Barrett 2001, 567; Pier 1998). This was evident in the declining unionization rates in the 1990s (after an initial increase between 1980 and 1991) and by the decline in the absolute number of union members after 1992—a fall of 15.5 percent between 1992 and

1998.[26] According to Barrett, the Aylwin reforms "signaled a modest advance in the legal protections afforded to Chilean workers. The overall thrust of the reforms, however, was to preserve the fundamental features of the Labor Plan" (2001, 568).[27]

Nonetheless, the government considered it important to portray the labor reform as an achievement of democratic government and as critical for its legitimacy (Haagh 2002, 89–90). Employer groups understood this and supported the reform as long as it did not represent any fundamental changes to the Pinochet-era legislation. The result was a democratic façade that left the unions disappointed in their erstwhile allies in government. For business, reaching an accord with labor meant getting labor's support for a market economy and firm-level bargaining. According to one member of the CPC, "Sure, we would talk about labor training and other matters, but that was just *bullshit*" (quoted in Barrett 2001, 584.)

The Government of Eduardo Frei (1994–2000)

Subsequent efforts under President Frei to amend the laws to expand labor rights protections also failed to overcome opposition from employers and the governing coalition. The original government initiative would have broadened the scope of bargaining, granted bargaining rights to transitory unions (e.g., miners, construction, port, agriculture);[28] made bargaining at supraenterprise levels obligatory; and repealed striker replacement legislation (Frank 2002, 43–44). The Senate rejected the reform initiative in 1995. It rejected the reform again in 1997, after two years of government-opposition talks in which major provisions of the government bill—interenterprise union bargaining and repeal of striker replacement—were dropped; and it was rejected for a third time in 1999 (Frank 2002, 43). On the last occasion, opposi-

26. Unionization rates were 11.5 percent in 1989, 15.3 percent in 1991, and 11.3 percent in 1998 (Barrett 2001, 568–69).

27. The U.S. government restored GSP benefits to Chile in 1991, after it determined that the country was "taking steps" to address worker rights. Chile would not ratify ILO Conventions No. 87 on Freedom of Association and Protection of the Right to Organize and No. 98 on the Right to Organize and Bargain Collectively until January 1999, making it one of the last major countries in Latin America to do so (Brazil had not yet ratified Convention No. 87, and Mexico had not ratified Convention No. 98). See http://www.ilo .org/ilolex/english/convdisp1.htm.

28. Transitory unions are unions of temporary, part-time, or seasonal workers, who make up the majority of workers in mining, construction, ports, and agriculture.

tion politicians accused the Concertación government of using the reform bill to bolster Lagos's presidential campaign. The president of the CPC, Walter Riesco, went so far as to say that the government's proposed reforms brought back memories of the Allende government.[29]

The government's inability to push through labor reform strained relations between the CUT and the Concertación. The CUT severed relations with the government in November 1994, restored them when the administration presented its package of reforms in January 1995, then broke off ties again after this proved unsuccessful (Barrett 2001, 590–91). The lack of progress in labor policy generated tensions within the labor movement as well and strengthened the left wing, represented by communist victories in several public-sector unions. The 1996 CUT elections reflected these tensions, as the socialist vice president of the CUT brokered a deal with the Communist Party and secured the election of a socialist president and communist vice president, thus splitting the Concertación coalition within labor and almost driving the rest of the Concertación from the confederation. Elections in 1998 produced another communist-socialist leadership split (reversing the positions this time) and a more confrontational CUT vis-à-vis government and business (Barrett 2001, 592).

Democratic Transition and the Failure to Expand Labor Rights

What accounts for the inability to expand labor rights during the democratic transition in Chile? Resistance by employers and conservative politicians was present to some degree in Brazil and Argentina as well. But in Chile the position of these sectors was especially unified and ideologically driven, given the earlier consolidation of market economic reforms and the memories of what a more powerful labor movement had meant to their interests under Allende.

Other factors were also at work in Chile. The labor movement entered the democratic transition from a position of considerable organizational weakness, even as it enjoyed political legitimacy (Drake 1996,

29. In 1999 two consecutive Senate votes resulted in a 23-23 standoff—with seventeen right-wing opposition and six designated senators against and twenty elected Concertación senators and three designated senators in favor. This result meant the legislation was defeated and, under Senate rules, could not be reconsidered for another year ("Tie Vote Assures No New Labor Law for At Least a Year," *Santiago Times*, 2 December 1999, http://www.tcgnews.com/santiagotimes).

137; Barrett 2001, 577). The economic restructuring, deindustrializa-
tion, and political constraints of the dictatorship had produced a fragmented labor movement whose frailties were institutionalized in the
1979 Labor Plan. Moreover, the dictatorship's attacks on the Chilean
labor movement were more devastating to labor than in either Argentina or Brazil (Barrera and Valenzuela 1986, 265).

In addition to labor's organizational and market weakness, the Chilean labor movement lacked strong political allies. Historically, Chilean
labor had been politically fragmented yet characterized by strong party
alliances with Christian Democrats, Socialists, and Communists (Angell
1972). But in the 1990s these parties lessened their commitment to
labor (Frank 2004, 99). Perhaps more important was the fact that members of the Concertación itself internalized the neoliberal arguments
about labor flexibility and economic performance (Drake 1996, 145).
Conservative politicians from the Christian Democratic Party were especially skeptical of efforts to reform labor laws in a more protective
direction (Frank 2004, 97).

During Chile's democratic transition, the labor movement was in the
difficult position of having to pursue labor rights both from an already
restricted legal base and with strong political constraints on labor activity. The fact that the economic model was a settled question and that
elites shared a commitment to defending the status quo kept labor demands subordinated at a time when "foundational" reforms in the area
of labor rights are otherwise typically possible.

CHILE AND PERU: QUEST FOR BALANCE IN THE 2000S?

Expectations for a significant labor reform returned with the government of Socialist Ricardo Lagos, who took office in March 2000. Like
his predecessors, Lagos called for dialogue between employers and
unions as a first step before sending an initiative to Congress, establishing a tripartite Council on Social Dialogue. The government also
stressed the importance of obtaining interenterprise union bargaining
and the repeal of striker replacement. It went so far as to label these
items nonnegotiable. However, the government soon removed these issues from the agenda when faced with opposition (Frank 2002).[30]

30. Other points of disagreement between employers and the government included
workday flexibility (the use of overtime), the scope of the Labor Directorate's powers, and

Lagos explained this retreat by saying that he preferred to work for what was attainable rather than risk complete failure by aiming too high.[31] The government's action generated protests from the CUT against business leaders' "indecent agenda,"[32] and warnings from Lagos's own coalition that the bill's passage through the legislature would now be difficult.[33]

Under the Lagos government, the CUT's strategy also shifted with regard to labor reform. Whereas in the early years of the new democracy under Aylwin, the CUT acted with relative restraint for the sake of easing a stable transition, it resorted more to mobilizations under Lagos and staged the country's first general strike in twenty years.[34] Internal political divisions explained part of this shift. The CUT's moderation during the transition was due in large part to its president, Manuel Bustos of the Christian Democrats, who helped mediate labor's relationship with the Concertación. Increasing discontent within the labor central ushered in a Communist president in 1998, Etiel Moraga, who took a more militant stance. Arturo Martínez, who ran as an independent socialist in 2000, continued this more combative posture, albeit in an increasingly fractured CUT.[35]

The hikes in unemployment and inflation in Chile in the late 1990s also influenced the labor reform process. In particular, the economic recession under Lagos provided fodder for those who believed that employment protection—and expanded labor rights—would generate labor market "rigidities" that would prove harmful to competition. The Lagos government turned from an emphasis on employment protection to "employment creation" (Frank 2002). The administration's reform package included provisions for part-time contracts, flexible work schedules, and probationary contracts for workers in small and medium-sized enterprises. Business leaders pointed to double-digit un-

---

the definition of a firm (to combat artificial divisions of a company in an effort to undermine union organization).

31. "CUT Leader Martínez Says October Protest May Be in the Making," *Santiago Times*, 27 September 2000, http://www.tcgnews.com/santiagotimes.

32. "CUT President Etiel Moraga Says Chile's Labor Situation Is Appalling," ibid., 1 August 2000.

33. "Unions and Leftists Protest Revised Proposals," ibid., 9 November 2000.

34. The general strike was held on 13 August 2003. See http://networks.org/?src=bbc:world:americas:3149541.

35. Luis Fromin, "CUT: Su pasado la persigue," *Qué Pasa*, 29 August 2003, http://www.quepasa.cl/revista/2003/08/29/t-29.08.QP.NEG.CUT.html.

employment rates when pressing, unsuccessfully, for postponement of a new labor reform initiative that they feared would extend worker protections.

The ILO had noted a number of concerns with Chile's labor laws, even after the reforms of the 1990s. Among these were restrictions on political party affiliation for union officials; problems with the procedures for calling strikes, restrictions on solidarity strikes, the ban on strikes in public services, the broad definition of essential services, the provision on striker replacements, and the broad powers granted to the Labor Directorate (Dirección del Trabajo) to supervise the books and financial and property transactions of associations (ILO-CEACR 2002). After 2000 the ILO reviewed two complaints against the government of Chile on the right to strike. One concerned strike restrictions for workers in companies providing essential services who were not directly involved in supplying these services. The second issue dealt with the hiring of replacement workers.[36]

Although the Lagos government did succumb to business pressure on its core issues of multifirm bargaining and striker replacement, the administration also tried to address some of the concerns of the ILO and worked with the ILO in the drafting of its reform proposal (U.S. Department of Labor 2003). Additional pressure in favor of labor rights protections came from trade negotiations with the United States and the European Union, which were occurring during reform talks.[37] The U.S. labor movement, among others, had expressed concern about Chilean labor laws. Chilean unions were reportedly using the trade negotiations to press the government for labor improvements (Frundt 1998, 95.)

Nonetheless, strong bias against expanded worker rights protections persisted within Chile, especially in the business community. The president of the CPC, Ricardo Ariztía, called the reform a "perverse project" and demanded that the government end its antibusiness bias.[38] Sebastian Edwards, a prominent Chilean economist, referred to the ILO as

36. While the Lagos government's initial proposal called for eliminating the strike replacement provision, the amendment was later dropped by the legislature (U.S. Department of Labor 2003, 9).

37. Carolina Soza J., "Eduardo Dockendorf: Las prioridades legislativas del semestre," *El Mercurio,* 25 August 2001, B-2.

38. The antibusiness agenda, according to Ariztía, included unemployment insurance, the law against tax evasion, and labor reform. See "Reforma laboral es un proyecto perverso que disminuirá el crecimiento," *Diario Estrategia,* 14 September 2001.

"a bunch of bureaucrats in Geneva" who should not dictate Chile's labor laws.[39]

The reform that did finally pass Congress in 2001 was a controversial piece of legislation that was modified more than one hundred times.[40] Employer organizations dubbed the new law the "anti-employment reform" and asked that its implementation be postponed (Craze 2001).[41] Labor unions were also dissatisfied, but they supported the bill's passage. CUT president Arturo Martínez conceded, "This is great progress considering workers will have access to defense mechanisms whenever their rights are violated. This is an important step in the democratization of labor relations, although there are still important topics to discuss."[42]

Among these "topics," the law did not dismantle what were regarded as the most significant constraints on collective rights: striker replacement and expanded bargaining rights. Instead, the new law increased the disincentives for employers to avoid or abuse employment regulations, and strengthened the capacity and authority of the Labor Directorate in pursuing cases of abuse. A key measure expanded the power of the Labor Directorate to apply higher fines in cases of unjust dismissal and to become a party to cases that involved unfair labor practices sent to labor tribunals. The government also agreed to double the number of labor inspectors in the Labor Directorate and add a total of 443 new employees (U.S. Department of State 2002b).

The new law increased protection in individual employment by addressing what many had seen as the extreme flexibility imposed during the dictatorship. The law limited overtime, reduced the length of a continuous work period, reduced the maximum workweek (to be phased in by 2005), and required employers to notify the Labor Directorate in writing if they wished to change the working hours of employees. The more balanced adjustment of labor laws may have reflected an effort to

39. Julio Nahuelhual, "Sebastián Edwards explica su cambio de voto," *La Tercera*, 2 January 2000, available at http://www.anderson.ucla.edu/faculty/sebastian.edwards/tercera.html.

40. The bill passed the Senate by a vote of 18 to 14, after Labor Minister Ricardo Solari's intense lobbying of the Christian Democratic senators. "Senate Approves Labor Reform Bill," *Santiago Times*, 12 September 2001, http://www.tcgnews.com/santiago times).

41. "Government to Enact Labor Reform: Business Community Pleads for Postponement of Law," ibid., 26 September 2001.

42. "Senate Approves Labor Reform Bill," ibid., 12 September 2001.

address a growing concern in Chilean society about job instability and precariousness (Frank 2002). Table 4.2 shows changes in Chilean labor laws throughout the three democratic administrations.

The 2001 law also made it easier for unions to form with a smaller number of workers and freed them from government regulation of their internal organization. Fines were increased for artificially dividing a company for the purpose of avoiding the obligations of the labor code or resisting unionization (U.S. Department of State 2002b). While employers could still replace strikers, it became more expensive to do so in that they were now required to pay a bond. Some provisions also increased the bargaining power of seasonal agricultural workers, although employers still had no obligation to bargain. Finally, a long-awaited unemployment insurance scheme was approved by Congress in 2001 (Haagh 2002, 106).

The experience of Chilean labor reform reflected the superior strength of employers and their alliance with powerful conservative groups in society, and the comparative weakness of Chilean unions. The consolidation of market reforms and of a flexible labor relations system during the dictatorship increased employer resistance to change. Recent labor law reforms reflect a persistence of this imbalance, but they also indicate something else: a shift of the pendulum away from extreme forms of employer flexibility toward greater levels of protection, especially for individual workers but also for workers trying to form unions. Although many of the laws remained weak in terms of their provisions, the government took steps toward improving the effective enforcement of those laws.[43]

In Peru, Fujimori's sudden departure in 2000 and his subsequent dismissal by Congress on the grounds of "moral incapacity" closed a peculiar chapter in Peruvian politics. While the country reeled from accounts of bribery, corruption, and abuses by Peru's national intelligence services, the head of the Senate, Valentín Paniagua, was thrust into the interim presidency. Part of Paniagua's term (November 2000–July 2001) and much of Alejandro Toledo's administration (July 2001–July 2006) saw new efforts to address ILO concerns with Peruvian labor law.

---

43. Even after the Lagos reform in 2001, the International Confederation of Free Trade Unions (ICFTU) continued to raise concerns about restrictions on freedom of association, bargaining, and strike rights (see Bureau of National Affairs 2003 and ICFTU 2003). The ILO also indicated a number of issues raised in previous reports that remained unchanged after the 2001 code (ILO-CEACR 2003).

TABLE 4.2 Comparison of Chilean Labor Laws, 1979–2001

Issue	Pinochet (1973–1990)	Aylwin (1990–1994)	Frei (1994–2000)	Lagos (2000–2006)
Individual				
Dismissal	At will.	Employer must justify in writing either failure to discharge duties or "necessities of firm."		If union-related, worker has choice between reinstatement with back wages or additional severance pay.
Severance	One month's pay per year of service up to five months.	One month's pay per year of service up to eleven months. Additional 20% if dismissal found to be unjustified by courts.	Workers unjustly dismissed under needs-of-firm clause receive severance + 30%. Other unfair dismissals + 80–100%.	
Work schedules				
Maximum workweek		Extend 48-hour workweek to new categories of workers.		Phase in reduction from 48 to 45 hours (by 2005).
Collective				
Collective bargaining	Allows for contracts and for convenios or "unregulated bargaining" (Art. 127).	Same.		Firms required to share financial information.
Level	Plant level only.	Multiemployer bargaining if by "mutual agreement" (Art. 90).		Same.

(continues)

TABLE 4.2 *Continued*

Issue	Pinochet (1973–1990)	Aylwin (1990–1994)	Frei (1994–2000)	Lagos (2000–2006)
Scope	Wages only (Art. 82).[1]	Same.	Joint commissions on health and safety (19345).	
Coverage	Parties to bargaining only.			Same.
Limits	Excludes public employees, enterprises with more than 50% public ownership, and firms less than one year old.			"Unregulated bargaining" applies to temporary workers, seasonal workers, apprentices, and part-time employees.[2] Seasonal agricultural workers may submit bargaining proposal.[3]
Strikes	Prohibited for public employees, essential services, temporary or seasonal workers. Solidarity strikes or strikes to demand compliance with contracts illegal.			
Striker replacement	Permitted.	Rules for replacing strikers from day one or after fifteenth day.		Employer must wait fifteen days to hire replacements, pay bond.[4]

Other	Automatic dismissal of strikers after sixty days.	Sixty-day provision abolished. Strike ends when 50% of striking workers drop out (Art. 159-1991).	Employer may lock out if strike affects more than 50% of company's employees or paralyzes essential activities of firm.
Organization	Firm level, interfirm, "independent workers," and seasonal workers' unions.	Same. Legalizes national unions, federations, and confederations.	Reduces number of workers needed to form unions.[5]
		Job security and leave extended to confederation leaders.	
		Number of workers required for unions in medium-sized firms reduced.	
			Public employee associations recognized (Law 19296).
Limits	Ban on unions within one year of firm's establishment.	Lifts ban on unions for seasonal agricultural workers.	
	Public administration denied right to unionize.	Same.	
	Open shop.	Same.	
Financing		Nonunion members to pay bargaining fee of 75% of union dues.	

TABLE 4.2 *Continued*

Issue	Pinochet (1973–1990)	Aylwin (1990–1994)	Frei (1994–2000)	Lagos (2000–2006)
		Confederations may arrange financing with affiliates.		
Enforcement			Expanded jurisdiction of Labor Directorate (19481).	Increase number of inspectors; Labor Directorate becomes party to cases that pass to tribunals.
				Fines raised for antiunion dismissals.
				Fines raised for artificial divisions of company to avoid unionization.

1. Bargaining over organization, direction, and administration of the firm is explicitly prohibited.

2. These workers are not allowed to strike, nor is the bargaining process subject to legal norms governing unfair labor and bargaining practices; only remuneration and general working conditions may be covered (U.S. Department of Labor 2003, 13).

3. If employer responds negatively, agricultural union may present a new plan the following season (Labor Code, Article 314, as amended by Law 19759).

4. The employer may hire replacements after first day of strike if employer's last offer contains the same conditions as the previous agreement (adjusted for inflation), provides for a minimum annual adjustment of wages based on inflation during the contract period, and provides a "replacement bond" equal to four times the wage of each replacement worker, to be divided among all the strikers (U.S. Department of Labor 2003, 9).

5. Eight workers form a quorum for firms with fewer than fifty employees. In firms with more than fifty employees, twenty-five workers are needed. If there is no existing union, however, a union can be formed with only eight workers for up to one year. A minimum of twenty-five workers is required for all other types of unions (Labor Code, Articles 227 and 228, as amended by Law 19759).

The regime's shift in focus toward bolstering labor protections occurred within a broader context of transition to democracy. Peruvians—citizens and politicians alike—saw the interim government as leading a transition from the "dictatorship" of Fujimori to a democratic regime. The goal was to reestablish democracy and the rule of law in Peru. One sign of this transition was the establishment of a Truth and Reconciliation Commission to investigate cases of human rights abuses under previous governments.

In this context, government and Congress saw fit to reevaluate previous policies and seek new consensus on reforms. In the labor arena this meant an examination of the previous decade's labor legislation and policies and a focus on "social dialogue" in the crafting of future reforms, which would seek a balance in labor relations and compliance with international labor standards.[44] A tripartite council was formed in January 2001 to review and discuss labor policies. In particular, Labor Minister Jaime Zavala insisted on the importance of reconstituting the Labor Ministry as an entity that enforced labor law, and he pushed for a labor inspection bill that would enable the ministry to begin to do this.[45]

In all, "sixteen observations" from the ILO for changes in Peruvian labor law became the focus of the government, as first the Paniagua and then the Toledo administrations tried to correct the abuses of the discredited Fujimori regime. According to Delia Muñoz, technical secretary of the new tripartite Consejo Nacional del Trabajo (or National Labor Council, CNT),[46] "the commitment here has been that we have to raise the issue of the 16 observations as a matter of the country's image."[47] Among the issues the ILO raised were the absence of sufficient protection against antiunion discrimination, the slowness of judicial procedures in the case of trade union complaints, the requirement of a "double majority" (a majority of workers and enterprises) for the

44. See Beatriz Alva Hart, "Urgente: Diálogo y conciliación laboral," *El Comercio,* 10 December 2000; Jaime Zavala Costa, "Diálogo social tripartito," ibid., 24 January 2001; Veronica Fernandini, "Menos costos y más empleo: Fórmula perfecta," ibid., 22 July 2001, B-1. Articles available at http://www.elcomercioperu.com/pe/online/.

45. "Se reglamentó ley de inspecciones laborales," ibid., 20 June 2001; "Inspectores laborales empiezan hoy a visitar las empresas," ibid., 2 July 2001; Decreto Legislativo 910, Ley General de Inspección del Trabajo y Defensa del Trabajador.

46. The National Labor Council was first established by Interim President Paniagua in January 2001 and later reinstated by President Toledo in September 2001.

47. "Trabajadores recibirían bono por productividad y alimentos," *El Comercio,* 23 January 2002, http://www.elcomercioperu.com/pe/online/.

conclusion of a collective agreement, and the unilateral powers of employers to introduce changes in working conditions.[48]

Other specific provisions of concern to the ILO included the denial of trade union membership during the probation period; the high requirement of a hundred members to form trade unions by branch of activity or occupation; the requirement that workers must be active members of a union and have been in the employ of the enterprise for at least one year to become eligible for trade union office; prohibition of political activities for trade unions; excessive restriction on the right of workers to call a strike; the obligation that trade unions compile reports that might be requested by labor authorities; the power of the labor authority to cancel registration of a trade union and the requirement that the union must wait six months after remedying cause of cancellation before reapplying for registration; the prohibition of federations and confederations of public services from forming part of organizations that represent other categories of workers; the power of the labor administration to establish minimum services when a strike was declared in essential public services; and the lack of sanctions against acts of interference by employers in trade union organizations, among others.[49]

In 2002 the ILO also noted the government's several efforts, as yet unsuccessful, to introduce and pass labor legislation that would address various ILO concerns. One of these was submitted to Congress in July 2000 but shelved by the labor committee of Congress one year later. A second bill was submitted to Congress in early 2002 (Anteproyecto de la Ley General de Trabajo) and routed through a tripartite forum for discussion and consensus.[50] The mandate of this tripartite CNT was to reach broad consensus among labor organizations, employers, and other interested parties on the outlines of the new labor code. In March 2004 the CNT presented to Congress the anteproyecto containing 440

48. "Observations made by the Committee on the Application of Standards, International Labour Conference (from 1990), ILC 2001/89th Session" (Peru), http://webfusion. ilo.org/public/db/standards/norms/libsynd.

49. "Comments made by the Committee of Experts on the Application of Conventions and Recommendations, Freedom of Association and Protection of the Right to Organise Convention, 1948 (No. 87), Peru," CEACR 2002, 73rd Session. See also "Application of Conventions and Recommendations (from 1990), Right to Organise and Collective Bargaining Convention, 1949 (No. 98), Peru," CEACR 2002, 73rd Session, http://webfusion .ilo.org/public/db/standards/norms/libsynd.

50. Comisión de Trabajo del Congreso de la República, Anteproyecto de la Ley General de Trabajo, Lima, February 2003.

articles dealing with individual and collective reforms. The labor minister claimed that consensus had been reached on approximately 70 percent of the articles and that the new proposal was in full compliance with ILO conventions.[51]

Several factors accounted for the focus on compliance with international labor standards in the elaboration of the new labor reform project. First, the labor commission in Congress was made up of politicians with ties to labor, who kept the pressure on the CNT to reach agreement.[52] Second, the technical committee that elaborated the anteproyecto consisted of lawyers from both labor and management sides who were able to reach consensus on all but two relatively minor points. They also agreed that the draft labor code should conform to ILO standards. To this end, the draft was sent to the ILO for review and commentary, and it came back improved. The draft then went to the tripartite CNT, where it was reviewed and modified until consensus was reached.[53] The parties were driven by the common understanding that the post-Fujimori democratic context required democratization of labor relations as well as of politics.

Nonetheless, the draft labor reform that the CNT submitted to Congress remained incomplete. Congress pressed the CNT to continue to work on reaching agreement on the remaining provisions of the bill. The labor minister also formed a set of "consultative commissions" made up of experts in labor and employment matters to identify the remaining provisions of the bill that required resolution and to advise the government more broadly on employment issues.[54] In June 2005,

51. The most controversial issues concerned the right to reinstatement and increase in severance pay in cases of unjust dismissal, "excessive protection" of union leaders, and branch-level collective bargaining, among others. "Entregan anteproyecto de Ley General de Trabajo al Congreso," *El Comercio,* 19 March 2004, http://www.elcomercioperu.com/pe/online/.

52. Marco Pascó Cosmópolis, member of the technical committee that drafted the anteproyecto, personal communication with author, Querétaro, Mexico, 15 September 2004.

53. Some of the original drafters of the proposal noted that the resulting consensus did not always improve the proposal, and felt it might be necessary to resubmit the final product to the ILO, in order to uncover possible gaps and contradictions. Adolfo Ciudad Reynaud, member of the technical committee that drafted the anteproyecto, personal communication with author, Querétaro, Mexico, 16 September 2004.

54. "Instalan Comisiones Consultivas de Trabajo y Promoción del Empleo," Oficina de Comunicación Social y Relaciones Públicas, Ministerio de Trabajo y Promoción del Empleo, Gobierno del Perú, 30 March 2004. The CNT also agreed to lay out a plan of action to eradicate the deficit of dignified and productive work, taking as a point of depar-

however, trade unions pulled out of the CNT, frustrated by the slow progress of reform talks and the delay in passing a new labor code in Congress.

Although the Toledo administration remained unable to implement a comprehensive labor reform bill by the end of 2005, it had earlier addressed several concerns of trade unions and the ILO. Among labor's demands, expressed during the presidential campaign, were an immediate end to arbitrary dismissals, a general wage increase, changes to the regulations governing AFPs, and reinstatement of workers dismissed during privatization of public enterprises.[55] Following through on a campaign promise to the unions, in February 2002 Toledo signed into law a bill requiring employers to pay overtime to employees who work more than eight hours a day, provide additional compensation for night work, and provide a forty-five-minute meal break during eight-hour shifts.[56] In July 2002 Congress passed a law on collective dismissals that would open the door to compensation for thousands of employees who had been fired unjustly under the Fujimori government (Law 27803). Several months later a constitutional tribunal ruled that the Spanish telecommunications company Telefónica had to rehire more than four thousand employees who had been fired for union activity (U.S. Department of State 2002b).[57] In December 2002 Congress passed a law (Law 27912) that explicitly addressed some of the ILO's concerns with the 1992 law on collective relations. The provisions of the new law, which had been discussed in the CNT, would allow workers in their probationary period to join unions, reduce the number of workers required to form a union, recognize and regulate the right to strike, and allow branch-level collective bargaining.[58]

---

ture the ILO Subregional Office for the Andean Region's Propuesta de Programa Nacional de Trabajo Decente 2004–2006 (Oficina Internacional del Trabajo 2003).

55. "Toledo afirma que respetará compromiso con trabajadores," El Comercio, 22 July 2001, A7; Guillermo Figueroa, "Toledo se reunió con la CGTP," ibid., 27 February 2001, http://www.elcomercioperu.com/pe/online/.

56. "Aprueban cambios en la ley de la jornada laboral," El Comercio, 26 January 2002, ibid. Among the concerns with this bill, which modified the Ley de Jornada de Trabajo, Horario y Trabajo en Sobretiempo (D.L. 854), was that it had not been discussed in the CNT and therefore consensus among the key social actors had not been reached. The Lima Chamber of Commerce thought it would raise costs. See "Podrían observar ley de la jornada laboral," ibid., 1 February 2002.

57. In December 2002 the Labor Ministry also published a list of 7,156 names of former public-sector employees who stood to benefit from the new collective dismissal law, with more names to be released as claims came forward and investigations continued.

58. El Peruano, 12 December 2002 and 27 September 2002, available at http://www.editoraperu.com.pe/edc/02/12/12/eco1.asp and http://www.editoraperu.com.pe/edc/02/09/27/der1.asp.

In March 2004 the Toledo government issued a decree (D.S. 003-2004-TR) creating a Registry of Union Organizations of Public Sector Employees so that public-sector unions could register.[59] The decree amended a November 2001 law (Law 27556) that restored the rights of state employees to unionize. In signing the decree, Toledo claimed that now all sixteen points of concern raised by the ILO had been addressed by the government. According to Juan José Gorriti, secretary general of the CGTP, "This decree ends a period in which the rights of Peruvian workers were trampled upon by the government. This decree is nothing more than recognition of the fundamental rights enjoyed by workers around the world" (Bureau of National Affairs 2004).

Despite this progress in addressing the labor rights deficits of the Fujimori regime, political instability under the Toledo administration hindered the government's ability to forge consistent labor policy and to oversee the passage of comprehensive labor law reform. Declining popular support for Toledo, antiprivatization protests (which led the government to declare a state of emergency in 2002), frequent cabinet reshuffling, charges of electoral fraud, and a long, as yet unfulfilled agenda of state and institutional reforms threatened to place labor issues on the back burner. Finally, the breakdown in talks within the CNT, along with the short lead time before the 2006 presidential elections, made it unlikely that the labor reform bill would pass before the end of Toledo's term.

CONCLUSION: RADICAL LEGACIES, REPRESSIVE FLEXIBILITY, AND THE SEARCH FOR BALANCE

Although both Chile and Peru established labor legislation earlier in the twentieth century, it was the later experience of radical pro-labor policies under the Allende regime in Chile and under the military in Peru that proved the critical turning point and produced a backlash. Allende's government was not able to change the Chilean labor code, but it did implement pro-labor policies and had an important impact on mobilization in the workplace and on unionization. These actions contributed to the sense of threat felt by conservative elites. In Peru, the military introduced favorable labor legislation that also expanded mobi-

59. In 1995 the Fujimori government deactivated the National Public Administration Institute, the registering agency for public employee unions.

lization by labor and the left. In both cases labor laws were later altered by governments that wanted to suppress labor action and create a more favorable environment for business. Although the timing differed—Pinochet introducing the Labor Plan in 1979 and Fujimori implementing changes in the 1990s—the effect on workers, and especially on trade unions, was similar: enhanced "flexibility" in an authoritarian political context.

Unions in both countries were dramatically weakened even prior to these changes in law. In Chile the repression of the dictatorship hurt the unions, whereas in Peru the severity of the economic crisis diminished union power well before Fujimori became president. With the return of democracy in Chile, unions remained weak political and social actors, while economic and political elites were committed to an economic model that further constrained workers. Yet, in an attempt to create a better balance in Chilean labor relations, efforts to expand labor rights protections became more pronounced in the early 2000s. In Peru a similar search for balance became possible after Fujimori's departure, even though, as in Brazil, the reform remains incomplete. Nonetheless, in the Peruvian context of "democratic transition," unions have found allies among prominent labor lawyers, government officials, and the ILO. Together they have begun to forge a consensus around labor rights.

Legacies of Revolution: Mexico and Bolivia

Mexico stands out in Latin America for the limited attention politicians have paid to reforming its labor laws. While other countries suppressed labor rights under authoritarian governments and adopted labor protections under democratic ones, Mexico's largely pro-worker legislation held up through decades of rule by the Partido Revolucionario Institucional (PRI). Similarly, when other countries were trying to make their labor legislation more flexible in response to economic opening, Mexican labor law went largely untouched despite Mexico's early commitment to structural economic reform, including extensive trade liberalization enshrined in the North American Free Trade Agreement, which Mexico signed in 1993.

In Bolivia, a largely protective body of labor legislation dating from the 1930s also survived without significant changes. By the end of the 1990s Mexico and Bolivia were among the very few countries in the region that had not carried out significant labor reforms. Since the mid-1980s Bolivia had also implemented market reforms that significantly liberalized its economy. These two countries exhibited the starkest contrast: between extensive economic liberalization, on the one hand, and the absence of labor law reform, on the other.

LEGACIES OF REVOLUTION

In Mexico a flexible and pragmatic relationship between state-sanctioned labor organizations and the state compensated in part for the protective character of labor law (Bensusán 2000). "Official" (pro-government) unions gained privileged access to state resources and enjoyed representational monopoly in exchange for controlling union members and mobilizing electoral support for the ruling party (Middlebrook 1995). Toward the end of the twentieth century, labor unions permitted a good deal of functional flexibility and generally restrained wage demands, while informal-sector employment remained at high levels. This political and institutional arrangement was rooted in an early pattern of incorporation of labor into the ruling party in the context of a nationalist, revolutionary regime.

In Bolivia, a mobilized labor movement became an important ally for political leaders and helped to move national politics to the left in the 1930s–1950s. A protective labor law and a constitution with a strong set of social rights were forged in the 1930s, and the 1952 nationalist revolution translated many of these rights into policy, much as President Lázaro Cárdenas did in Mexico in the 1930s. Although the labor-party link had weakened by the late 1950s, labor's autonomous strength persisted until the 1980s. Despite a policy of extensive economic liberalization since the mid-1980s, labor laws were not fundamentally altered. This was due in part to labor's mobilization capacity and strong opposition to change, but also to the difficulties with enforcement, structural flexibility evident in a large informal sector, and political crises, which postponed labor reform.

Labor Law and the Revolutionary State in Mexico

Throughout most of the twentieth century, industrial relations in Mexico were characterized by strong state involvement and labor unions with close ties to the ruling party.[1] These features originated in the 1930s under the presidency of Lázaro Cárdenas (1934–40) and persisted throughout the twentieth century. Also significant was the corporatist makeup of the ruling party, which included functional representation for labor, peasant, and "middle" sectors (and until 1946, the military). During this time the Mexican labor movement unified organizationally if not yet ideologically. The Confederación de Trabajadores de México (CTM) was formed in 1936 and eventually affiliated with the Party of the Mexican Revolution, the forerunner to the PRI (Middlebrook 1995; Collier and Collier 1991; Garrido 1982).[2]

The state's strong degree of involvement in labor affairs grew out of a protracted process of political centralization and stabilization that began after the Mexican Revolution (1910–17). The years after the revolution were rife with political factionalism as rival leaders sought to gain control. The peasantry and, to a lesser extent, urban labor were a mobilized force during the revolution and ensuing years.[3] In the 1930s President Cárdenas appealed to these sectors with progressive rural and labor reforms. This earned Cárdenas the political support he needed to break the hold that former president Plutarco Elías Calles had wielded over Cárdenas's predecessors. Toward the end of his administration, however, Cárdenas sought increasing control over the labor and peasant movements. Subsequent governments also sought this control through an elaborate system of "inducements and constraints" embedded in Mexico's labor laws and institutions (Collier and Collier 1979; Middlebrook 1995).

Mexican labor law is based on Article 123 of the 1917 Mexican constitution and in the 1931 Federal Labor Law. In spite of changes to both documents over the years, core principles and legislation have remained largely unaltered since their founding, in sharp contrast with most other countries in the region.[4] The constitution's treatment of

1. Parts of this discussion draw on Bensusán and Cook (2003).

2. The earliest version of what would become the PRI was the National Revolutionary Party in 1929, followed by the Party of the Mexican Revolution in 1938 under President Cárdenas. The party was renamed the PRI in 1946 under President Miguel Alemán.

3. In the 1920s labor leader Luis Morones occupied a top cabinet post in the government of President Calles (1924–28) as Minister of Industry, Commerce, and Labor, reflecting a degree of labor influence in government rarely seen since.

4. The most recent changes, as well as the greatest number of amendments to the Federal Labor Law, occurred in the 1970s.

labor issues was strongly favorable to workers and served as a model for other countries in the elaboration of their labor codes early in the twentieth century.[5] At the time of its passage in 1917, Article 123 was easily the most advanced labor charter in the world. The Federal Labor Law of 1931 provided a more expansive and detailed treatment of labor matters.[6] It also set up a number of obstacles to independent unions by granting the state a role in overseeing the formation and actions of trade unions, a role in deciding labor-management and intraunion conflicts, and the discretionary authority to interpret constitutional labor protections through its control of tripartite labor boards and tribunals (Bensusán 2000). Despite the generally protective character of labor legislation, the strong state role in labor relations allowed successive governments to modify and even violate these protections in order to adapt to changing demands of a more market-oriented economy, especially during the 1980s and 1990s.

The Mexican government's involvement in labor relations also extends beyond the law. Traditionally the Mexican political system has been highly centralized, with enormous power residing in the executive branch despite formal separation of powers (Garrido 1989; Meyer 1977; Cornelius 1996). Direct intervention by the executive branch has been common in labor disputes and strikes, with presidential involvement in the highest-profile cases. This role of the federal government has been further enforced and complicated by labor's alliance with the PRI. Until recently, party and state were thoroughly intertwined. Although the defeat of the PRI in the 2000 presidential elections helped to break this link, the strong government presence in labor relations remains the system's core feature, and calls for a diminished state role have gained force in discussions of labor reform.

5. The 1917 constitution established the right to organize and to strike as a "natural right of man," and also established the right to an eight-hour day, a living wage, overtime, maternity leave, and profit sharing, among other things (Bensusán 2000).

6. Mexican law provides for several kinds of labor organization, including firm-level unions, craft unions, industrial unions, and national industrial unions. It also allows for regional, state, and national federations and state and national confederations, and permits plant-level, company, and sector-wide collective bargaining. The constitution creates two categories of legislation, "A" and "B." The former applies to most private-sector workers and the latter to public employees. The primary difference between the two is that "B" legislation puts strong constraints on union formation, bargaining, and strikes. A central demand of unions and reformers is to terminate this legal distinction and extend the terms of category "A" to all workers (Zazueta and de la Peña 1984; Bensusán and Alcalde 2000a).

Most unions cooperated in this system because they also received a range of benefits. Pro-government unions gained representation on several government agencies, including the Mexican Social Security Institute and the National Minimum Wage Commission, and were given substantial control over others, such as the National Worker Housing Institute (INFONAVIT) and the Workers' Bank (Banco Obrero) (Burgess 2004, 66–67). These institutions provided labor organizations with sizeable economic resources and benefits that leaders could distribute to their membership, cementing patronage networks within unions and confederations. Along with these subsidies, the main labor organizations also received privileged access to government officials and limited influence over public policy.

Unions' involvement in these state institutions stemmed from their alliance with the PRI. At the root of this alliance was an exchange in which unions delivered votes for PRI candidates in return for privileged state access and economic and political resources, including union representation in political office. Union leaders routinely obtained seats in Congress and top positions in the party at national, state, and local levels. Labor's strong organized support for PRI candidates, especially for president, along with its unwavering backing of the executive on controversial national policy matters, gave labor substantial political influence.

Perhaps the person most responsible for this strategy was Fidel Velázquez, who headed the CTM from 1941 to 1947 and again from 1950 until his death in 1997 at age ninety-seven. Velázquez presided over the Mexican labor movement through ten presidential administrations, and for many years he had a hand in determining who would occupy the highest office. Velázquez was instrumental in turning the CTM into a close ally of the PRI and in steering the labor movement through difficult economic times while clamping down on worker demands.

Features of Mexico's Labor Law

Despite the favorable and protective nature of much Mexican labor legislation, the system's constraints and restrictions derive from the law's implementation. Many of the controls on labor were, and still are, implemented through decisions of the labor conciliation and arbitration boards. These boards are made up of labor, business, and government representatives and operate at federal and local (state) levels.[7] The boards handle most industrial relations matters, including union registration, enforcement of contract provisions, elections to determine which union holds title to the collective agreement, strikes, and.individual and collective grievances and disputes (Middlebrook 1995, 61).

Most criticism of the system in recent years has focused on the labor boards. One critique relates to the board's composition: Since there is a government representative on the board, and since the union representative has tended to be from a pro-government union, labor boards rarely find in favor of independent unions or union challengers to one of the official unions. It is difficult for independent unions to gain registry, legal certification for strikes, or the ability to challenge incumbent unions for title to the contract on fair grounds.

The highly technical and ambiguous nature of the law gives the boards significant discretionary power when making decisions about the legality of strikes or union registration. The boards deny union registration for failure to comply with any part of a long list of requirements; technical criteria are often cited when the real reasons for rejecting a union's registration bid are political.[8] The boards can declare strikes "nonexistent" or "illicit" according to ambiguous criteria that are often politically manipulated. Elections to determine which union has the majority and is therefore entitled to represent workers in bargaining are typically stacked against challengers, and threats and intimidation of voters are commonplace. The labor boards contain labor militancy by controlling strike activity and the formation of independent unions.[9]

Laws governing internal union activities formally support union autonomy, allowing unions to draw up their own statutes and internal

7. Mexican unions are divided into local and federal jurisdictions depending on the nature of the economic activity and whether the union's membership spans more than one state. This union status determines whether the union must appear before local or federal boards. Most maquiladora unions are under local (state) jurisdiction. The local boards handle union registration in local jurisdictions. Unions in federal jurisdictions must register with the Ministry of Labor and Social Welfare (Zazueta and de la Peña 1984).

8. The law sets out a detailed list of requirements for union registration. Unions must have a minimum of twenty members and they must submit notarized copies of minutes from the organizational assembly and from the meeting where union leadership was elected, a list of members' names and addresses, and a copy of the union statutes (Middlebrook 1995, 64).

9. For more on the functions of the labor conciliation and arbitration boards, see Middlebrook (1995), Bensusán (2000), and Commission for Labor Cooperation (2000).

regulations and to elect their own officers (Middlebrook 1995, 67). Yet the lack of regulations on the conduct of union elections or on member approval of collective bargaining agreements has not strengthened union democracy. Instead it has made it more difficult to secure contracts that benefit members, led to undemocratic leadership selection, and encouraged union leaders' neglect of member needs.[10] For decades union members have protested undemocratic (rigged or coerced) union elections (de la Garza 1991; Cook 1996).

This lack of regulation, together with the makeup of the labor boards, has also led to a widespread practice that has become a core concern of independent unions and labor rights advocates in recent years. In many small enterprises and in the maquiladora sector, union leaders or unscrupulous labor lawyers arrange collective agreements with employers without workers' knowledge. These "protection contracts" provide the minimum protection required by law or sometimes below the minimum and are rarely updated. The collective agreements are registered with the labor authorities. Workers are frequently unaware of such arrangements until they try to form their own union and get employers to sign a collective contract, when they learn that a union and contract are already in place. Workers must then submit to a *recuento*—an election to determine which of the two unions, the new one formed by the workers or the unknown "incumbent" union, has majority support and hence which will have title to the contract.[11] In 2000 the president of the local labor conciliation and arbitration board of Mexico City estimated that about 90 percent of all registered contracts in Mexico City were protection contracts.[12]

Protection contracts are also difficult to combat because the labor conciliation and arbitration boards do not maintain a public registry of

10. Numerous reporting requirements provided the government with opportunities to intervene, including the selection of union leaders, should unions fail to meet their obligations or other irregularities arise.

11. While Mexican law allows more than one union to form in a workplace in the private sector, only one union is granted representation rights to bargain on behalf of members. Even so, labor boards often reject registration of additional unions in the workplace. Recent events and court cases have begun to alter this practice of permitting only one union in a workplace. See the Mexican Supreme Court cases described below, as well as the Fisheries Union and Maxi-Switch submissions filed under the NAALC (Cook et al. 1997; and http://www.dol.gov/dol/ilab/public/programs/nao/main.htm, under "submissions").

12. *La Jornada,* 2 November 2000, 42. On protection contracts, see Bensusán, García, and von Bülow (1996); La Botz (1992); Bouzas Ortíz and Gaitán Riveros 2001; Bensusán and Alcalde (2000b); de la Garza (2000); and Xelhuantzi (2000).

union contracts.[13] It is impossible for unions, workers, or other members of the public to determine whether a protection contract exists or the nature of its terms. Hence a key demand for legal reform entails the establishment of a public registry of unions and contracts operated by these boards (Bensusán 2001; Bensusán and Alcalde 2000b; Xelhuantzi-López 2000).

Another common mechanism that allows unions to maintain internal control is the "exclusion clause" in collective agreements. The exclusion clause regarding "entry" calls for a union shop; the employer agrees to hire only union members. The exclusion clause regarding "separation" obligates the employer to fire any workers who have been expelled by the union. This clause strengthens the union's position by inhibiting employer efforts to destabilize the union or create employer-dominated unions. However, the clause is used most commonly by union officials to control internal dissent, since workers can be expelled—and therefore fired—for disloyalty to the union (Middlebrook 1995, 96; Bensusán and Alcalde 2000b).[14]

Labor and the Revolutionary State in Bolivia

In Bolivia, the labor movement began to emerge as an important political force in the 1930s, after the disastrous Chaco War (1932–35) with Paraguay destroyed the old regime and radicalized a new generation of middle-class intellectuals, young officers, workers, and indigenous peasants. Although Bolivia's industrial working class was small (in this way it mirrored Mexico's prerevolutionary situation), the silver and tin mines produced the most cohesive and militant sector of the labor movement. The postwar period in Bolivia thus gave rise to new, politi-

13. An exception was the local board of the federal district (Mexico City, under PRD leadership), which has made information on collective agreements public since 2000. While no specific legal distinction singles out protection contracts, analysts have identified as likely protection contracts those which are not revised every two years, or in which wages are not revised annually, since Mexican law permits contract negotiations every two years on conditions of employment and annually on wages (de la Garza 2000).

14. There has been some disagreement among labor reform advocates as to whether the exclusion clause should be permitted. Both official and some independent unions have found this provision useful in controlling internal dissent and limiting employer domination of worker organization. Nonetheless, this provision is an obstacle to voluntary union affiliation and in 2001 was found unconstitutional by the Mexican Supreme Court. Relatively high union density figures in Mexico should be seen in the context of this quasi-obligatory or involuntary union membership status.

cized groups and to the creation of new political parties in direct rejection of the traditional party and elite system that had led the country to war (Degregori 1998).

The young officers who overthrew the government in 1936 did so with the direct support of the miners and these new sectors of the country. While national-socialist tendencies were strong and came from the parties and politicians linked to the regime, the powerful presence of the labor movement drove the new civilian-military government to the left. In May 1936 the country's first labor ministry was created, and a trade union leader from the printers' union was named labor minister. In what was called a government of "military socialism," the regime pursued nationalist policies that broke decisively with the orientation of previous governments. A key move was the nationalization, without compensation, of Standard Oil in March 1937 and the creation of a state oil company, Yacimientos Petrolíferos Fiscales Bolivianos (YPFB), a full year before President Cárdenas nationalized the oil companies in Mexico. As in Mexico, a corporatist model for the legislature in which there would be functional representation was also considered, but later abandoned (Klein 1982, 202, 204).

In the late 1930s two of the most significant political developments took place: the elaboration of a new, national-statist constitution in 1938, followed by a labor code in 1939. The 1938 National Convention was filled with radical delegates from veterans' associations and labor. Much like the 1917 Mexican constitution, the new Bolivian charter contained a set of social provisions regarding individual working conditions, organization of unions, and the right to strike (Sandoval 1997, 20). Also like the Mexican constitution, it firmly established the state's role as regulator of the economy and the agent responsible for the economic welfare of the population. Individual property rights were secondary to property as a "social right," to be protected and overseen by the state (Malloy 1970, 92). The Bolivian constitution of 1938 thus fit within the emerging tradition of "social constitutionalism" in Latin America, initiated with the Mexican charter of 1917 (Klein 1982, 205–6).

The constitution was followed in 1939 by a protective and state-centered labor code. Decreed by Colonel Germán Busch shortly after an "autocoup" in which he declared a dictatorship, the "Busch Code" was nonetheless hailed as "a major piece of national legislation" (Klein 1982, 208). Drafted under an earlier government with a trade unionist labor minister, the labor code established the pro-labor character of the new government and had far-reaching political repercussions (Lora 1977, 182). The code reflected the Busch government's efforts to secure the support of the labor movement—a common theme in Bolivian politics in this era—which itself was pressuring for regulation of the "social rights" established in the constitution.

As in Mexico and other countries, the 1939 labor code[15] established individual protections such as the eight-hour day, forty-eight-hour week, limits on night work, and overtime regulations. It also established one union per enterprise and required a minimum of 50 percent of the workers in the sector in order to form industrial unions. The right to strike was recognized but was also regulated and controlled by the state, and arbitration was required in cases of labor-management conflict. It also limited the number of foreign workers to 15 percent of total employees in a firm, a provision Guillermo Lora calls "unnecessary" because of the limited presence of foreign workers, but one which clearly pandered to the nationalist sentiments of the population (Lora 1977, 182). As in Mexico, most provisions of the 1939 labor code remained in place throughout the twentieth century and even into the twenty-first.[16]

Throughout the 1940s the national-socialist and left-radical political tendencies coexisted in uneasy tension, together with traditional political elites and the more conservative army officers who represented their interests. The miners' movement emerged as an important political resource for the new political parties that were trying to secure their base. The Stalinist Partido de Izquierda Revolucionaria (PIR), the Trotskyist Partido Obrero Revolucionario (POR), and the national-socialist Movimiento Nacionalista Revolucionario (MNR) all had adherents in the labor movement and tried to mobilize support from the miners for nationalization of the tin mines. Support for nationalization came from diverse sectors, including a radicalized middle class that threw its backing behind the MNR (Klein 1982, 213).

The MNR's first, if brief, foray into government came in 1943 as part of a military junta. However, mounting pressure from the United States

15. The labor code was approved by decree in 1939 and raised to the category of law in 1942; its regulatory decree was issued in 1943 (Goldín 1999, 9).
16. Since 1943 there have been more than twenty-five hundred complementary "dispositions" that include laws, supreme decrees, and resolutions at varying levels (Goldín 1999, 9).

in the context of World War II forced the MNR, which harbored a fascist wing, out of the governing coalition. The party nonetheless retained ties with the regime and worked closely with Juan Lechín, leader of the Federación Sindical de Trabajadores Mineros de Bolivia (FSTMB), whose creation the MNR supported in 1944 (Klein 1982, 218–19).

Lechín was instrumental in securing the labor movement's ties with the MNR in the prerevolutionary period of the 1940s and through the 1952 revolution. He was a popular and charismatic leader and, like Fidel Velázquez in Mexico, he became the key interlocutor for the labor movement with the state in the ensuing decades. In contrast to Mexico, however, the role of Lechín and the miners was to drive the MNR further to the left. In the prerevolutionary *sexenio* of 1946–52, labor helped to rid the MNR of its fascist elements and demanded that the party support its radical program, which included armed struggle against the regime. In ways that parallel the Mexican case, Lechín's tie to the MNR (along with mistakes committed by the PIR) helped to undermine the more radical leftist parties that had allied with labor in the past, making the MNR the main party of labor and the left. The alliance between the MNR, labor, and the middle class was further cemented at the end of the decade after the MNR attempted armed insurrections against the regime, which at that point was controlled by traditional political elites in the Republican Party (Klein 1982, 222, 224).

In April 1952 three days of fighting between the army and civilians (including the miners) led to the overthrow of the government and the installation of an MNR-labor administration under Víctor Paz Estenssoro and Hernán Siles Zuazo. Thus began "the most important revolution in Latin America since the 1910 Mexican Revolution" (Degregori 1998, 214). With the army virtually destroyed, popular urban and rural militias became a new power base for the regime. Citizenship expanded practically overnight as literacy was removed as a requirement for voting. Worker and peasant unionization grew at a fast pace, and in 1953 an agrarian reform law abolished the latifundia and created a new class of communal peasant landowners (Klein 1982, 235). The regime established a state capitalist economic model and set out a project of "national integration" that redefined indigenous peoples as peasants, much as the Mexican Revolution had done decades earlier (Degregori 1998, 214).

Labor was a direct beneficiary of the regime. The Central Obrera Boliviana (COB), an overarching labor confederation with Lechín at its head, was formed with the full support of the new government only weeks after it took power. Although the COB claimed to be politically neutral, it was in fact closely allied with the regime and played an important role in driving the government further to the radical left, at least in the first few years. While the MNR leadership hoped to control labor, "the COB became a semi-sovereign institution that challenged the MNR's every move" (Gamarra and Malloy 1995, 403). The COB named three ministers to the new cabinet; Lechín was given the Ministry of Mines and Petroleum. In October 1952 the tin mines were nationalized without compensation and placed under the control of a new state agency, the Corporación Minera de Bolivia, COMIBOL. Mineworkers became co-administrators of the mines: They received two out of seven seats on the board of COMIBOL and had veto power in any decisions affecting workers (Klein 1982, 232–34).

The degree of labor influence in the 1952 government was unprecedented and marked a "radical turning point" (Degregori 1998, 214). The MNR government in turn used its support of the miners and the COB to secure and strengthen its power base. Initially, the idea of the MNR was to create a hegemonic single-party regime similar to the Mexican PRI. The MNR leadership especially admired the PRI's ability to establish social control (Gamarra and Malloy 1995, 403). Over time, however, the more moderate MNR leaders aimed to restrain the COB and its radical demands. They sought to attract foreign capital and protect private property, and eventually the government was forced to accept an IMF stabilization plan in a bid to win back middle-class supporters. The IMF plan created rifts between labor and the party, as the government cut food subsidies and held down wages. In order to generate counterweights to labor, MNR leaders Paz and Siles cultivated a relationship with the new peasant sector, which evolved into a relatively conservative political force. President Paz Estenssoro also took advantage of the intense U.S. dislike of Lechín to further isolate him and keep him from the presidency by rebuilding the army and permitting a greater U.S. military presence in Bolivia (Klein 1982, 242, 244).

By the end of the decade, the "revolutionary" phase of the regime was over. Lechín joined forces with Siles Zuazo to oppose Paz's run for a third presidential term, and broke with the MNR. The army then overthrew Paz in 1964 and installed General René Barrientos Ortuno as dictator. Thus began a series of dictatorial administrations of varying political tendencies. The Barrientos regime was hostile to labor. It outlawed the FSTMB and COB, suppressed all strikes, and stationed troops at the mines (Klein 1982, 247). Barrientos was followed by two relatively moderate and populist military governments (1969–71), which restored legality to the unions and withdrew the troops. Despite government efforts to regain labor support, labor did not offer its backing.

This tolerance of labor soon came to an end with the repressive military dictatorship of General Hugo Banzer (1971–78). Banzer's government came closest to reflecting the characteristics of bureaucratic-authoritarian regimes that had set up elsewhere in the region in this same period (Klein 1982, 255–56; Gamarra and Malloy 1995, 407). Banzer outlawed the labor unions and all parties to the left of the MNR (the "traditional" MNR was a partner in his government). His administration resorted to torture, assassination, and the jailing and exile of political party leaders. In 1974 Banzer expelled the MNR from his government and ruled as an all-military, nonparty government.

Protests against the Banzer government grew strong in 1976, as national strikes, including a two-month miners' strike, took hold of the country. Banzer closed the universities, which were centers of opposition to the dictatorship. By the late 1970s he had lost the support of the nationalist middle class for failing to negotiate an outlet to the sea with Chile's Pinochet. This erosion of support, coupled with the election of President Jimmy Carter in the United States (who insisted on respect for human rights as a condition of aid), led Banzer to announce a return to elections in 1980. In December 1977 Banzer's handling of a hunger strike by the wives of exiled mine union leaders forced the regime to hold elections in 1978, two years earlier than planned. Workers returned from exile, seized the trade unions from government appointees, and rebuilt them, often reinstating the same leaders they had before Banzer's coup (Klein 1982, 262).

ECONOMIC LIBERALIZATION AND THE LABOR REFORM DEBATE IN MEXICO

For decades Mexico's economic development model had reinforced the alliance between the party/state and official labor unions. Between 1950 and 1970, the period known as "stabilizing development," the economy grew an average of 7.8 percent annually and annual inflation averaged 3 percent (Lustig 1998, 14–15). Wages increased steadily (Middlebrook

1995, 214–15). As in the rest of Latin America, the Mexican economy was guided by import-substitution industrialization. The state became extensively involved in the economy, domestic industries received tariff protection and government subsidies, and the industrial urban labor force was an important component of the domestic market. Official labor organizations also were consolidated during this period, as the government intervened on their behalf against challengers from independent unions or democratic currents within unions.

Signs that this economic model was breaking down emerged in the 1970s, but it was not until the 1980s that an economic crisis of greater proportions took hold. In 1982 Mexico became the first Latin American nation to default on its debt, initiating a regional debt crisis. Real wages plummeted during this decade. Government subsidies for items such as basic foodstuffs and spending for health and education fell sharply (Lustig 1998, 80–81). While the entire region was plunged into economic crisis, Mexico stood out for the dramatic drop in real wages and for the relatively few strikes conducted by organized labor.[17] This was attributed to the role played by the unions, who moderated their demands sharply and curbed labor protest throughout the decade.

The 1980s were a turning point for labor. While labor organizations curtailed wage demands and limited protest, government and employers began widespread industrial restructuring in response to the economic crisis. This restructuring led in turn to layoffs, plant closures, and reorganization of work and production, as employers tried to adjust to the weakened but more competitive economy and the government prepared to sell off state-owned industries (Zapata 1995). This process also had the effect of eliminating many independent and democratic trade unions that had emerged in several industries during the labor insurgency of the 1970s (Roxborough 1984; de la Garza 1991; Cook 1996). Auto assembly plants in which independent unions had become established in the 1970s were shut down in the 1980s, sometimes after protracted strikes, and new ones set up in greenfield sites in the north, where auto companies signed bargaining agreements with the CTM rather than with independent unions (Tuman 1998).[18]

17. The cumulative drop in the minimum wage between 1983 and 1988 was 48.5 percent, 38 percent in industrial wages (Lustig 1998, 68–69).

18. In other cases, plants were shut down during a strike and were later reopened with a new workforce and new collective agreement. On unions and restructuring in the Mexican auto industry, see Carrillo (1990); Middlebrook (1991); La Botz (1992); Bayón (1997);

The economic crisis weakened all labor unions, but independent unions were hit hardest by industrial restructuring and never regained a presence in manufacturing.[19] Pro-government labor organizations, especially the CTM, also faced difficulties. Relations with members became more strained, as unions were unable to deliver material benefits as they had in the past. This strained relationship in turn affected union leaders' ability to deliver worker docility and votes for the PRI—the latter point became especially evident in the 1988 presidential elections, when many workers apparently voted for the leftist opposition candidate. Yet in the 1980s the CTM was able to secure its presence in the dynamic, export-oriented automobile industry as well as in other manufacturing areas (Middlebrook 1995, 272–75; Bensusán 1997, 15; de la Garza 1993, 155; Tuman 1998). Official unions continued to rely on legal mechanisms and state and employer support to dominate in the maquiladora sector, which expanded significantly in the 1980s.[20] Despite a general weakening of labor's market power and political influence, official unions actually expanded their presence in key export sectors of the economy and managed to purge most independent union competitors.

The shift to neoliberal economic policies during the 1980s and 1990s led Mexican governments to abandon their earlier protection of labor in favor of employers. The state supported de facto flexibility, including employer restructuring of the workplace and collective agreements, making the immediate need for legal reform less pressing. Wages served as a vehicle of flexibility during this period through wage suppression in annual accords among government, business, and labor. The role of the CTM in containing wage demands and militancy among members

---

Morris (1998); Tuman (1998); Bayón and Bensusán (1996); and Juárez Núñez and Babson (1999).

19. The scant availability and reliability of official data on union membership have until very recently made it difficult to know exact rates or to track long-term trends in union density. One of the most widely cited independent studies on union structure and union membership used data collected in 1978 to estimate union density. According to this study, 16.2 percent of all wage and salary earners were unionized; 27.9 percent of all workers *eligible* to be organized belonged to unions (Zazueta and de la Peña 1984, 64–67). Data from a more recent comprehensive survey on household incomes indicate that unionization rates fell between 1984 and 1996 from 24.4 percent of eligible workers to 15.9 percent (or from 14.5 percent to 9.7 of the economically active population). For more data and discussion on unionization rates, see Bensusán and Alcalde (2000a).

20. In 1980 employment in maquiladoras stood at 117,759; by 1990 it had reached 439,198. The 1990s also saw rapid growth. In 1999 employment in maquiladoras, at both border and inland plants, reached 1,131,316 (Rendón and Salas 2000, 66–67).

was also crucial in providing employers greater flexibility and control over the workplace than the law mandated—a sort of "corporatist flexibility" (Bensusán and von Bülow 1997, 195).

The governments of Carlos Salinas (1988–94) and Ernesto Zedillo (1994–2000) oversaw two important developments in the 1990s: the extension and consolidation of structural economic reforms and the gradual liberalization of the political system. Both developments affected the labor movement. While trade liberalization and privatization had begun in the 1980s, President Salinas's negotiation of NAFTA promised to lock in structural economic reforms that favored the market. In spite of modest economic recovery in the early 1990s, workers' real wages remained below their 1980 levels (Lustig 1998). Real wages continued to fall in the 1990s, especially after 1995, when the peso was devalued by 40 percent. By the end of the decade jobs were unstable, informal-sector employment had grown, and the greatest formal-sector job expansion was in the manufacturing assembly plants, or maquiladoras, where wages were low and genuine unions virtually nonexistent.[21]

The economic crisis of 1994–95 hastened the fragmentation of the official labor movement headed by the CTM. In 1995 labor groups critical of the CTM's passive acceptance of economic policy met to discuss alternatives to the official structure. With Fidel Velázquez's death in June 1997, the importance of these efforts increased. By November 1997 a new central of labor organizations, the Unión Nacional de Trabajadores (UNT), had formed. The labor movement then coalesced around three major centers: the CTM and other organizations of the umbrella Labor Congress, containing the majority of workers; the UNT, headed by the telephone union, university unions, and social security workers' union; and the May 1 Inter-Union Coordinating Committee, made up of an array of more radical labor and community groups.[22] The UNT hoped to become the alternative to the Labor Congress and to displace the official sector of the labor movement.

21. The subduing of labor was a key component of the Salinas government's economic strategy. See Americas Watch (1990); La Botz (1992); Cook (1995); Bensusán and León (1991).

22. For a more detailed discussion of the emergence of these groups and their strategies, see Bensusán and Cook (2003).

The Labor Reform Debate in Mexico

As in other countries, economic opening and increased global competition brought national attention back to the subject of Mexico's protective labor legislation. Employers argued that the law was too restrictive and interfered with their ability to remain competitive in the new economic environment. Unions called for reform in several instances, seeking even stronger protections. Although the Mexican government did not reform labor law under either Salinas or Zedillo, both administrations raised the issue, prompting political parties and affected interest groups to respond. Under the Salinas administration, the possibility that labor reform would escape the PRI's control in Congress (the first where leftist opposition was strongly represented), together with the CTM's staunch opposition, ensured that the issue would never reach Congress (Middlebrook 1995).

In 1992 a Salinas government initiative created the possibility of productivity bonuses for workers in exchange for concessions in functional flexibility at the workplace (Bensusán and von Bülow 1997).[23] Later, President Zedillo's Plan Nacional de Desarrollo (National Development Plan, PND) for 1995–2000 set the tone for a change in labor law and labor relations based on consensus. One of Zedillo's labor ministers, José Antonio González Fernández, came closest to pushing labor reform by reminding labor and employer groups that President Zedillo had the authority to send an initiative on labor law to the Congress but would prefer that the process be based on "consensus and dialogue" (Contreras 1998).

As early as 1989 employer organizations had begun to demand changes in the Federal Labor Law and Article 123 of the Mexican constitution. Many of business's proposals emphasized employer flexibility and cost reduction as well as limits on labor's political influence, rather than any measures that might democratize industrial relations. The proposals from two important business organizations, the Confederación Patronal de la República Mexicana (Employers' Confederation of the Mexican Republic, COPARMEX) and the Consejo Coordinador Empresarial (Business Coordinating Council, CCE), bear this out.

---

23. This was the Acuerdo Nacional para la Elevación de la Productividad y la Calidad (ANEPC) signed by government, labor, and employer organizations.

Employers wanted to hire workers under temporary and part-time contracts; pay by the hour (the minimum wage is a daily rate); reduce dismissal costs; subject strike decisions to a vote by workers; introduce probationary periods in employment (via training or apprenticeship contracts); promote employees according to performance and knowledge rather than by seniority exclusively; prohibit the closed shop and union shop; require arbitration upon the request of one of the parties in conflict; allow individual workers to determine whether to join the union; prohibit union leaders from holding union and political office simultaneously and prevent collective affiliation to political parties; eliminate the exclusion clause; allow workers and employers to negotiate wages and work schedules directly (within a forty-eight-hour workweek); reduce overtime costs; eliminate various categories of craft unions; increase the minimum number of workers required to form a union (the number was twenty); eliminate law contracts (industry-wide contracts that exist in sectors such as sugar and textiles); and prohibit solidarity strikes (COPARMEX 1989; CCE 1994; Bensusán and von Bülow 1997, 208).

The most significant instance of employer-labor "dialogue" in the 1990s took place during the Zedillo administration in 1995–96. In the wake of the peso crisis and high unemployment, COPARMEX began to talk about the need for dialogue on *la nueva cultura laboral* (the new employment culture), leaving aside for the moment the question of legal reform. COPARMEX and the CTM agreed to engage in a series of talks. Nine working groups, composed of representatives from labor and employer organizations, met over the course of approximately a year and drafted agreements on each of nine issues.[24] The agreements were mostly limited to general principles or points of consensus rather than specific references to existing law or explicit recommendations to change the law, with few exceptions.

The first public document to emerge from this process, "Principios de la Nueva Cultura Laboral," was a brief consensus statement of principles elaborated by the Technical Committee in August 1996. Critics of the process cited labor's poor negotiation skills, the fact that the agreements did not reflect real changes on the ground, and the fact that

24. These issues were (1) principles of labor ethics; (2) employment; (3) remuneration; (4) training and education; (5) productivity, quality, and competitiveness; (6) the role of the firm in society; (7) rights and obligations; (8) conflict and labor justice; and (9) rural labor policy.

independent unions did not play more of a role in the discussions. Aides close to the COPARMEX-CTM negotiations downplayed the criticism and claimed that this was the first step in a long process of dialogue. Although no further action was taken at the time, government, employer, and some labor groups continued to refer to "the new employment culture" through the end of Zedillo's term and even into the Fox administration.

The new employment culture accords foreshadowed future bargains between employer and labor organizations. Its "corporatist compromise" entailed granting increased flexibility to employers in exchange for conserving the status quo on unions' organizational prerogatives and collective rights. According to an observer close to the talks, labor made concessions on issues such as merit-based promotion, increased flexibility in the workplace, and lower benefit costs for employers, in exchange for retaining the closed shop, union autonomy (and the right to engage in politics), and exclusive representation (exclusivity of the title to the collective bargaining agreement). Employers had wanted to see concessions in the areas of lower dismissal costs, elimination of exclusion clauses, reform of strike laws, and limits to union participation in politics, but unions managed to prevent changes in these areas.

Opposition political parties also played an important role in the debate over labor reform. Indeed, the most comprehensive labor reform proposals came from the two main opposition parties, the center-right Partido Acción Nacional (PAN) and the left Partido de la Revolución Democrática (PRD). Despite the fact that these initiatives came from parties at opposite ends of the political spectrum, they shared a common goal. Both proposals aimed to alter the corporatist character of Mexican industrial relations by increasing the autonomy of unions, ensuring representative workers' organizations, and "democratizing" labor institutions (Bensusán 2001; Garavito Elías 2001).

The PAN proposal was the first of the initiatives for labor law reform submitted to Congress (Senado de la República 1995). Commissioned by a PAN senator and drafted by two respected labor lawyers, the PAN proposal was widely discussed and commented upon in the press and in academic symposia.[25] It was presented to the Senate in July 1995. Even though it was tabled in committee, renewed discussions of labor

25. For example, see Aguilar et al., *Legislación laboral: El debate sobre una propuesta* (1996).

reform in the late 1990s brought the PAN initiative back into public debate.

Despite a common perception to the contrary, given the conservative ideological orientation of the PAN, the PAN proposal was not a faithful reflection of employers' demands. It did not call for minimizing employer obligations, weakening workers' rights, or lowering employers' costs (Bensusán 1996, 7). It contained "liberal" provisions that would break with corporatist features such as union monopolies, with institutional and legal supports that encourage antidemocratic internal practices, and with the state's tutelary role and powers of intervention. It called for changes that would challenge union bureaucracies: the elimination of exclusion clauses; the establishment of workplace committees separate from trade unions; and transparent election procedures. The proposal also contained improvements for workers in work schedules and benefits, and stipulated worker participation in strategic decisions at the firm level through rank-and-file-elected "factory councils" (co-mités de empresa) or plant delegates.[26] These committees would also be responsible for administering the collective bargaining agreement, called here "collective pacts on working conditions."

The result of the PAN project would be to make unions work harder to keep their membership, a development that would be consistent with democratization but that some unions resisted. Indeed, the tone of the PAN proposal was less than sympathetic toward unions overall. Rather, the initiative stressed protection of individual workers against the corrupt and authoritarian tendencies of unions. This did not necessarily reflect sympathy toward employers. The proposal retained many of the law's existing employer obligations and in some cases increased their costs (vacation time, vacation pay, and the end-of-year bonus or agui-naldo). However, it also contained significant nods in the direction of flexibility, notably through eased adoption of temporary contracts, longer probationary periods, and easier dismissal terms.

Other notable features of the PAN proposal were an expanded scope of bargaining topics at the workplace and an obligation that employers

26. The last provision was one of the proposal's most controversial aspects for trade unions. While it theoretically demanded democratic participation by rank-and-file workers at the firm or plant level, nothing in the proposal stipulated that such committees must include union members. Unions feared that employers would use factory committees to sow discord among workers and undermine support for the union, making it easier to form company unions or even nonunion plants.

share company financial information with employees, considered essential if workers were to bargain effectively for wage and benefit gains based on productivity. The PAN proposal left open the possibility of collective agreements by industry, something akin to the law contracts that exist in some sectors in Mexico, but without central government oversight (Bensusán 1996, 7). Finally, the PAN proposal took the resolution of labor conflicts out of the executive branch (through the local and federal boards and tribunals) and placed this responsibility in the hands of the judiciary through the creation of *jueces de lo social,* judges specially trained to rule on labor conflicts. The goal was to rid the boards of their tripartite structure and political bias, which was a key obstacle to registering independent unions, among other things.

Observers believed there was very little chance that either unions or employers would accept the proposal. The PAN initiative threatened those who benefited from long-standing corporatist arrangements and was rejected by organizations such as the CTM. From employers' perspective, the proposal did not go far enough in lowering their costs or freeing their hands. Some leftist analysts and independent labor unions rejected the proposal because they claimed it would leave unions too unprotected before employers and would fragment Mexican unions. Others protested that it was too "neoliberal." Still, labor analysts and advocates viewed many elements of the PAN proposal positively. At the very least, the debates surrounding the proposal opened some of the most entrenched and undemocratic elements of Mexican labor law to public scrutiny.

By 1998 several important developments had reopened the debate on labor law reform. One was the reorganization of the labor movement after Fidel Velázquez's death. More important was the fact that, after the congressional elections in July 1997, the lower house of Congress had an opposition majority for the first time (though it was divided between the leftist PRD and the conservative PAN). This meant that Congress would no longer rubber-stamp executive initiatives and that President Zedillo would have to negotiate with the opposition in Congress for passage of his legislative proposals.

Encouraged by this chain of events, the PRD also commissioned a labor law reform proposal (PRD 1998).[27] The PRD proposal bore sev-

27. The party did not immediately submit the proposal to Congress when it was crafted as a draft discussion document in 1998, but key elements of it were later incorporated into a joint initiative by the PRD and UNT and submitted to Congress in 2002.

eral similarities to the PAN initiative, which raised the possibility of consensus on key points (see Table 5.1). The greatest changes in the PRD proposal related to the system of collective representation and bargaining, in particular the areas of union autonomy, union and bargaining structure; internal functioning of unions; workplace representation; and the system of labor justice.[28]

The chief aim of the PRD proposal was to "democratize" the industrial relations system. It intended to accomplish this through "counterweights and balances," focusing on democracy, autonomy, and the "full citizenship rights of workers" (PRD 1998, x). In contrast to the PAN, the proposal acknowledged that unions must be allowed to retain power in order to protect labor standards and rights.[29] The intent was to introduce sufficient "liberal" elements to break the corporatist links between unions and government in order to force unions to become more responsive to their members. To accomplish this, the proposal called for removing government from union affairs, especially its involvement in union registration and its authority to "intervene" during strikes and to determine wage increases.[30]

Although the PRD plan proposed radical change in the areas of collective labor relations and labor justice, it nevertheless reaffirmed the existing law's protective orientation toward individual workers. In the areas of working conditions and benefits the initiative largely maintained existing terms. In other cases it strengthened the levels and scope of protection of workers and increased employer obligations by requir-

28. Like the PAN proposal, the PRD's called for removing the labor court system from the executive branch and placing it under the judiciary, and for eliminating its tripartite structure.

29. The PRD proposal allowed unions to maintain the exclusion clause in union contracts as long as members voted to authorize their leaders to include it in their collective bargaining agreements.

30. Other important changes recommended in the PRD proposal included establishing one single minimum wage level throughout the country (there were several) and giving Congress the authority to set the minimum wage; establishing a forty-hour workweek with fifty-six-hour pay; allowing unions to determine their bargaining structure and levels rather than having this set by law; eliminating section B of the labor code, thereby granting public-sector workers a full set of collective rights; deregulating the area of strikes; extending federal jurisdiction in labor matters throughout the country (including over states and municipalities); and calling for a range of measures aimed at benefiting female employees, including nondiscrimination in employment, prohibition of pregnancy tests as a condition of employment, and affirmative action. The draft proposal tabled some important topics for later discussion, among them part-time work, occupational health and safety, and child labor (Bensusán 2000).

TABLE 5.1   Comparison of PAN and PRD Labor Reform Proposals in Mexico

Goals	PAN Proposal (1995)	PRD Proposal (1998)
Protection, flexibility, and productivity	Improvements in conditions of work; greater numerical and functional flexibility, flexibility in work schedules and compensation (through bargaining/unilateral); bargain over productivity, training, and gain sharing at workplace (with delegates-factory councils) and sector levels	Improvements in conditions of work; protect job stability; replace minimum wage commission with independent institute; bargain over flexibility: functional, wage, and schedules; bargain over productivity, training, and profit sharing at workplace (with delegates and factory councils), sector and national levels; create tripartite industry chambers
Autonomy and union registration		
End state intervention in formation and activities of unions	Simplify union registration and eliminate restrictions	Simplify union registration and create public registry of unions and collective contracts; free choice in type and level of union organization, including international unions
Representation and genuine collective agreements		
1. End employer discretion over choice of union to bargain 2. Rules for fair competition among union choices before and after collective agreements (public representation elections with secret ballot and guarantees of impartiality)	1–2. Bargain collective pacts with elected workplace representatives (procedures to prevent employer interference)	1–2. Bargain with union with participation of worker delegates (or factory council); employers must notify employees if a union wants to negotiate a collective agreement (in case of dispute, a secret ballot representation election must be held)

(continues)

TABLE 5.1 *Continued*

Goals	PAN Proposal (1995)	PRD Proposal (1998)
3. Protection against antiunion and discriminatory employer actions	3. Not mentioned	3. Penalties for antiunion and discriminatory employer practices
4. Greater member participation in collective bargaining	4. Through elected workplace representatives	4. Worker delegates and union representatives participate
5. Change in obligatory union affiliation requirements	5. Prohibit obligatory union affiliation	5. Option (1) workers vote on exclusion clause in assembly; option (2) prohibit exclusion clause by separation
Internal democracy	No changes	Sets principle that union democracy must be promoted
1. Greater member participation		1. Require union assemblies every six months, at least
2. Secret, universal, and direct election for union leadership		2. Secret, universal, and direct ballot
3. Minority representation rights		3. Not mentioned
4. Increase effective rights of members (publicize union statutes)		4. Must deposit copy of statutes
5. Accountability		5. Must make financial statements available to members
Liberalization of right to strike	Strike goal is defense of collective interests	Same
	New requirement: prior strike vote by assembly	
	Type of strike: definite or indefinite	Same
	Essential services: service providers or by judgment of administrative authority	Normal service providers according to law
	Strike end: arbitration sought by either party after thirty days of strike	Not mentioned
Independent system of labor justice	"Social" judges in the judiciary	Labor judges in the judiciary

SOURCE: Bensusán (2000, 451–53).

ing a greater number of paid vacation days, expanded year-end bonus payments, and granting longer paid-leave periods for women employees after giving birth. There were few concessions to employer demands for flexibility.

For their part, unions were divided on whether and how much change in labor law they wanted to see. The unions represented by the CTM and the umbrella Labor Congress had largely stood by Federal Labor Law and Article 123, although there were times when they wanted to strengthen their pro-union provisions. Independent unions varied in their positions. The independent Frente Auténtico del Trabajo (FAT) was the most supportive of the PRD proposal, since it called for many of the same changes that the FAT had championed over the years. The UNT came out in favor of some provisions in the PRD proposal—namely, a public registry of union registration and further provisions to end the practice of establishing protection contracts.[31] In late 2002 the UNT joined the PRD in presenting a labor reform proposal to Congress.

Of central concern to most unions and employer organizations as the labor reform issue seemed to move toward debate in Congress was that they, the "social actors," would be marginalized from the debate.[32] This concern was behind labor and employer criticism of the political party reform proposals as well as the efforts to unite around a set of initiatives under the Zedillo government. The government tried to assure labor and employer organizations that no reform would pass without prior consensus of the parties most directly affected. Yet consensus was not easy to achieve.

BOLIVIA'S "LIBERAL REVOLUTION" AND THE DECLINE OF LABOR POWER

Bolivia's "economic transition" followed the return to democratic civilian government. Although labor regained political influence in the dem-

31. Other independent unions, such as the Sindicato Mexicano de Electricistas (SME), maintained that both greater democracy and greater flexibility were possible within the parameters of the existing law and constitution. The SME and its allies, an expanded coalition of fifty-two unions, together with the Frente Sindical Mexicano (composed of dissident currents from the electrical, telephone, railroad, teachers, and oil workers' unions), vowed to fight the parties' proposals and any changes in the labor law or Article 123 (Bensusán and von Bülow 1997, 220).

32. José Domínguez, assistant to Juan Millán, secretary general of the PRI, interview by author, 29 October 1996, Mexico City.

ocratic transition years (1978–82),[33] it then lost considerable power in the hyperinflationary crisis of President Siles Zuazo's term (1982–85), despite labor's effectiveness in combating government austerity policies (Gamarra 1994, 107; Gamarra 1997, 374). The MNR government of Víctor Paz Estenssoro (1985–89), however, marked a clear turning point in Bolivia's economic orientation and the decline of union power (Sandoval 1997, 24).

President Paz Estenssoro introduced the "new economic policy" (*Nueva Política Económica,* NPE), lauded as the most important set of reforms since 1952 and "among the boldest in Latin America's movement toward liberalism" (Morales 1994, 129). The NPE consisted initially of shock therapy: freezing wages, cutting public-sector employment, reducing the fiscal deficit, and devaluing the currency. The goals of the NPE were liberalization of the economy, development of the private sector as the central actor in the economy, and the recovery of state control over state enterprises that had been "captured" by labor and other groups (Gamarra 1997, 373). Paz Estenssoro's efforts to dramatically cut hyperinflation of 26,000 percent proved successful, and the ensuing four years of economic growth and low inflation were dubbed "the Bolivian miracle" (Gamarra 1994, 105).

This miracle was not possible without repression, however. In an effort to curb labor opposition to the NPE, the administration called a state of siege and banished hundreds of labor leaders, including COB leader Juan Lechín. A pact between the ruling MNR and the conservative opposition Acción Democrática Nacionalista (ADN) provided congressional support for the state of siege and for the government's economic reforms. Later, a new electoral reform law created a majority coalition in Congress and achieved congressional sanction of two more states of siege (Gamarra 1994, 107, 109). In addition to this open repression of the labor movement, Supreme Decree 21.060 (which served as the legal foundation for the NPE), issued in 1985, also increased employer flexibility in dismissals and introduced a number of other flexible changes, thereby bypassing the job stability provisions of the labor code (Sandoval 1997, 23–24).

The advent of neoliberalism under civilian elected governments created a hostile context for the Bolivian labor movement. Although labor

---

33. This was a period of rapid government turnover, in which seven military governments and two civilian governments held power (Gamarra 1997, 366).

had broken its ties to the MNR, it remained a powerful political force, as the government's persistent efforts to undermine and contain it demonstrate.[34] Market reforms had to overcome labor resistance, as well as opposition from sectors of the left represented in Congress. To this end, "pacts" arranged between the government and political parties offered political patronage and alternation in the presidency in exchange for support of government economic policies and political repression of labor. The irony, of course, was that this was orchestrated by the same party, the MNR, and the same individual, Paz Estenssoro, that had been an ally of the labor movement in the national revolution of 1952!

The government of Jaime Paz Zamora (1989–93), of the left Movimiento de Izquierda Revolucionaria (MIR), proved to be no exception to this pattern. The "Patriotic Accord" between the MIR and the ADN established political stability and permitted the continuation of neoliberal economic policies (Gamarra 1994, 123). The government of Paz Zamora passed laws permitting joint ventures in mining and hydrocarbons and privatization of state enterprises.[35] In addition, the government proceeded with trade liberalization and passed legislation guaranteeing the free flow of capital, including foreign companies' repatriation of profits (Gamarra 1994, 113).[36] As with Paz Estenssoro, the Paz Zamora government used presidential decrees to circumvent Congress and avoid public discussion of policies (Morales 1994, 131). Paz Zamora also continued his predecessor's tactic of employing a state of siege to control labor opposition. In November 1989 hundreds of union leaders were arrested and banished to remote jungle towns. This time, however, Congress did not back the move; the "Patriotic Accord" had not managed to include the two-thirds needed to approve the siege (Gamarra 1994, 112). Popular opposition against the government's policies—especially foreign investment and privatization—grew, and eventually the government was forced to back down in the face of pressure by opposition parties, regional civic committees, and the COB.

In 1993 the MNR returned to power in a coalition government under

---

34. Nonetheless, Gamarra remarks that labor's overuse of the strike eroded its legitimacy. When twenty-three thousand mineworkers were fired during the Siles Zuazo government, the COB was barely able to gain enough support to hold a general strike (1997, 374).

35. These were the Mining Actualization Law, the Hydrocarbons Law, and the Investment Code, approved in 1990–91 (Morales 1994, 142).

36. Both the Paz Estenssoro and the Paz Zamora governments greatly increased the access of the IMF and the World Bank to internal decision making (Morales 1994, 132).

the leadership of Gonzalo Sánchez de Losada (1993–97), who had been "super" minister of economic planning under Paz Estenssoro's NPE. Sánchez de Losada continued the previous governments' neoliberal policies and, faced again with hyperinflation, turned to shock therapy. This austerity conflicted with the new administration's stated aim of creating a "social market economy."[37] The policies also proved difficult to implement, as opposition from labor and other sectors grew. President Sánchez de Losada's government clashed with labor, university students, coca growers, regional organizations, and opposition parties throughout his term. In 1995 the COB led a number of strikes. The president dealt with these the way previous democratic governments had—by declaring a state of siege for two consecutive ninety-day periods between April and October 1995 (Gamarra 1997, 387, 391).

The growing popular dissatisfaction with neoliberalism in Bolivia became starkly evident in the two later presidential administrations. Under President Hugo Banzer (1997–2001), who ran as a civilian this time, the attempted privatization of water utilities in Cochabamba through their sale to a French water company sparked a civil conflict of international renown in 2000. The government declared martial law and arrested the protest leaders. One of them, Oscar Olivera, a trade union leader, became an international symbol of popular resistance to globalization. Later, under a second term by Sánchez de Losada (2002–3), the country erupted in protest when it became known that Bechtel planned to build a pipeline through Chile to ship Bolivian natural gas overseas. The so-called "gas war" left more than eighty people dead and produced a general strike. In October 2003 Sánchez de Losada resigned the presidency, leaving his vice president, Carlos Mesa, in charge of the government. Although labor was a major player in both of these conflicts, the uprisings became generalized throughout the population (U.S. Department of State 2004).

The Labor Reform Debate in Bolivia

As in other countries, economic liberalization in Bolivia brought discussion of broader institutional reform, including the reform of the coun-

---

37. A key component of this social market economy would be the "capitalization" of state enterprises, whereby the state would contribute assets and a private investor would contribute capital, with sole management control and 50 percent of the stock to go to the investor and the rest to be distributed among all Bolivians over the age of eighteen. Revenue from the sale of state enterprises was also to be placed in a pension fund for Bolivians over the age of eighteen (Gamarra 1997, 385).

try's labor laws. The core labor code in Bolivia had not been significantly altered since it was first developed in 1939. Nonetheless, by some estimates as many as 4,200 legal dispositions had been attached to the labor code over the years, some addressing new labor relations situations or setting out exceptions, and encompassing laws, decrees, regulations, and ministerial resolutions. The result was a confusing and contradictory mass of labor regulation, much of which was ignored. Economic reformers and labor advocates alike therefore shared the sense that the labor code needed updating. Where these groups parted ways was on the extent to which protective regulation needed to be relaxed and the role of the state minimized.

The proposals for labor law reform in Bolivia began to emerge in the early 1990s and responded to two sets of pressures, liberalization and the ILO. Since 1985 the Bolivian government had pledged to the ILO that it would draft a new proposal for labor law. The ILO's Committee of Experts had focused on seven points that required change in order to bring Bolivian law into compliance with Convention No. 87 on freedom of association. In 1993 the government produced a draft labor reform document, following a visit by a mission of the ILO and the IADB, which it presented to the COB in an "offer to consult," an invitation the COB refused, according to the government (ILO-ILCCR 1995). The state of emergency called by the government in 1995 made further discussions impossible. The government blamed the COB's "lack of resolve" for the delay in reforming the labor code. In particular, it claimed that the COB rejected any reform that would make possible the presence of more than one union in a firm or work center (ILO-ILCCR 1998). The government also defended itself in exchanges with the ILO, indicating that many of the laws the ILO said needed changing were in fact unenforced (ILO-ILCCR 1995). In 1996 a social dialogue program was begun with the assistance of the ILO regional office and the IADB. The government complained that the COB attended only one session, despite the fact that no union leaders remained in detention or confinement (ILO-ILCCR 1997).

Although the Banzer administration renewed the government's pledge to reform the labor code via tripartite consultation, it also failed to bring about any results. In October 1997 the ILO sent a direct contacts mission to Bolivia and emerged with a set of recommendations (including draft legislation) for change to comply with requirements of ILO Conventions 87 and 98. The government reactivated the social dialogue program in an effort to develop a proposal through consultation to reform the labor code. In January 1998 the Banzer government signed a letter of intent with the IMF indicating its intention to draft a proposal for labor law reform by December of that year (CEDLA 1998). Although the government did not have a proposal ready by December, it continued to support development of proposals through 1999. In 2000 the Cochabamba water protests created a political crisis that halted government efforts to enact labor reform. By mid-2004 the issue had not reemerged in any significant way. Indeed, the 2004 communication of the ILO's Committee of Experts noted that the same points it had raised for many years remained unaddressed (ILO-CEACR 2004).

Despite the lack of progress on labor law reform, some of the proposals and ideas of the late 1990s are still likely to find their way into future changes. The ILO recommendations were quite specific. They included reducing state control over union activities, including eliminating the government's authority to dissolve unions; establishing legal protection for workers against employer antiunion discrimination; enacting protections from employer intervention in workers' organizations; and removing penal sanctions in the event of general and solidarity strikes (Goldín 1999, 23–24; ILO-ILCCR 1998).[38]

An ILO consultant's 1999 report for the Bolivian government took up these recommendations and developed others. For instance, it recommended developing a unitary labor code that would incorporate and render consistent the numerous other sources of labor regulation established since the 1940s. The report also suggested making the law inclusive by taking into account various new forms of work relations that have developed in recent decades that are not contemplated by the law, including wage labor in agriculture. It placed considerable emphasis on the need for improved state enforcement of the law, arguing that what was needed was "more state intervention in the oversight of legal enforcement, less in regulation" (Goldín 1999, 7). The report promoted autonomy of the parties, including the self-resolution of conflicts, and

---

38. The parties had agreed on the need to reform the law to address these points. Among the points on which consensus among the social partners had not been reached were the right to organize for public servants; the possibility of establishing more than one union in an enterprise; the removal of nationality and residence requirements for trade union leaders; lifting restrictions on the right to strike, including removing the prohibition of solidarity strikes and permitting strikes in the banking sector, and doing away with compulsory arbitration as a means of ending strikes.

said the state should facilitate and promote a culture of negotiation and bargaining. And, of course, it argued that the law must be adapted to conform to ILO conventions, especially those relating to freedom of association and the right to organize.

Earlier, in March 1997, the Unidad de Análisis de Políticas Sociales y Económicas (UDAPE), an economics research unit established by the government to advise it on public policy, published an analysis and set of recommendations for labor law reform that came closer to the view of employer groups. It claimed to stake out a middle ground between employer and labor perspectives, one based on economics that also recognized the important role played by labor institutions. UDAPE criticized existing law for its deterrent effect on private investment owing to the uncertainty its laws generated. It also condemned high labor costs, suggested by the range of requirements regarding severance, *desahuicio* (the penalty for not giving three months' notice before dismissal), maternity leave, and restrictions on work schedules for women, among other things (UDAPE 1997, 13).

The document also stated that the government's role in labor relations needed to be curtailed, and that a number of changes regarding collective rights and protections were in order. Among these, the report promoted the establishment of union pluralism within a workplace so that workers could have a choice of affiliation; limited coverage of the collective bargaining agreement (e.g., so that it would not apply to new employees); the establishment of procedures to govern union activities (e.g., secret ballot elections, terms for union leaders); the promotion of firm-level collective bargaining, with bargaining at other levels to be entered into voluntarily (i.e., no obligation to bargain at multiemployer level); provisions that allowed minority groups of workers to leave a strike and accept the employer's offer if they wish, and others (UDAPE 1997, 26–29). The UDAPE report made no mention of the ILO or of the need for labor code reforms to conform to ILO conventions.

Although UDAPE's analysis claimed to occupy a middle ground, its closer proximity to the position of neoliberal reformers was evident in its suggestion that controversial Supreme Decree 21.060 be raised to the status of law so as to ensure its continuity (UDAPE 1997, 25). The labor movement attributed much of the employer community's evasion of the labor code to the loopholes established by D.S. 21.060, which was first decreed in 1985 by the Paz Estenssoro government (1985–89) (CEDLA 1998, 7). The decree eliminated the legal requirement for government authorization of dismissals and enabled employment through short-term contracts. It also spurred employer abuses of the probationary period, home work, subcontracting, and the establishment of fake microenterprises so as to avoid laws regarding unionization (Goldín 1999).

Other contributions to the labor law reform debate came from the Centro de Estudios para el Desarrollo Laboral y Agrario (CEDLA), an NGO that issued sophisticated analyses of labor market and rural conditions as well as of social and economic policy. CEDLA rejected the "modernization" arguments of liberal reformers and argued that what was needed was *actualización*—an updating—of the law, but one that did not jettison the core principles on which the original labor code was founded. These included a role for state intervention, worker protection, and the inalienability of worker rights (CEDLA 1998, 15–17). CEDLA criticized the UDAPE view of a "third way" that focused on labor institutions, insisting that its proposals were more similar to those of the "traditional economic" or employer perspective that focused on such matters as labor costs over the need for worker protection. CEDLA also rejected the "liberal" view that more autonomy for the parties was enough to ensure the exercise of rights. This presupposed an equality among the parties that simply did not exist. Instead, the role for the state should be intervention in the form of protection for the weaker party—workers and unions. CEDLA viewed with special concern proposals for union pluralism; limited coverage of collective bargaining agreements; firm-level union organization; limits on strikes; striker replacement; allowing workers to "opt out" of a strike by negotiating individually with the employer; and legal recognition of other forms of worker representation aside from unions (CEDLA 1998, 11–12).

At the same time, CEDLA agreed with reformers on the need to unify legislation on labor; to clearly define what a labor relationship is and distinguish among its various forms; to include agricultural labor;[39] to update laws regarding women and minors; to promote autonomy of the parties in collective bargaining; to distinguish more clearly between individual and collective contracts; to make unionization possible for seasonal or temporary employees and in workplaces with fewer than twenty workers; and to develop consistency among various bodies of

---

39. A 1996 agrarian reform law extended the protection of the national labor law to all paid agricultural workers.

law affecting areas such as social security, occupational health and safety, the law on minors, and so forth. As a strategic move, CEDLA also proposed creating a "Platform for Labor Rights" that would encompass a broad sector of society and form a counterweight to reform pressures by government and international financial institutions (CEDLA 1998, 20–24).

Differences between the UDAPE and CEDLA documents related to the causes of unemployment, the informal sector, and the lack of enforcement of labor laws. While UDAPE attributed the enforcement gap to the "obsolescence of labor institutions," thus justifying their "modernization," CEDLA and other labor advocates attributed this to lack of political will and resources. In any case, there was broad agreement that lax enforcement was a problem. Although labor laws and regulations were on balance favorable to workers, the lack of enforcement allowed employers to shun many of these standards (U.S. Department of State 2002a). The National Labor Court took so long to decide cases that by the time it did, the issue was moot. Labor courts faced a backlog of cases that hindered their ability to aid aggrieved workers, as in much of the rest of the region.

The lack of enforcement of labor protections contributed to the poor labor conditions and severe labor market deficiencies Bolivian workers faced. Seventy percent of the economically active population, notably many women and children, worked in the informal sector. Although labor law had not changed, job instability increased and flexibility occurred "on the margins" within firms. Liberalization had brought about the decline of public employment, the most important stable job source for many Bolivians. Underemployment—insufficient use of the existing labor force—was pervasive. Rural work conditions were especially poor, as trade liberalization and competition reduced production levels in the countryside. Much new hiring was done through temporary contracts. In 1994 only 14 percent of the formal private-sector contracts registered with the government in that year were "indefinite" contracts; 68 percent were fixed-term contracts, and 18 percent were for short-term, specific projects (*por obra terminada*) (CEDLA 1998, 6n4).

While the lack of enforcement usually hurt workers, in some instances it helped them. Legal restrictions on strikes and unionization often went unenforced. For example, although the labor code denied civil servants the right to unionize, nearly all government workers belonged to unions. The labor code also banned strikes in public services, including banks, but strikes in the public sector did occur. A penal code sanction against striking government workers in public safety was not applied in practice. Solidarity strikes were illegal, but the government had "neither prosecuted those responsible nor imposed penalties" (U.S. Department of State 2002a). Although the state did engage in violent repression of workers, strong worker organizations in Bolivia were apparently able to take advantage of lax enforcement of legal restrictions, engaging in strikes and unionization where the law prohibited it.

MEXICO'S "DEMOCRATIC TRANSITION": LABOR REFORM UNDER FOX

Mexico arrived late to a process that most other countries in Latin America had already experienced by the 1990s: the transition from authoritarian rule to democracy. But Mexico's political transition differed from those in the Southern Cone, where electoral democracies emerged from military dictatorships. Mexico's authoritarian regime was a civilian government headed by the same political party for more than seventy years. In other countries, the end of dictatorship was clearly signaled by "founding" elections whose rules were negotiated by all the parties (O'Donnell et al. 1986). In contrast, Mexico had undergone a gradual process of political opening over many years, culminating in the elections that produced the victory of Vicente Fox of the opposition PAN in July 2000.

Competitive party politics in state and local elections had existed since the 1980s, and opposition parties already had experience governing at these levels. In 1997 the PRI lost its majority in the lower house of Congress for the first time, which broke the control the executive had over Congress. Nonetheless, many observers believed that Mexico could initiate a transition to a democratic regime only when the largest prize—the presidency—was ceded to the opposition in a clean electoral contest. Only then could the party begin to be extricated from state institutions, and the PRI's extensive network of resources, power, and control be dismantled.

As in other countries, the political transition also returned the issue of labor law reform to the national agenda. Mexico once again faced the prospect of reforming its labor legislation, but now in the context of a legitimate democratic government and more extensive political and institutional reforms. Unlike other countries in the region, however, Mexico faced a simultaneous challenge—from neoliberalism and democratization—in addressing reform of its labor laws.

Vicente Fox campaigned on a platform that included changes in Mexico's corporatist labor laws, support for union democracy, and wage increases. In June 2000, while still a presidential candidate, Fox signed on to a document developed by a distinguished group of labor experts, intellectuals, human rights activists, and congressional representatives. The goal of the document, titled "Agreement on Twenty Commitments to Freedom, Union Democracy, and Enforcement of Individual and Collective Rights for the Labor Agenda and Government Program," was to place institutional and democratic reform of labor relations on the agenda of presidential and congressional candidates prior to the July 2000 elections. It was a succinct list of proposals focused on establishing just working conditions, union democracy and freedom of association, legitimate collective bargaining agreements, and improvements in the labor justice system.

The premise of the document was that key legal and institutional reforms were needed to ensure development of a democratic labor movement, which could in turn press for workers' rights. Among the specific proposals were a public registry of unions and collective agreements, independent of the executive branch; secret, universal, and direct election of union officers; worker ratification of collective agreements; secret, universal, and direct elections during recuentos—elections held to determine which union has the majority and therefore title to the collective agreement; inclusion of labor issues within the mandate of the Human Rights Commission, and more (Carrillo Alejandro 2001, 31–33). Although Fox signed the document as a candidate, his administration failed to make these proposals a centerpiece of the labor reform agenda.

After his electoral victory, President Fox set up a transition team that included labor experts and trade unionists who developed proposals on how to proceed on labor reform and what elements a reform should include. The team called for a working group on labor reform made up of parties, government, and key social actors that would agree on the principal institutional changes required within the context of a broader pact for political transition and state reform. The parties were to agree on a set of commitments and behaviors that would build a climate of consensus and trust and that could ease the transition from an "authoritarian" to a "democratic" model of labor governance. The proposal also called for establishing the industrial relations base to move toward an economic model that was not based primarily on exports but that instead included a growth strategy based on the domestic market. This implied an industrial relations model in which unions were real representatives of workers, and in which cooperation and consensus (not complicity) among employers, unions, and government would steer the country on a path of "high-road" development.[40]

Despite these early actions, the Fox administration's approach to labor exhibited continuity with past practices and even increased conservatism. Perhaps the clearest sign of this was Fox's appointment of Carlos Abascal to head the Labor Ministry. Abascal, a deeply religious and socially conservative businessman, was a former head of COPARMEX, Mexico's most important employer association. As president of COPARMEX Abascal had spearheaded the "new employment culture" talks with organized labor, and his views on industrial relations reflected the Catholic values that defined the agenda of those meetings. In addition to Abascal, who filled the Labor Ministry with businesspeople, much of the rest of Fox's cabinet was composed of individuals from the business community. This represented a break with the past, when business wielded influence from outside government, and it gave the administration a corporate orientation.[41]

As labor minister, Abascal insisted that labor reform must be based on consensus among the "productive sectors" (employers and labor unions) before discussion in Congress. In June and July 2001, the Labor Ministry put together a commission and working groups made up of employer and union representatives to discuss labor reform (Secretaría del Trabajo y Previsión Social 2001). The idea was to arrive at some consensus on labor reform that could then be eased into Congress as a government initiative. The commission, or "Central Table of Decisions," was composed of eleven employer and eleven labor representatives, three of them from the UNT and the rest from the "official" sector.

40. See "Proyecto de un acuerdo político para la transición en el mundo del trabajo," supplement no. 49 of *Trabajo y Democracia Hoy* 10 (58) (2000). On a labor transition agenda, see also Bensusán (1996).

41. The presence of individuals with links to the Monterrey business community has been noted with special interest, since company unions are prevalent in that region and define the labor relations culture. It is significant, for instance, that the head of the federal conciliation and arbitration board was an employment-relations lawyer from Monterrey. On Monterrey-based corporations and labor relations, see Pozas (1993). On the role of employers in Mexican politics see Valdés (1997).

Yet given the conservative positions of the CTM-CT on labor reform, coupled with employers' preference for the "corporatist flexibility" that characterized labor relations, it was unlikely that the commission would produce the institutional reforms needed to create a democratic model of labor governance, despite the UNT's best efforts to move the process in this direction. One significant constraint in the talks—as well as a limitation to democratic reform—was that constitutional changes were to be taken "off the table." The UNT eventually withdrew from the commission out of frustration with the direction in which the talks were heading and the consistent sidelining of its proposals.

In late October 2002 the UNT joined with the PRD in presenting a labor reform initiative to Congress.[42] The proposal included most of the features of the original PRD project that called for a radical restructuring of the traditional labor system. It called, for example, for abolition of the tripartite labor boards, to be replaced by labor judges; abolition of the tripartite National Minimum Wage Commission and its replacement by an independent institute that would make recommendations to Congress; an independent public registry of unions *and* collective bargaining agreements; secret ballot vote in representation elections *and* union elections; and stronger protection for women workers, among other things.

The proposal that ultimately came out of the labor-employer commission (dubbed the "Abascal project") reached Congress in December 2002. This proposal included many of the employers' demands for increased flexibility in exchange for the status quo regarding corporatist unions' autonomy and monopoly. However, employers also succeeded in securing a number of provisions that generally undermined labor rights, including an expansion of the reasons for rejecting a union's petition for registration, and increased power to deny or delay the use of the strike. Flexibility measures included a lengthened (six-month) employee probation period, and a provision enabling overtime work compensated not by overtime pay but by "comp time." Issues that had received much publicity, such as a national registry and secret ballot, were present in the initiative but in ways that limited their significance.[43] For instance, the labor-employer proposal called for a national

42. For a broader discussion of the UNT-PRD proposal, see La Botz and Alexander (2003).

43. There is no provision in Mexican law for secret ballot vote in union leadership elections or during representation elections (recuentos). In the case of union elections, the method is left to each union to decide and is stated in its statutes. This gave rise to several

registry of unions but not of collective bargaining agreements, thus making the identification of protection contracts more difficult, and for secret ballot elections in representation elections but not in internal union elections, a concession to "official" union leaders.

This "initiative of the sectors" was sent for analysis to a joint congressional committee made up of deputies and senators from the labor commissions of both houses. Approval of the initiative was blocked by the PRD, which insisted on a number of changes, including the inclusion of secret ballot election of union leaders and a public registry of bargaining contracts. The head of the Senate labor commission, a member of the PRI and the CTM, countered that internal union leadership selection processes should be left to each union to determine and not dictated by law. The Labor Ministry, meanwhile, hinted that it was sympathetic to forming some type of public registry as a way of combating the proliferation of protection contracts (Martínez 2003). A smaller group of legislators continued to meet to try to establish some bases for consensus among the three major parties. By mid-2004, however, it looked as if the joint congressional committee, led by an alliance of the PAN and the PRI, would be considering an initiative based largely on the Abascal project, which excluded the key demands of the PRD and UNT: secret ballot elections and an independent public registry of union contracts.

In December 2004 members of the joint labor committee of Congress and Labor Minister Abascal put forth their proposal to Congress in the hope that it would be considered on a "fast track" in either December or at the beginning of the 2005 session. While employers and leaders of the CTM and CT supported the proposal, criticism from labor law experts, the PRD, and other labor unions was strong. The proposal also attracted attention within U.S. labor and human rights circles. Human Rights Watch issued a press release strongly criticizing the Abascal project for its setbacks in the areas of the right to strike, organize, and bargain collectively (Human Rights Watch 2005). In February 2005, the Washington Office on Latin America (WOLA) and U.S., Canadian, and Mexican labor unions also signed on to a NAFTA labor complaint on the proposed reform (WOLA 2005).

---

cases under the NAALC claiming that the absence of secret ballot elections in representation elections violates workers' freedom of association. See Bacon (2001); Human Rights Watch (2001); and http://www.dol.gov/dol/ilab/public/programs/nao/main.htm.

The labor reform project that was put before the Mexican Congress raised concerns in several areas. The proposal facilitated employer flexibility in hiring and dismissals by legalizing short-term contracts (three-month training contracts) and introducing a thirty-day probation period in indefinite employment contracts. It also proposed changes within the workplace, such as comp time, flexible work schedules, broad-banding, rescheduling days off, and the possibility of promotion by merit and skill rather than seniority. While many unions opposed these measures, they were similar to those introduced in the rest of the region, and indeed reflected changes that in many instances had already been implemented on the ground.

More troubling were proposed changes in the area of collective labor relations. These amounted to restrictions on collective rights and largely reflected employers' wishes (with some nods to official union leaders' interests). Among the proposed changes were increased procedural requirements for securing a collective bargaining agreement, which Human Rights Watch called "burdensome" and "prejudicial." The process of challenging an existing union (to gain title to the collective agreement) would be rendered even more difficult and would require documents from the tripartite labor board, which traditionally opposed independent union challenges. Going on strike in order to pressure an employer to sign a contract entailed a similar set of onerous requirements, including submitting the names and signatures of all union members and authorization by the labor board that these workers were indeed members of the union. With regard to internal union elections, the proposal stated that the vote could be secret or open, enabling unions to continue current forms of leadership selection. The public registry of unions was included here, but not that of collective agreements. The proposal also failed to address discrimination against pregnant women in the hiring process, even though it prohibited employers from firing or pressuring a worker to resign because of her pregnancy.[44]

In February 2005 labor leaders from the CT and CTM who were members of the lower house's Labor Commission criticized the Abascal project and refused to back the labor reform initiative, reducing the

44. According to analyst Enrique de la Garza, the proposal was also greatly limited in its vision of a labor relations system for the twenty-first century, as it contemplated neither worker involvement in productivity improvement nor the extension of protections to new categories of workers, nor did it acknowledge the mixed record of flexibility measures in other countries in terms of their impact on worker productivity (de la Garza Toledo 2005).

likelihood, once again, that the proposal would come before Congress in that legislative session. Labor leaders referred to the importance of labor's support for the PRI in upcoming elections, and warned that the labor reform project, if passed, would harm both labor's interests and the PRI's prospects (Vergara 2005). The Labor Ministry downplayed the disagreements and claimed that consensus could still be reached.

In September 2005 the Labor Ministry issued another version of the Absacal proposal that removed several of the more controversial provisions concerning collective relations.[45] It even reinserted the original term for employer, *patrón,* in place of the new term, *empleador,* which had been a key point of contention with the unions. Nonetheless, it retained a number of flexible provisions regarding promotion and scheduling and ignored the UNT's demands for a public registry of collective agreements and secret ballot in union elections (Barba 2005). Some critics observed that the project now represented a "minimal" reform that was unlikely to produce significant changes and that certainly did not amount to the structural reform that was needed (Garduño 2005). Labor Minister Salazar Sáenz said that the PRI and PAN had reached agreement on the reform project, from which the most controversial items had been removed "because they were not going to be approved." Still, he insisted that the initiative would not be a *"reforma light"* (Muñoz Ríos 2005). Yet by late 2005 even a watered-down version of the labor reform bill seemed unlikely to pass Mexico's Congress, and the 2006 presidential elections made passage during Fox's administration ever more remote.

The government's initial insistence on "consensus" between employer and labor organizations on the terms of labor reform had the effect of marginalizing the political parties' democratic reform proposals in Congress. This resistance to address democratic reform was evident in previous examples of employer-labor consensus. The new employment culture accords showed that the peak employer and official labor organizations would only reach agreement on a "corporatist compromise." Labor would seek corporatist guarantees: monopoly of representation, union autonomy (meaning no change in rules on internal politics of unions, such as a requirement for secret ballot elections), and the exclusion clause, provisions that enabled these labor unions to de-

---

45. The Labor Ministry was now headed by Francisco Javier Salazar Sáenz, who took over from Abascal in June 2005, when the latter became Fox's interior minister.

fend against challenges from independent unions. Employers would gain changes in laws affecting internal and external flexibility and lowering social-wage costs. In addition, employers would retain the security of working with unions that were relatively effective at containing member demands and keeping out more representative and possibly more militant unions. This compromise was a blueprint for a minimal reform that did not have democratization at its core.

Despite this limited outcome with regard to labor reform, some signs of opening in labor relations were evident under the Fox administration. For example, the Fox government did not resort to administrative intervention (a practice known as the *requisa*) in the airline Aeroméxico when the Association of Flight Attendants, a UNT member, called a strike in June 2001.[46] The result after only three days was a contract favorable to the union. In another surprise development, the Mexican Supreme Court determined in the case of thirty-one sugar mill workers[47] that the exclusion clause in the collective agreement violated the constitution's guarantee of freedom of association.[48] The potential significance of this decision is vast.[49]

Another source of pressure for labor reform came from the international arena. NAFTA negotiations incorporated a parallel agreement on labor issues (the North American Agreement on Labor Cooperation, or NAALC) that enabled citizens of Mexico, Canada, and the United States to file complaints relating to governments' ineffective enforcement of

46. The requisa, or government takeover of installations, had been applied frequently by previous governments during strikes in the airline and telephone industries and has always been a point of contention between government and the more militant unions in these industries. See Conesa and Larrañaga (1989).

47. The sugar mill workers had formed a new union and separated from the national sugar workers' union, which in turn demanded that the workers be dismissed from their jobs under the industry-wide contract's exclusion clause.

48. The end of the exclusion clause (the equivalent of the "closed shop" in U.S. terms) would enhance freedom of association, but in all likelihood it would also erode union power and control in the workplace. In the absence of the exclusion clause, employers may find it easier to set up company unions or to divide workers.

49. Under Mexican law four additional findings are required before the decision becomes binding on lower courts. Once the decision becomes binding on lower courts ("obligatory jurisprudence"), the exclusion clause would not be prohibited, but workers against whom the clause would apply would be able to challenge it in the court, and if employers fired workers expelled from the union, they might be subject to penalties for unjust dismissal. The likelihood is that such clauses would become more infrequent, thus removing a key principle of corporatist labor relations: for unions, quasi-obligatory membership, and for employers, union control over members in the workplace.

labor legislation. Between 1994 and 2004 approximately thirty cases had been filed in the three countries; thirteen of these involved violations taking place in Mexico.[50] Labor advocates have questioned the effectiveness of these case filings, yet in many instances the use of the NAALC drew attention to persistent labor rights violations, and in some cases the publicity itself helped to end abusive practices.[51] More important, Mexican unions and nongovernmental groups used the NAALC filings to press for reform within Mexico. Some cases coincided with Mexican Supreme Court decisions questioning the constitutionality of Mexican labor law and practice.[52] Yet the labor reform proposal under consideration in Congress in 2005 responded hardly at all to the numerous complaints issued under the NAALC on freedom of association and the right to organize. Instead, the proposal itself inspired another NAALC complaint.

Indeed, international forces brought contradictory pressures to bear on labor reform debates. While the NAALC, ILO, and the Office of the United Nations High Commissioner for Human Rights focused on labor rights violations, the World Bank, OECD, and IMF pressed for greater flexibility. These latter groups pushed for short-term contracts and "less costly" hiring and dismissal provisions, which would enable the formal sector to absorb the informal economy. They saw the "new employment culture" talks as a positive development, and urged the passage of law that would implement those accords (OCDE 2000).

Mexico: Transition Without Reform

The context of democratic political transition, the extensive public debate on labor reform, the existence of concrete proposals, and interna-

50. The NAFTA labor accord has served as a vehicle for cross-border labor collaboration, given the requirement that cases must be filed in a different country from the one in which the violation occurred. This has led to joint strategizing around NAALC campaigns, helping to cement transnational solidarity (Cook 1997; Damgaard 1999; Alexander 1999; Wells 1999). The change in leadership of the AFL-CIO in 1995 has also led to a more involved relationship with a range of Mexican unions (Beaty 1999; Hermanson 2001).

51. On the NAFTA labor side agreement and for details on cases filed, see Bensusán (1996); Compa (1999); Damgaard (1998); Cook et al. (1997); Alexander (1999); and Dombois et al. (2003). Also see the website of the U.S. Department of Labor, National Administrative Office, at http://www.dol.gov/dol/ilab/public/programs/nao/main.htm.

52. For instance, in 1996 and again in 1999 the Mexican Supreme Court found in several specific public-sector cases that laws or statutes stipulating that workers must belong to a specific union violate the constitutional guarantee of freedom of association. On the implications of Supreme Court decisions, see Bouzas Ortíz (1999).

tional pressure deriving from NAALC cases and other cross-border campaigns provided the pressures and context for changes that would expand protection of labor rights. How, then, to explain the Fox government's failure to push for democratic labor reform in Mexico?

Several factors may explain continuities in labor and employment relations despite political opening. First, Mexican political analysts are quick to point out that what transpired in Mexico was not a political transition but simply an alternation of power. Critics claimed that Fox chose to pursue continuity in economic policy rather than focus on political and institutional reforms that would mark a true break with the past. One reason for this was that the Fox government put aside any reforms that might threaten the PRI's interests in the hopes of gaining PRI support for other measures in Congress.[53] The strategy was a costly one for President Fox, whose party lost votes in the 2003 midterm elections. The Fox government was ultimately unable to carry out the kinds of changes the electorate expected and that would have distinguished a PAN government from one run by the PRI.

Second, the sequence of transitions, whereby economic transition occurred before democratization, may have limited the possibilities for democratic labor reform. Economic liberalization strengthened employer groups relative to trade unions, and NAFTA tied Mexico's economy more closely to that of the United States. The U.S. economic downturn in the early 2000s slowed a Mexican growth trend that was critical for the Fox government's reform plans. Employers' claims that "rigid" laws harmed Mexican competitiveness began to resonate in Mexico. NAFTA also limited the political opportunities for a more expansive wage policy. The Fox government continued former administrations' wage policies and maintained ties with traditional unions, which also guaranteed wage restraint. The importance of low-cost production strategies was evident in the government's promotion of maquiladora expansion into the interior of Mexico as a job-creation strategy. Because of the central role of foreign investment, NAFTA also limited tolerance for labor conflict and its costs, which would probably increase were "real" unions able to challenge official unions in export industries.

Third, the leadership of the traditional labor sector showed an ability to adapt to new political circumstances, despite a history of fierce criti-

53. Among these were reforms of "the state" and fiscal, energy, and labor reforms. A controversial social security reform was passed with PRI support in 2004.

cism of the PAN. The continued importance of the traditional labor organizations to employers and to the state reflects the fact that the CTM
and other corporatist labor organizations were becoming firmly entrenched in key export sectors of the economy (especially oil, automo-
biles, and maquiladoras) just as they were losing their effectiveness as
get-out-the vote machines for the PRI (Middlebrook 1995; de la Garza
1993, 155; Tuman 1998). In the 1980s and early 1990s, the stability of
the political bargain between labor and the PRI masked official labor's
industrial strength and its remarkable ability to adapt to the new economic environment of the 1990s. Indeed, the CTM's declining role in
the PRI over the past decade has forced it to become more flexible and
pragmatic in its alliances at the level of state government and in the
workplace, even as it has continued to voice support for the PRI at
election time.[54]

Finally, a sizeable segment of the labor movement has retained its
alliance with the PRI. As long as the PRI remains a significant presence
in Mexican politics, labor's relationship with the party is likely to continue and the party is likely to defend the demands of the traditional
labor sector. Faced with the PRI's plurality and the PAN's declining presence in Congress after 2003, the Fox government was forced to seek an
alliance with the PRI. The result has been a failure to advance on democratic labor reform despite Mexico's "democratic" transition.

CONCLUSION: REVOLUTIONARY LEGACIES, DE FACTO FLEXIBILITY, AND THE LIMITS OF LABOR REFORM

The two countries that experienced nationalist revolutions early in the
twentieth century remained unable to realize the promise of their progressive labor laws at the end of the century. Mexico and Bolivia shared
a legacy of labor's alliance with the state in the context of a nationalist
revolution. In both cases labor served as an important political ally during intraelite conflict. Labor unions were rewarded in both instances
with privileged access to government and involvement in ruling parties,
as well as with policies benefiting workers.

In Mexico this labor-state alliance survived important economic and

---

54. Evidence of this pragmatic adaptability could be seen in the behavior of CTM unions
and federations in states governed by the PAN in the 1990s (Bensusán and Reygadas 2000).

political challenges, and labor facilitated the ruling party's adoption of market reforms as well as its increasingly unfavorable labor policies in the 1980s and 1990s. Despite the PRI's loss in the 2000 presidential elections and the emergence of an independent UNT, official unions in Mexico remained influential. They collaborated with employers and government in a new labor reform project that would introduce greater legal flexibility while reaffirming unions' monopoly status and limiting institutional changes that would aid independent unions. Even with the existence of protective labor laws, the corporatist flexibility supported by the unions made employer demands for labor reform less urgent than in other countries. High levels of informality also created a situation of de facto flexibility in employment. This made it possible for employer groups to await a more favorable political context in which to codify changes and press for reform.

Labor's alliance with the state in Bolivia was far less consistent, but the labor movement remained a strong political and social actor, at least into the 1980s. Labor in Bolivia also experienced a good deal more autonomy than in Mexico, aided in part by the relative weakness of the state and political institutions in Bolivia compared with Mexico's. The combination of the state's political weakness and labor's active resistance to unfavorable policies made reform efforts relatively costly. The Bolivian story, therefore, is one more of institutional weakness than was the case in Mexico. Yet in both countries, and especially in Bolivia, de facto flexibility was an important factor in slowing strong demands for labor reform. With nearly 70 percent of its working population in the informal sector, and the widespread failure to enforce labor laws, the demands for labor flexibility in Bolivia were less urgent. In the early 2000s, even international financial institutions began to argue against the adoption of flexibility reforms in contexts that were already quite flexible but still lacking in basic enforcement and rights protection.

The Future of Labor Reform:
Between Flexibility and Rights?

As more countries around the world revise their labor laws in response to the challenges of globalization, the questions this study addresses take on broader significance. What explains the diversity of reform processes and policy outcomes within the same geographical region? How important are international pressures versus domestic factors in explaining reform? Will reforms shift from their strong focus on flexibility during the 1990s toward a greater balance between flexibility and rights in the twenty-first century?

This book has aimed to answer these questions by looking at the politics of labor law reform in six Latin American countries. All six countries faced pressures to make their labor laws more flexible, pressures generated by a mix of increased economic competitiveness, the stipulations of international financial agencies, and legislation originally crafted to respond to a different set of political and economic challenges. Chile and Peru did flexibilize quite extensively, but under authoritarian conditions. Argentina and Brazil saw mixed outcomes, as relatively strong labor movements staved off government attempts to introduce reforms. The result was some flexibility in employment regulations, but far less in collective legislation. Mexico and Bolivia have not implemented labor law reform as of the early 2000s, despite domestic demands for greater flexibility and an extensive national debate on reform projects.

I have attributed cross-pair differences in reform outcomes to differences in legal frameworks and political legacies, which in turn shaped different levels of labor strength, signaling varying degrees of effective resistance to reform. Under the state corporatist legacy of both Argentina and Brazil, unions acquired legal protections that helped to sustain them, as well as a social and political presence that enabled them to shape labor reforms during democratic transition. The result—a stronger set of labor rights and protections—provided a more advantageous position from which to resist government flexibility reforms during the 1990s, when labor was weakened overall by market-oriented changes. In Argentina, government used the threat of collective reforms to extract concessions on employment flexibility. In Brazil, flexibility in employment regulation also advanced, while proposals for collective reform remained stalled in the face of widespread political resistance.

The more extreme employment flexibility and restrictions on collective rights seen in Chile and Peru grew out of a strong political reaction to the pro-worker radical regime legacies of Allende in Chile and the Velasco Alvarado military government in Peru. Advances in unionization, wages, and labor and social policy were reversed by the Chilean dictatorship in the 1970s and 1980s. In Peru the severity of the debt crisis and the presence of governments less friendly to workers' interests weakened the labor movement, leaving it unable to resist the market reforms and labor restrictions of the Fujimori years. In both countries the weakness of labor as a social and political actor facilitated the erosion of legal protections.

At no point did Chilean and Peruvian labor laws provide the monopoly representation, centralized union structure, or subsidies that unions in Brazil and Argentina enjoyed. When antilabor regimes came to power, unions could not avail themselves of legal or institutional resources in order to protect themselves. The result was a loss of rights and protections, making any effort at redress later on much more difficult and largely dependent on the initiative of other sectors of society rather than on unions alone.

Mexico and Bolivia are the anomalies in the region. Whereas Mexico's state corporatist features provided trade unions with resources and protections similar to those in Argentina, it was Mexico's revolutionary state legacy that best explained the absence of reform in the 1990s. In Mexico, labor's strong alliance with the ruling party eventually led to a quid pro quo: Labor would countenance flexibility, particularly within firms, and keep industrial peace, while the state protected "official" unions from competition and guarded labor's legal prerogatives. In addition to this corporatist flexibility pact, the large informal economy and enforcement weaknesses generated de facto labor market flexibility and lessened the urgency of employer demands for labor law reform. Indeed, the largely protective nature of labor legislation that derived from this revolutionary legacy was in part responsible for the informality and extralegality that characterized both Mexican and Bolivian labor relations, as employers and government strove to lower costs and avoid rules.

Bolivia's greater political instability relative to Mexico created a somewhat different dynamic. Nonetheless, Bolivian labor initially shared Mexican labor's alliance with a nationalist revolutionary regime. As a result, labor's strong presence in politics and society, a largely protective labor code, and labor's militancy (especially that of the miners' union) helped the trade union movement retain veto power over aspects of social and labor policy even as it lost strength in the 1980s. The large degree of informality in the economy and the lax enforcement of existing labor laws also enabled a degree of de facto flexibility in the Bolivian labor market. Even so, as in Mexico, pressures remained in Bolivia for labor reform that would codify some of this flexibility while updating individual protections.

Domestic actors clearly responded to international pressures to reform labor laws. Just as the economic context of import-substitution industrialization in the mid-twentieth century led to worker protections, state corporatism, and political party alliances with labor, the shift of recent decades toward greater global competitiveness has favored regulatory flexibility, greater autonomy, and weaker party ties. Yet while international pressures shaped the context for labor law change in these countries and even set the agenda of states in the region, they did not cast the political dynamics or determine the outcome of reform. Instead, domestic factors drove reform dynamics, and their interaction with international forces was frequently unpredictable.

In fact, this study's focus on legal frameworks and political legacies reveals an important degree of path dependency in determining labor reform outcomes. In most of these cases, initial labor incorporation and accompanying labor legislation produced a lasting legacy, defining institutions and practices and shaping actors' strengths and weaknesses for years to come. Whether these initial events favored trade unions by providing resources for protection of their organizational interests became an important determinant of labor's ability to resist attacks on those legal protections decades later.

In this regard, state corporatism appears to have provided the best institutional setting for labor's organizational survival during its most difficult decade—the 1990s. Despite its frequent portrayal as an archaic configuration of institutions and relations, corporatism remained important under neoliberalism, at least for large union organizations in Mexico and Argentina, and to a lesser extent Brazil. In contrast, nations with weaker labor movements (and weaker legal and institutional protections) were more vulnerable to flexibility pressures, whether these came from domestic or international actors.

The implications of these legacies for the future of labor rights are less clear. Corporatist settings may provide relative stability to labor organizations, but they do not necessarily afford the best environment for expanding labor rights. Stronger unions coming out of corporatist legacies may be less inclined to embrace international labor standards, especially those regarding freedom of association, given the monopoly advantages many unions gained from early corporatist legislation. The greater tendency of such unions to enjoy political party alliances also increases the likelihood that they will work to sustain their advantages over competing unions. On the other hand, weaker labor unions might be more willing to embrace international labor standards and rights for all workers, since international standards usually pose a distinct advantage over existing conditions. Weaker unions pressing for increases in protection may also be seen as less of a threat by employer organizations and others, making it easier to address issues of rights in labor reform. This was the situation in the early part of the Toledo administration in Peru. In Central America, however, weak unions were susceptible not only to pro-labor rights interventions but also to global market pressures that undermined enforcement and commitment to labor standards.

BETWEEN FLEXIBILITY AND RIGHTS: THE SEARCH FOR BALANCE

Past studies of market-oriented policy reform have tended to focus on how elites may implement their desired reforms most effectively. Many studies of labor reform have treated it as largely a technical matter and therefore simply a question of convincing society of the reform's broader benefits while overcoming resistance by unions. Given the high stakes of legal and institutional change, however, successful reform involves far more than a good public relations campaign. Both the content of the reforms and the way in which they are implemented matter for their sustainability.

In Latin America, where labor reforms were imposed, they proved unsustainable. Most of the flexibility-driven reforms of the labor market in the 1990s failed in some respect, whether in meeting reform goals, gaining public acceptance, or coexisting with basic rights. Argentina reversed its flexibility laws in 1998; Brazil's reforms remained marginal and ineffective; Chilean labor reforms afforded inadequate rights protections and undermined human capital development; and Peru's flexibility reforms destroyed labor rights.

Even where governments tried to discuss reform in tripartite settings, talks foundered because of preset agendas and lack of trust. In the market reform decade of the 1990s, governments resisted systemic changes in labor laws and industrial relations institutions that would have addressed existing labor market problems in a more integrated and complementary manner. Instead, changes were piecemeal, fragmented, and resisted by unions or employers. Attempts at tripartism and consensus failed as it became clear that the objective was to impose an agenda rather than to address problems that affected all actors. Collective rights in particular were either attacked or ignored, placing unions on the defensive and creating an unfavorable context for discussions of institutional reform.

This narrow and aggressive approach to labor reform in the 1990s produced some unintended outcomes. In some countries, such as Argentina, there emerged a backlash to labor reforms that had been implemented in the name of flexibility. In other countries, such as Brazil, Chile, and Peru, there were attempts to strike a better balance between flexibility and rights in new rounds of reform. These initial efforts to address labor reform through social dialogue appeared especially promising in Brazil and Peru. In these cases, governments recognized labor's collective interests as legitimate and strove to protect these during reform discussions. The Peruvian and Brazilian experiments in multipartite dialogue in the 2000s also presented examples of a more integrated approach. The entire labor relations system became the subject of discussion, so that attention could be paid to how the different parts interacted and so that no one group would be singled out to bear most of the costs of reform. The Chilean system, by contrast, retained nonnegotiable pockets of employer authority and privilege that continued to hinder the search for consensus and integration, even as legal reforms around the margins improved conditions for labor unions.

The search for a balance between flexibility and rights has been aided by a shift in the global debate over labor rights, especially by the enhanced visibility and role of the ILO. As the link between labor rights protection and global trade becomes more accepted by governments and international organizations, trade unions and labor advocates in Latin America and other regions can draw on the moral authority, legitimacy, and technical resources offered by organizations like the ILO to press for improvements in labor rights protections at home. Latin American unions have been filing complaints with the ILO for years. Yet it is the convergence of labor rights' new legitimacy in international discourse with more favorable national political environments that is most likely to create an amenable context for rights-oriented labor reforms.

In recent years several developments have produced this more favorable political environment in Latin America. The failure of neoliberal economic reforms to generate growth and employment in the 1990s, and their association in some countries with corrupt and semiauthoritarian governments, provoked a backlash or at least generated strong skepticism of market-oriented reforms in several countries. This shift away from a predominant focus on market reform was reflected in the election in the early 2000s of leftist governments in Argentina, Brazil, Uruguay, Ecuador, and, to a lesser extent, Chile. Although these governments did not abandon the market-oriented policies of their predecessors, they were more oriented toward redistributive policies and friendlier to trade unions (if not directly aligned with them). The early results were a more favorable political environment for organized labor and greater potential for a more balanced labor policy.

Still, a more balanced outcome in labor reform has yet to emerge. By late 2005, neither Peru nor Brazil had concluded reform discussions, much less passed new legislation, and other issues threatened to sideline the labor debate once more. In Argentina, where unions prevailed upon party allies to rescind the laws passed under de la Rúa, it is not clear that the result has been a "balance" as much as it has been a return to pre-Menem labor legislation. That this occurred in a weaker economic and employment environment, where informality, unemployment, and poverty all increased dramatically, underscores the persistent need to address some of the disjunctures between law and reality in Argentina. Despite claims that the government of Hugo Chávez in Venezuela has a leftist policy orientation, trade unions in that country have come under attack and basic rights of freedom of association have been undermined. Moreover, in Mexico, Congress remains unable to pass labor reform that addresses constraints on freedom of association, in particular the inability of independent unions to form and pursue their members' interests. Finally, recurrent political crises in Bolivia have hindered efforts to adjust labor laws and policies to address the reality of a large informal sector.

What would a better balance between flexibility and rights look like? Although a full exploration of policy options and their corresponding debates is beyond the scope of this book, some basic elements can be outlined here. A key issue is how to extend social protections (including income insurance, training, and employment assistance) to workers who are outside the formal sector, or who spend their lives moving between informal and formal employment. Addressing this issue requires something other than weakening protections and lowering stability for formal-sector workers, policies that have not been shown to work. Approaching the problem requires reviewing the entire array of labor market institutions, sharing the costs of transition or adjustment, and providing compensation for unrecoverable losses. Most important, perhaps, and most difficult, it requires the engagement of collective actors such as trade unions. At a minimum, this means providing meaningful forums for tripartite negotiation/social dialogue. But it also means a commitment to protect collective labor rights. In the past, attacks on unions under the guise of corralling "special interests" undermined an important channel of employee representation and worker citizenship. It also placed the strongest unions on the defensive, so that they were unwilling or unable to engage in strategic innovation, such as broadening their demands to include those who are excluded from formal labor markets. The extension of security to all workers in a more flexible labor market should come through strengthened collective rights.

Most countries in Latin America have yet to start down this road. Yet the recent shift toward enhanced international attention to labor rights, coupled with more favorable domestic politics in some countries, makes achieving a balance between flexibility and rights more possible in the 2000s than it was in the previous decade. It remains uncertain whether governments, employers, and unions in Latin America will take up the task of reforming labor laws and institutions in a way that strikes this balance. The aim of this book has been to elucidate the path they have traveled so far.

References

Acuña, Carlos H. 1994. "Politics and Economics in the Argentina of the Nineties (Or, Why the Future No Longer Is What It Used to Be)." In *Democracy, Markets, and Structural Reform in Latin America*, ed. William C. Smith, Carlos H. Acuña, and Eduardo A. Gamarra, 31–33. Miami: North-South Center Press.

Adler, Glenn, and Eddie Webster, eds. 2000. *Trade Unions and Democratization in South Africa, 1985–1997*. London: Macmillan.

Aguilar, Javier, Graciela Bensusán, Rosa Albina Garavito, Marco Gómez, Jorge González, Patricia González, Octavio Lóyzaga, Luisa Mussot, Mario Ortega, Patricia Ravelo, Armando Rendón, Jesús Rodríguez, and Sergio Sánchez. 1996. *Legislación laboral: El debate sobre una propuesta*. México, D.F.: Universidad Autónoma Metropolitana-Xochimilco, Fundación Friedrich Ebert.

Aidt, Toke, and Zafiris Tzanattos. 2003. *Unions and Collective Bargaining: Economic Effects in a Global Environment*. Washington, D.C.: World Bank.

Alexander, Robin. 1999. "The UE-FAT Strategic Organizing Alliance." In *Confronting Change: Auto Labor and Lean Production in North America/Enfrentando el cambio: Obreros del automóvil y producción esbelta en América del Norte*, 2d ed., ed. Huberto Juárez Núñez and Steve Babson, 525–33. Puebla, Puebla, México: Benemérita Universidad Autónoma de Puebla and Wayne State University Labor Studies Center.

Amadeo, Edward, Ricardo Paes e Barros, José Márcio Camargo, and Rosane Mendonça. 1995. "Brazil." In *Reforming the Labor Market in a Liberalized Economy*, ed. Gustavo Marquez, 35–78. Washington, D.C.: Inter-American Development Bank.

Angell, Alan. 1972. *Politics and the Labour Movement in Chile*. London: Oxford University Press.

———. 1979. "Peruvian Labour and the Military Government Since 1968." Working Paper no. 3. London: University of London, Institute of Latin American Studies.

Bacon, David. 2001. "Secret Ballot Denied in Vote at Duro Maquiladora." *Mexican Labor News and Analysis* 6 (3). Available at http://www.ueinternational.org/vol6no3.html.

Balbi, Carmen Rosa. 1997. "Politics and Trade Unions in Peru." In *The Peruvian Labyrinth: Polity, Society, Economy*, ed. Maxwell A. Cameron and Philip Mauceri, 134–51. University Park: Pennsylvania State University Press.

Barba, Héctor. 2005. "Cuadro comparativo: Cambio de redacción en artículos de la iniciativa PRI, PAN, PVEM." Available at http://www.fatmexico.org/analisis/reforma%20laboral%2020%20de%20agosto.05.doc.

Barrera, Manuel. 1998. "Macroeconomic Adjustment in Chile and the Politics of the Popular Sectors." In *What Kind of Democracy? What Kind of Market? Latin America in the Age of Neoliberalism*, ed. Philip D. Oxhorn and Graciela Ducatenzeiler, 127–49. University Park: Pennsylvania State University Press.

Barrera, Manuel, and J. Samuel Valenzuela. 1986. "The Development of Labor Movement Opposition to the Military Regime." In *Military Rule in Chile: Dictatorship and Oppositions*, ed. J. Samuel Valenzuela and Arturo Valenzuela, 230–69. Baltimore: Johns Hopkins University Press.

Barrett, Patrick S. 2001. "Labour Policy, Labour-Business Relations, and the Transition to Democracy in Chile." *Journal of Latin American Studies* 33 (3): 561–97.

Bayón, María Cristina. 1997. *El sindicalismo automotriz mexicano frente a un nuevo escenario: Una perspectiva desde los liderazgos*. México, D.F.: FLACSO and Juan Pablos, ed.

Bayón, María Cristina, and Graciela Bensusán. 1996. "El poder sindical y la reestructuración productiva en México." *Revista Latinoamericana de Estudios del Trabajo* 2 (4): 111–38.

Beaty, Tim. 1999. "Vínculos sindicales." In *Libertad sindical*, ed. José Alfonso Bouzas Ortíz, 231–33. México, D.F.: UAM/UNAM/FAT/AFL-CIO.

Bensusán, Graciela. 1996. "Un nuevo pacto laboral: Ejes y problemas de la agenda." In *México: Una agenda para fin de siglo*, ed. Alberto Aziz Nassif, 137–73. México, D.F.: La Jornada Ediciones/Centro de Investigaciones Interdisciplinarias en Ciencias y Humanidades, UNAM.

———. 1997. "Contratos de protección en México." *Nexos* 234 (June): 17–21.

———. 2000. *El modelo mexicano de regulación laboral*. México, D.F.: Universidad Autónoma Metropolitana-Xochimilco, Fundación Friedrich Ebert, and Facultad Latinoamericana de Ciencias Sociales.

———. 2001. "La libertad sindical y los derechos colectivos en las propuestas del PAN (1995) y el PRD (1998)." In *Democracia sindical*, ed. José Alfonso Bouzas, 155–66. México, D.F.: UAM/UNAM/FAT/AFL-CIO.

———, ed. 2006. *Diseño legal y desempeño real: Instituciones laborales en América Latina*. México, D.F.: Miguel Angel Porrúa and Universidad Autónoma Metropolitana-Xochimilco.

Bensusán, Graciela, and Arturo Alcalde. 2000a. "Estructura sindical y agremiación." In *Trabajo y trabajadores en el México contemporáneo*, ed. Graciela Bensusán and Teresa Rendón, 163–92. México, D.F.: Miguel Angel Porrúa.

———. 2000b. "El régimen jurídico del trabajo asalariado." In *Trabajo y trabajadores en el México contemporáneo*, ed. Graciela Bensusán and Teresa Rendón, 127–61. México, D.F.: Miguel Angel Porrúa.

Bensusán, Graciela, and Maria Lorena Cook. 2003. "Political Transition and Labor Revitalization in Mexico." In *Labor Revitalization: Global Perspectives and New Initiatives*, ed. Daniel B. Cornfield and Holly J. McCammon, 229–67. Oxford: Elsevier JAI.

Bensusán, Graciela, Carlos García, and Marisa von Bülow. 1996. *Relaciones laborales en las PYMES de México*. México, D.F.: Friedrich Ebert Stiftung.

Bensusán, Graciela, and Samuel León, eds. 1991. *Negociación y conflicto laboral en México*. México, D.F.: Friedrich Ebert Stiftung/FLACSO.

Bensusán, Graciela, and Luís Reygadas. 2000. "Relaciones laborales en Chihua-hua: Un caso de abatimiento artificial de los salarios." *Revista Mexicana de Sociología* 52 (2): 29–57.

Bensusán, Graciela, and Marisa von Bülow. 1997. "La reforma institucional del corporativismo sindical: Las experiencias de Brasil y México." *Perfiles Latinoamericanos* 6 (11): 185–229.

Bergquist, Charles. 1986. *Labor in Latin America: Comparative Essays on Chile, Argentina, Venezuela, and Colombia*. Stanford: Stanford University Press.

Bermeo, Nancy. 1994. "Sacrifice, Sequence, and Strength in Successful Dual Transitions: Lessons from Spain." *Journal of Politics* 56 (3): 601–27.

Birdsall, Nancy, Carol Graham, and Richard H. Sabot. 1998. "Virtuous Circles in Latin America's Second Stage of Reforms." In *Beyond Trade-Offs: Market Reform and Equitable Growth in Latin America*, ed. Nancy Birdsall, Carol Graham, and Richard H. Sabot, 1–28. Washington, D.C.: Inter-American Development Bank and Brookings Institution Press.

Blank, Rebecca M., and Richard B. Freeman. 1994. "Evaluating the Connection Between Social Protection and Economic Flexibility." In *Social Protection Versus Economic Flexibility: Is There a Tradeoff?* ed. Rebecca M. Blank, 21–42. Chicago: University of Chicago Press.

Bouzas Ortíz, José Alfonso. 1999. "Libertad sindical: Impacto de la jurisprudencia de la Suprema Corte de Justicia en las organizaciones de trabajadores." In *La jurisprudencia y la libertad sindical: México, 1999*, ed. Francisco Pérez Arce Ibarra, 93–99. México, D.F.: Secretaría de Gobierno, Subsecretaría de Trabajo y Previsión Social.

Bouzas Ortíz, José Alfonso, and María Mercedes Gaitán Riveros. 2001. "Contratos colectivos de trabajo de protección." In *Democracia sindical*, ed. José Alfonso Bouzas, 49–66. México, D.F.: UAM/UNAM/FAT/AFL-CIO.

Boyer, Robert. 1987. "Labor Flexibilities: Many Forms, Uncertain Effects." *Labour and Society* 12 (1): 107–29.

"Brasil: Concluido debate de reforma sindical." *Correio Sindical Mercosul* 4 (169) (21 October–10 November 2004): 1–2. Available at http://www.sindicatomercosul.com.br/download_up/CSM%20169.pdf.

Bronstein, Arturo S. 1995. "Societal Change and Industrial Relations in Latin America: Trends and Prospects." *International Labour Review* 134 (2): 163–86.

———. 1997. "Labor Law Reform in Latin America: Between State Protection and Flexibility." *International Labour Review* 136 (1): 5–26.

Buchanan, Paul G. 1995. *State, Labor, Capital: Democratizing Class Relations in the Southern Cone*. Pittsburgh: University of Pittsburgh Press.

Buchanan, Richard. 1989. "The Future of Brazilian Labor Law Under the Federal Constitution of 1988." *Comparative Labor Law Journal* 10 (2): 214–42.

Bureau of National Affairs. 1996. "Privatization, Automation, Weaken Once-Powerful Labor Unions in Brazil." *Daily Labor Report* 142 (24 July), C1.

———. 2003. "Chile Should Streamline Labor Tribunals, Boost Organizing Protections, ICFTU Says." *Daily Labor Report* 235 (8 December), A7.

————. 2004. "Public Employees in Peru Granted Bargaining Rights." *Daily Labor Report* 57 (25 March), A14.

Burgess, Katrina. 2004. *Parties and Unions in the New Global Economy.* Pittsburgh: University of Pittsburgh Press.

Camargo, José Márcio. 1997. "Brazil: Labour Market Flexibility and Productivity, with Many Poor Jobs." In *Labour Productivity and Flexibility,* ed. Edward J. Amadeo and Susan Horton, 37–64. Hampshire, UK: Palgrave Macmillan.

Camargo Chávez, Carlos, Benjamín Grossman Parrondo, and María Isabel Arauco. 1998. *Apuntes para el debate: Sobre la reforma de la legislación laboral en Bolivia.* La Paz: Centro de Estudios Laborales-Ayuda Obrera Suiza.

Cameron, Maxwell A., and Philip Mauceri. 1997. "Conclusion: Threads in the Peruvian Labyrinth." In *The Peruvian Labyrinth: Polity, Society, Economy,* ed. Maxwell A. Cameron and Philip Mauceri, 223–43. University Park: Pennsylvania State University Press.

Campana Zegarra, David. 1999. *Libro blanco sobre la violación de los derechos humanos laborales y sindicales en el Perú, 1990–1999.* Lima: Centro de Asesoría Laboral del Perú/Organización Regional Interamericana de Trabajadores.

Cardoso, Adalberto Moreira. 1999. *Sindicatos, trabalhadores e a coqueluche neoliberal: A era Vargas acabou?* Rio de Janeiro: Editora Fundação Getulio Vargas.

————. 2000. "Brazilian Central Union Federations at the Crossroads." Paper prepared for the "Workshop on National Labor Confederations in Brazil and South Korea," University of California, Berkeley, 13–14 May.

Carrillo, Jorge, ed. 1990. *La nueva era de la industria automotriz en México.* Tijuana: Colegio de la Frontera Norte.

Carrillo Alejandro, Patricia. 2001. "La libertad sindical en la agenda de los 20 compromisos." In *Democracia sindical,* ed. José Alfonso Bouzas, 49–66. México, D.F.: UAM/UNAM/FAT/AFL-CIO.

Centro de Estudios para el Desarrollo Laboral y Agrario (CEDLA). 1998. "Por la defensa del derecho del trabajo: Fundamentos para una propuesta de actualización de la legislación laboral." Working Paper no. 14, July. La Paz, Bolivia: CEDLA.

Chacaltana, Juan, and Norberto García. 2001. *Reforma laboral, capacitación y productividad: La experiencia peruana.* Documento de Trabajo no. 139. Lima: Oficina Internacional del Trabajo.

Ciudad, Adolfo. 2002. *Reformas laborales y procesos de integración en los países de la OEA: 1980–2000.* Lima: Oficina Internacional del Trabajo.

Collier, Ruth Berins. 1982. "Popular Sector Incorporation and Political Supremacy: Regime Evolution in Brazil and Mexico." In *Brazil and Mexico: Patterns in Late Development,* ed. Sylvia Ann Hewlett and Richard S. Weinert, 57–109. Philadelphia: Institute for the Study of Human Issues.

Collier, Ruth Berins, and David Collier. 1979. "Inducements Versus Constraints: Disaggregating 'Corporatism.'" *American Political Science Review* 73 (4): 967–86.

———. 1991. *Shaping the Political Arena: Critical Junctures, the Labor Movement, and Regime Dynamics in Latin America*. Princeton: Princeton University Press.

Commission for Labor Cooperation. 2000. *Labor Relations Law in North America*. Washington, D.C.: Secretariat of the Commission for Labor Cooperation.

Compa, Lance. 1973. *Labor Law and the Legal Way: Collective Bargaining in the Chilean Textile Industry Under the Unidad Popular*. Working Paper no. 23. New Haven: Yale Law School, Program in Law and Modernization.

———. 1999. "NAFTA's Labour Side Agreement Five Years On: Progress and Prospects for the NAALC." *Canadian Labour and Employment Law Journal* 1 (1): 1–30.

Compa, Lance, and Jeffrey S. Vogt. 2001. "Labor Rights in the Generalized System of Preferences: A 20-Year Review." *Comparative Labor Law and Policy Journal* 22 (2–3): 199–238.

Conaghan, Catherine M. 1988. *Restructuring Domination: Industrialists and the State in Ecuador*. Pittsburgh: University of Pittsburgh Press.

Conesa, Ana María, and Eduardo Larrañaga. 1988. "El derecho de huelga en quiebra." *El Cotidiano* 25 (September–October): 66–70.

Confederación Patronal de la República Mexicana (COPARMEX). 1989. "Propuestas preliminares que la Coparmex presenta para la discusión de un anteproyecto de Nueva Ley Federal del Trabajo." June. Mimeograph. In author's possession.

Consejo Coordinador Empresarial (CCE). 1994. "Propuestas del sector privado." July. Mimeograph. In author's possession.

Contreras, José. 1998. "La reforma laboral llegará hasta donde los involucrados quieran: González Fernández." *La Crónica*, 9 September. Available at http://www.cronica.com.mx.

Cook, Maria Lorena. 1995. "State-Labor Relations in Mexico: Old Tendencies and New Trends." In *Mexico Faces the 21st Century*, ed. Donald E. Schulz and Edward J. Williams, 77–95. Westport, Conn.: Praeger.

———. 1996. *Organizing Dissent: Unions, the State, and the Democratic Teachers' Movement in Mexico*. University Park: Pennsylvania State University Press.

———. 1997. "Regional Integration and Transnational Politics: Popular Sector Strategies in the NAFTA Era." In *The New Politics of Inequality in Latin America: Rethinking Participation and Representation*, ed. Douglas A. Chalmers, Carlos M. Vilas, Katherine Hite, Scott B. Martin, Kerianne Peister, and Monique Segarra, 516–40. New York: Oxford University Press.

———. 1998. "Toward Flexible Industrial Relations? Neo-Liberalism, Democracy, and Labor Reform in Latin America." *Industrial Relations* 27 (3): 311–36.

———. 2002. "Labor Reform and Dual Transitions in Brazil and the Southern Cone." *Latin American Politics and Society* 44 (1): 1–34.

Cook, Maria Lorena, Morley Gunderson, Mark Thompson, and Anil Verma. 1997. "Making Free Trade More Fair: Developments in Protecting Labor Rights." *Labor Law Journal* 48 (8): 519–29.

Cook, Maria Lorena, Kevin J. Middlebrook, and Juan Molinar Horcasitas. 1994. "The Politics of Economic Restructuring: Actors, Sequencing, and Coalition Change." In *The Politics of Economic Restructuring: State-Society Relations and Regime Change in Mexico,* ed. Maria Lorena Cook, Kevin J. Middlebrook, and Juan Molinar Horcasitas, 3–52. U.S.-Mexico Contemporary Perspectives Series no. 7. La Jolla: University of California, San Diego, Center for U.S.-Mexican Studies.

Corbo, Vittorio. 1985. "Chilean Economic Policy and International Economic Relations Since 1970." In *The National Economic Policies of Chile,* ed. Gary M. Walton, 107–44. London: JAI Press.

Córdova, Efrén. 1989. "From Corporatism to Liberalisation: The New Directions of the Brazilian System of Industrial Relations." *Labour and Society* 14 (3): 251–69.

———. 1996. "The Challenge of Flexibility in Latin America." *Comparative Labor Law Journal* 17 (2): 314–37.

Cornelius, Wayne A. 1996. *Mexican Politics in Transition: The Breakdown of a One-Party-Dominant Regime.* La Jolla: University of California, San Diego, Center for U.S.-Mexican Studies.

———. 1999. "Subnational Politics and Democratization: Tensions Between Center and Periphery in the Mexican Political System." In *Subnational Politics and Democratization in Mexico,* ed. Wayne A. Cornelius, Todd A. Eisenstadt, and Jane Hindley, 3–16. La Jolla: University of California, San Diego, Center for U.S.-Mexican Studies.

Cortázar, René, Nora Lustig, and Richard H. Sabot. 1998. "Economic Policy and Labor Market Dynamics." In *Beyond Trade-Offs: Market Reform and Equitable Growth in Latin America,* ed. Nancy Birdsall, Carol Graham, and Richard H. Sabot, 183–212. Washington, D.C.: Inter-American Development Bank and Brookings Institution Press.

Cox Edwards, Alejandra. 1997. "Labor Market Regulation in Latin America: An Overview." In *Labor Markets in Latin America: Combining Social Protection with Market Flexibility,* ed. Sebastian Edwards and Nora Claudia Lustig, 127–50. Washington, D.C.: Brookings Institution Press.

Craze, Matthew. 2001. "Labor Reform: A Step in the Right Direction?" *Journal of the Chilean American Chamber of Commerce.* Available at http://www .amchamchile.cl/publicaciones/thejournal/labor_reform.htm (accessed 15 November 2002).

Crivelli, Ericson. 1998. "O projeto da CUT para a transição da estrutura sindical corporativa." Paper presented at seminar titled "A Política da CUT para Conquistar um Sistema Democrático de Relações de Trabalho." CUT-Nacional, São Paulo, Brazil, 16–17 March.

Damgaard, Bodil. 1998. "Cinco años con el Acuerdo Laboral Paralelo." Paper presented at a meeting of the Latin American Studies Association, Chicago, 24–26 September. Available at http://136.142.158.105/LASA98/Damgaard .pdf.

———. 1999. "Labor Standards, Income Distribution, and Free Trade." *Integration and Trade* 3 (7–8): 39–85.

Degregori, Carlos Iván. 1998. "Ethnicity and Democratic Governability in Latin

America: Reflections from Two Central Andean Countries." In *Fault Lines of Democracy in Post-Transition Latin America,* ed. Felipe Agüero and Jeffrey Stark, 203–34. Miami: North-South Center Press.

De la Cuadra, Sergio, and Dominique Hachette. 1991. "Chile." In *Liberalizing Foreign Trade: The Experience of Argentina, Chile, and Uruguay,* vol. 1, ed. Demetris Papageorgiou, Michael Michaely, and Armeane M. Choksi, 169–319. Cambridge, Mass.: Basil Blackwell.

De la Garza, Enrique. 1991. "Independent Trade Unionism in Mexico: Past Developments and Future Perspectives." In *Unions, Workers, and the State in Mexico,* ed. Kevin J. Middlebrook, 153–84. La Jolla: University of California, San Diego, Center for U.S.-Mexican Studies.

———. 1993. *Restructuración productiva y respuesta sindical en México.* México, D.F.: Instituto de Investigaciones Económicas, UNAM.

———. 2000. "La contratación colectiva." In *Trabajo y trabajadores en el México Contemporáneo,* ed. Graciela Bensusán and Teresa Rendón, 193–209. México, D.F.: Miguel Angel Porrúa.

De la Garza, Enrique, and Alfonso Bouzas. 1998. "Flexibilidad del trabajo y contratación colectiva en México." *Revista Mexicana de Sociología* 60 (3): 87–122.

De la Garza Toledo, Enrique. 1997. "La flexibilidad del trabajo en América Latina." *Revista Latino-americana de Estudos do Trabalho* 3 (5): 129–57.

———. 2005. "La polémica sobre la reforma laboral en México." Available at http://www.iztapalapa.uam.mx/amet/debate/polemica.doc.

Dombois, Rainer, Erhard Hornberger, and Jens Winter. 2003. "Transnational Labor Regulation in the NAFTA—A Problem of Institutional Design? The Case of the North American Agreement on Labor Cooperation Between the USA, Mexico and Canada." *International Journal of Comparative Labour Law and Industrial Relations* 19 (4): 421–40.

Dombois, Rainer, and Ludger Pries, eds. 1993. *Trabajo industrial en la transición: Experiencias de América Latina y Europa.* Caracas: Fundación Friedrich Ebert de México, Colegio de Puebla, Editorial Nueva Sociedad.

Drake, Paul W. 1996. *Labor Movements and Dictatorships: The Southern Cone in Comparative Perspective.* Baltimore: Johns Hopkins University Press.

Durand, Francisco. 1997. "The Growth and Limitations of the Peruvian Right." In *The Peruvian Labyrinth: Polity, Society, Economy,* ed. Maxwell A. Cameron and Philip Mauceri, 152–75. University Park: Pennsylvania State University Press.

Edwards, Sebastian. 1995. *Crisis and Reform in Latin America.* New York: Oxford University Press.

Edwards, Sebastian, and Nora Claudia Lustig, eds. 1997. *Labor Markets in Latin America: Combining Social Protection with Market Flexibility.* Washington, D.C.: Brookings Institution Press.

Elliott, Kimberly, and Richard B. Freeman. 2003. *Can Labor Standards Improve Under Globalization?* Washington, D.C.: Institute for International Economics.

Ellner, Steve. 1993. *Organized Labor in Venezuela, 1958–1991: Behavior and Concerns in a Democratic Setting.* Wilmington, Del.: Scholarly Resources.

Epstein, Edward C. 1993. "Labor and Political Stability in the New Chilean Democracy: Three Illusions." *Economía y Trabajo* 1 (2): 45–64.

Epstein, Edward C., and David Pion-Berlin, eds. 2006. *Broken Promises? The Argentine Crisis and Argentine Democracy.* Lanham, Md.: Lexington Books.

Erickson, Kenneth P. 1977. *The Brazilian Corporative State and Working-Class Politics.* Berkeley and Los Angeles: University of California Press.

Ermida Uriarte, Oscar. 1995. "El futuro del derecho de trabajo y las relaciones laborales." In *Sindicalismo latinoamericano: Entre la renovación y la resignación,* ed. Maria Silvia Portella de Castro and Achim Wachendorfer, 47–56. Caracas: ILDES-FES Brasil and Nueva Sociedad.

———. 2000. "La flexibilidad laboral." *Escenario* 2 (3) (December). Available at http://www.escenario2.org.uy/numero3/uriarte.html.

Eróstegui T., Rodolfo. 1996. *Economía, sindicato y conflicto laboral.* La Paz: ILDIS, Friedrich Ebert Stiftung.

Etchemendy, Sebastián. 1995. "¿Límites al decisionismo? El poder ejecutivo y la formulación de la legislación laboral (1983–1994)." In *Política y sociedad en los años del menemismo,* ed. Ricardo Sidicaro and Jorge Mayer, 127–53. Buenos Aires: Universidad de Buenos Aires, Facultad de Ciencias Sociales.

———. 2001. "Constructing Reform Coalitions: The Politics of Compensations in Argentina's Economic Liberalization." *Latin American Politics and Society* 43 (3): 1–35.

———. 2004. "Repression, Exclusion, and Inclusion: Government-Union Relations and Patterns of Labor Reform in Liberalizing Economies." *Comparative Politics* 36 (3): 273–90.

Etchemendy, Sebastián, and Vicente Palermo. 1997. "Conflicto y concertación: Gobierno, congreso y organizaciones de interés en la reforma laboral del primer gobierno de Menem." Working Paper no. 41. Buenos Aires: Universidad Torcuato di Tella.

Fórum Nacional do Trabalho (FNT). 2004. *Relatório final da Comissão de Sistematizacão do Fórum Nacional do Trabalho: Organizacão sindical, negociacão coletiva, sistema de composição de conflitos.* March. Available at http://www.cut.org.br/sno/RELATORIO_COMISSAO_SISTEMATIZACAO _FNT.pdf.

———. 2005. *Reforma Sindical: Proposta de emenda à Constituição-PEC 369/ 05, Anteprojeto de Lei.* Brasília: Ministério do Trabalho e Emprego.

Frank, Volker K. 2002. "The Elusive Goal in Democratic Chile: Reforming the Pinochet Labor Legislation." *Latin American Politics and Society* 44 (1): 35–68.

———. 2004. "Politics Without Policy: The Failure of Social Concertation in Democratic Chile, 1990–2000." In *Victims of the Chilean Miracle: Workers and Neoliberalism in the Pinochet Era, 1973–2002,* ed. Peter Winn, 71–124. Durham: Duke University Press.

Freije Rodríguez, Samuel, Keila Betancourt, and Gustavo Márquez. 1995. *Mercado laboral: Instituciones y regulaciones.* Caracas: IESA.

Freitas, Carlos Eduardo. 2000. "Precarização e leis do trabalho nos anos FHC." São Paulo: CUT, Secretaria de Política Sindical.

French, John D. 2001. *Afogados em leis: A CLT e a cultura política dos trabalha-dores brasileiros.* Trans. Paulo Fontes. São Paulo: Editora Fundação Perseu Abramo.

Frundt, Henry J. 1998. *Trade Conditions and Labor Rights: U.S. Initiatives, Dominican and Central American Responses.* Gainesville: University Press of Florida.

Gacek, Stanley A. 1994. "Revisiting the Corporatist and Contractualist Models of Labor Law Regimes: A Review of the Brazilian and American Systems." *Cardozo Law Review* 16 (1): 21–110.

Gamarra, Eduardo A. 1994. "Crafting Political Support for Stabilization: Politi-cal Pacts and the New Economic Policy in Bolivia." In *Democracy, Mar-kets, and Structural Reform in Latin America,* ed. William C. Smith, Carlos H. Acuña, and Eduardo A. Gamarra, 105–27. Miami: North-South Center Press.

———. 1997. "Hybrid Presidentialism and Democratization: The Case of Bo-livia." In *Presidentialism and Democracy in Latin America,* ed. Scott Mainwaring and Matthew Soberg Shugart, 363–93. Cambridge: Cam-bridge University Press.

Gamarra, Eduardo A., and James M. Malloy. 1995. "The Patrimonial Dynamics of Party Politics in Bolivia." In *Building Democratic Institutions: Party Systems in Latin America,* ed. Scott Mainwaring and Timothy R. Scully, 399–433. Stanford: Stanford University Press.

Garavito Elías, Rosa Albina. 2001. "La libertad sindical en los proyectos de re-forma laboral (PAN-PRD)." In *Democracia sindical,* ed. José Alfonso Bou-zas, 141–53. México, D.F.: UAM/UNAM/FAT/AFL-CIO.

García V., Carlos. 1993. "El sindicalismo mexicano frente al modelo neoliberal." In *Modelo neoliberal y sindicatos en América Latina,* ed. Holm-Detlev Köhler and Manfred Wannöffel, 165–93. México, D.F.: Fundación Fried-rich Ebert.

Garduño, Roberto. 2005. "Promueve la STPS una reforma laboral mínima en lugar de la ley Abascal." *La Jornada,* 21 August.

Garrido, Luis Javier. 1982. *El partido de la revolución institucionalizada.* México, D.F.: Siglo XXI Editores.

———. 1989. "The Crisis of Presidencialismo." In *Mexico's Alternative Political Futures,* ed. Wayne A. Cornelius, Judith Gentleman, and Peter H. Smith, 417–34. La Jolla: University of California, San Diego, Center for U.S.-Mexican Studies.

Geddes, Barbara. 1995. "The Politics of Economic Liberalization." *Latin Ameri-can Research Review* 30 (2): 195–214.

Gill, Indermit S., Claudio E. Montenegro, and Dorte Dömeland, eds. 2002. *Crafting Labor Policy: Techniques and Lessons from Latin America.* Washington, D.C.: World Bank/Oxford University Press.

Giugale, Marcelo M., Olivier Lafourcade, and Vinh H. Nguyen. 2001. *Mexico: A Comprehensive Development Agenda for the New Era.* Washington, D.C.: World Bank.

Goldín, Adrián O. 1999. *Para reformar la Ley General del Trabajo (documento de trabajo).* January. Mimeograph. In author's possession.

Graham, Carol. 1998. *Private Markets for Public Goods: Raising the Stakes in Economic Reform.* Washington, D.C.: Brookings Institution Press.

Graham, Carol, and Moisés Naím. 1998. "The Political Economy of Institutional Reform in Latin America." In *Beyond Trade-Offs: Market Reform and Equitable Growth in Latin America,* ed. Nancy Birdsall, Carol Graham, and Richard H. Sabot, 321–62. Washington, D.C.: Inter-American Development Bank and Brookings Institution Press.

Haagh, Louise. 2002. "The Emperor's New Clothes: Labor Reform and Social Democratization in Chile." *Studies in Comparative International Development* 27 (1): 86–115.

Haggard, Stephan, and Robert R. Kaufman. 1995. *The Political Economy of Democratic Transitions.* Princeton: Princeton University Press.

Hall, Michael M., and Hobart A. Spalding Jr. 1986. "The Urban Working Class and Early Latin American Labour Movements." In *The Cambridge History of Latin America.* Vol. 4, *1870–1930,* ed. Leslie Bethell, 325–65. Cambridge: Cambridge University Press.

Hermanson, Jeff. 2001. "Algunas reflexiones en torno a la globalización y la solidaridad sindical internacional." In *Democracia sindical,* ed. José Alfonso Bouzas, 119–26. México, D.F.: UAM/UNAM/FAT/AFL-CIO.

Hirata, Helena. 1998. "Alterações do perfil do mercado de trabalho na França." *Debate e Reflexões: Sindicato e Relações de Trabalho, Desafios no Limiar do Século* 21 (5). São Paulo: Escola Sindical São Paulo-CUT.

Human Rights Watch. 1990. *Human Rights in Mexico: A Policy of Impunity.* Americas Watch Report. Los Angeles: Human Rights Watch.

———. 2001. *Trading Away Rights: The Unfulfilled Promise of NAFTA's Labor Side Agreement.* April. Available at http://www.hrw.org/reports/2001/nafta/.

———. 2005. Letter to Deputy Francisco Javier Barrio Terrazas, Deputy Emilio Chuayffet Chemor, Deputy Pablo Gómez Alvarez, and Deputy Manlio Fabio Beltrones Rivera of the Mexican Chamber of Deputies. 9 February. Available at http://hrw.org/english/docs/2005/02/09/mexico10156.htm.

Hunter, Wendy. 1998. "Civil-Military Relations in Argentina, Brazil, and Chile: Present Trends, Future Prospects." In *Fault Lines of Democracy in Post-Transition Latin America,* ed. Felipe Agüero and Jeffrey Stark, 299–322. Miami: North-South Center Press.

Inter-American Development Bank (IADB). 1998. *Facing Up to Inequality in Latin America.* Economic and Social Progress in Latin America, 1998–1999 Report. Washington, D.C.: Inter-American Development Bank.

International Confederation of Free Trade Unions (ICFTU). 2003. *Internationally Recognised Core Labour Standards in Chile: Report for the WTO General Council Review of the Trade Policies of Chile.* 2 and 4 December. Geneva: ICFTU.

International Labor Office. 1999. "Report of the Director General, Fourteenth American Regional Meeting, Lima, Peru, 24–27 August." Available at http://www.oitamericas99.org.pe.

———. 2002. *Globalization and Decent Work in the Americas.* Report of the Director-General. Fifteenth American Regional Meeting, Lima, December.

Available at http://www.ilo.org/public/english/standards/relm/rgmeet/pdf/
am15-dg.pdf.

International Labor Organization (ILO). 1997. *World Labour Report 1997–98:
Industrial Relations, Democracy and Social Stability.* Available at http://
www.ilo.org/public/english/dialogue/ifpdial/publ/wlr97/annex/.

International Labor Organization, Committee of Experts on the Application of
Conventions and Recommendations (ILO-CEACR) (Argentina). 2001. "Individual Observation Concerning Convention No. 87, Freedom of Association and Protection of the Right to Organise, 1948, 2001." Available at
http://www.ilo.org/ilolex/.

———(Chile). 2002. "Comments Made by the Committee of Experts on the
Application of Conventions and Recommendations—Freedom of Association and Protection of the Right to Organise Convention, 1948 (No. 87),
Chile, 2002, 73rd Session." Available at http://webfusion.ilo.org/public/db/
standards/normes/libsynd/index/cfm?hdroff = 1.

———(Bolivia). 2004. "Individual Observation Concerning Convention No. 98,
Right to Organise and Collective Bargaining, 1949, 2004." Available at
http://www.ilo.org/ilolex/.

International Labor Organization, International Labor Conference Committee
(ILO-ILCCR). 1995. "Examination of Individual Case Concerning Convention No. 87, Freedom of Association and Protection of the Right to Organise, 1948, Bolivia." Available at http://www.ilo.org/ilolex/.

———. 1997. "Examination of Individual Case Concerning Convention No. 87,
Freedom of Association and Protection of the Right to Organise, 1948,
Bolivia." Available at http://www.ilo.org/ilolex/.

———. 1998. "Examination of Individual Case Concerning Convention No. 87,
Freedom of Association and Protection of the Right to Organise, 1948,
Bolivia." Available at http://www.ilo.org/ilolex/.

James, Daniel. 1988. *Resistance and Integration: Peronism and the Argentine
Working Class, 1946–1976.* Cambridge: Cambridge University Press.

Jones, Mark P. 1997. "Evaluating Argentina's Presidential Democracy, 1983–
1995." In *Presidentialism and Democracy in Latin America,* ed. Scott
Mainwaring and Matthew Soberg Shugart, 259–99. Cambridge: Cambridge University Press.

Keck, Margaret E. 1989. "The New Unionism in the Brazilian Transition." In
Democratizing Brazil, ed. Alfred Stepan, 252–96. New York: Oxford University Press.

———. 1992. *The Workers' Party and Democratization in Brazil.* New Haven:
Yale University Press.

Kingstone, Peter R. 1999. *Crafting Coalitions for Reform: Business Preferences,
Political Institutions, and Neoliberal Reform in Brazil.* University Park:
Pennsylvania State University Press.

Klein, Herbert S. 1982. *Bolivia: The Evolution of a Multi-Ethnic Society.* New
York: Oxford University Press.

Kochan, Thomas A., Harry C. Katz, and Robert B. McKersie. 1994. *The Transformation of American Industrial Relations.* Ithaca: ILR Press, Cornell
University.

Köhler, Holm-Detlev, and Manfred Wannöffel, eds. 1993. *Modelo neoliberal y sindicatos en América Latina.* México, D.F.: Fundación Friedrich Ebert.

La Botz, Dan. 1992. *Mask of Democracy: Labor Suppression in Mexico Today.* Boston: South End Press.

La Botz, Dan, and Robin Alexander. 2003. "Mexico's Labor Law Reform: Employers' Rights vs. Associational Rights." *Guild Practitioner* 60 (3): 149–61.

Levitsky, Steven. 2003. *Transforming Labor-Based Parties in Latin America: Argentine Peronism in Comparative Perspective.* Cambridge: Cambridge University Press.

Levitsky, Steven, and Lucan A. Way. 1998. "Between a Shock and a Hard Place: The Dynamics of Labor-Backed Adjustments in Poland and Argentina." *Comparative Politics* 30 (2): 171–92.

Locke, Richard, and Kathleen Thelen. 1995. "Apples and Oranges Revisited: Contextualized Comparisons and the Study of Comparative Labor Politics." *Politics and Society* 23 (3): 337–67.

Lora, Eduardo. 1997. "A Decade of Structural Reforms in Latin America: What Has Been Reformed and How to Measure It." Working Paper, Green Series, no. 348. Washington, D.C.: Inter-American Development Bank, Office of the Chief Economist.

———. 2000. "What Makes Reform Likely? Timing and Sequencing of Structural Reforms in Latin America." Working Paper no. 424. Washington, D.C.: Inter-American Development Bank.

Lora, Eduardo, and Carmen Pagés. 1997. "La legislación laboral en el proceso de reformas estructurales de América Latina y el Caribe." *Documentos del Trabajo.* Washington, D.C.: Inter-American Development Bank, Office of the Chief Economist.

Lora, Guillermo. 1977. *A History of the Bolivian Labour Movement, 1848– 1971.* Cambridge: Cambridge University Press.

Loveman, Brian. 1979. *Chile: The Legacy of Hispanic Capitalism.* New York: Oxford University Press.

Lustig, Nora. 1998. *Mexico: The Remaking of an Economy.* 2d ed. Washington, D.C.: Brookings Institution Press.

Madrid, Raúl L. 2003a. "Labouring Against Neoliberalism: Unions and Patterns of Reform in Latin America." *Journal of Latin American Studies* 35: 53–88.

———. 2003b. *Retiring the State: The Politics of Pension Privatization in Latin America and Beyond.* Stanford: Stanford University Press.

Mainwaring, Scott. 1997. "Multipartism, Robust Federalism, and Presidentialism in Brazil." In *Presidentialism and Democracy in Latin America,* ed. Scott Mainwaring and Matthew Soberg Shugart, 55–109. Cambridge: Cambridge University Press.

Mainwaring, Scott, and Matthew Soberg Shugart, eds. 1997. *Presidentialism and Democracy in Latin America.* Cambridge: Cambridge University Press.

Malloy, James M. 1970. *Bolivia: The Uncompleted Revolution.* Pittsburgh: University of Pittsburgh Press.

Márquez, Gustavo, and Carmen Pagés. 1998. "Ties That Bind: Employment Protection and Labor Market Outcomes in Latin America." Paper given at the annual meeting of the Board of Governors, Inter-American Development Bank and Inter-American Investment Corporation, Cartagena de Indias, Colombia, 15 March.

Marshall, Adriana. 1995. "Employment Protection Reforms in South America: Effective Instruments to Manage Employment?" FOCAL/CIS Discussion Papers. Toronto: University of Toronto, Centre for International Studies.

———. 1996. "Weakening Employment Protection in Latin America: Incentive to Employment Creation or to Expand Instability?" *International Contributions to Labour Studies* 6: 29–48.

Martínez, Fabiola. 2003. "Frena negociaciones propuesta del PRD para que líderes sindicales sean electos por voto secreto." *La Jornada*, 15 June. Available at http://www.jornada.unam.mx.

Martínez, Javier, and Alvaro Díaz. 1996. *Chile: The Great Transformation.* Washington, D.C.: Brookings Institution Press.

McGuire, James W. 1995. "Political Parties and Democracy in Argentina." In *Building Democratic Institutions: Party Systems in Latin America,* ed. Scott Mainwaring and Timothy R. Scully, 200–246. Stanford: Stanford University Press.

———. 1997. *Peronism Without Perón: Unions, Parties, and Democracy in Argentina.* Stanford: Stanford University Press.

Mericle, Kenneth S. 1977. "Corporatist Control of the Working Class: Authoritarian Brazil Since 1964." In *Authoritarianism and Corporatism in Latin America,* ed. James M. Malloy, 303–38. Pittsburgh: University of Pittsburgh Press.

Meulders, Daniele, and Luc Wilkins. 1987. "Labour Market Flexibility: Critical Introduction to the Analysis of a Concept." *Labour and Society* 12 (1): 3–17.

Meyer, Lorenzo. 1977. "Historical Roots of the Authoritarian State in Mexico." In *Authoritarianism in Mexico,* ed. José L. Reyna and Richard Weinert, 3–22. Philadelphia: Institute for the Study of Human Issues.

Middlebrook, Kevin J. 1991. "The Politics of Industrial Restructuring: Transnational Firms' Search for Flexible Production in the Mexican Automobile Industry." *Comparative Politics* 23 (3): 275–97.

———. 1995. *The Paradox of Revolution: Labor, the State, and Authoritarianism in Mexico.* Baltimore: Johns Hopkins University Press.

Ministerio de Trabajo y Promoción del Empleo. Oficina de Comunicación Social y Relaciones Públicas. 2004a. "Autorizan al Ministerio de Trabajo y Promoción del Empleo crear el registro de organizaciones sindicales de los servidores públicos" (Lima). 24 March. Available at http://www.mintra.gob.pe.

———. 2004b. "Autorizan revisión de la tercera lista de ex trabajadores considerados para ser compensados por el Estado" (Lima). 10 March. Available at http://www.mintra.gob.pe.

Ministério do Trabalho e Emprego. 2005. *Reforma sindical: Perguntas e respostas.* Brasília: Ministério do Trabalho e Emprego.

Morales, Juan Antonio. 1994. "Democracy, Economic Liberalism, and Structural

Reform in Bolivia." In *Democracy, Markets, and Structural Reform in Latin America,* ed. William C. Smith, Carlos H. Acuña, and Eduardo A. Gamarra, 129–48. Miami: North-South Center Press.

Morris, James O. 1966. *Elites, Intellectuals, and Consensus: A Study of the Social Question and the Industrial Relations System in Chile.* Cornell International Industrial and Labor Relations Report no. 7. Ithaca: Cornell University, New York State School of Industrial and Labor Relations.

Morris, John T. 1998. "Economic Integration and the Transformation of Labor Relations in the Mexican Automotive Industry." In *Transforming the Latin American Automobile Industry: Unions, Workers, and the Politics of Restructuring,* ed. John P. Tuman and John T. Morris, 113–47. Armonk, N.Y.: M. E. Sharpe.

Munck, Gerardo L. 1998. *Authoritarianism and Democratization: Soldiers and Workers in Argentina, 1976–1983.* University Park: Pennsylvania State University Press.

Munck, Ronaldo. 2004. "Introduction." *Latin American Perspectives* 31: 3–20.

Muñoz Ríos, Patricia. 2005. "Apoyan PRI y PAN la reforma laboral." *La Jornada,* 21 September. Available at http://www.jornada.unam.mx.

Murillo, María Victoria. 1997. "Union Politics, Market-Oriented Reforms, and the Reshaping of Argentine Corporatism." In *The New Politics of Inequality in Latin America: Rethinking Participation and Representation,* ed. Douglas A. Chalmers, Carlos M. Vilas, Katherine Hite, Scott B. Martin, Kerianne Peister, and Monique Segarra, 72–94. New York: Oxford University Press.

———. 2001. *Labor Unions, Partisan Coalitions, and Market Reforms in Latin America.* New York: Cambridge University Press.

———. 2005. "Partisanship Amidst Convergence: The Politics of Labor Reform in Latin America." *Comparative Politics* 37 (4): 441–58.

Murillo, María Victoria, and Andrew Schrank. 2005. "With a Little Help from My Friends: Partisan Politics, Transnational Alliances, and Labor Rights in Latin America." *Comparative Political Studies* 38 (8): 971–99.

Nelson, Joan M. 1994. "Overview: How Market Reforms and Democratic Consolidation Affect Each Other." In *Intricate Links: Democratization and Market Reforms in Latin America and Eastern Europe,* ed. Joan M. Nelson, Jacek Kochanowicz, Kálmán Mizsei, and Oscar Muñoz, 1–36. New Brunswick, N.J.: Transaction Publishers.

Nelson, Joan M., Jacek Kochanowicz, Kálmán Mizsei, and Oscar Muñoz. 1994. *Intricate Links: Democratization and Market Reforms in Latin America and Eastern Europe.* New Brunswick, N.J.: Transaction Publishers.

O'Donnell, Guillermo, Philippe Schmitter, and Laurence Whitehead, eds. 1986. *Transitions from Authoritarian Rule.* Baltimore: Johns Hopkins University Press.

Oficina Internacional del Trabajo. 1995. *Las relaciones laborales en el Cono Sur: Estudio comparado.* Informe Relasur, Colección Informes OIT, no. 44. Madrid: Ministerio de Trabajo y Seguridad Social.

———. 2003. *Perú: Propuesta de Programa Nacional de Trabajo Decente, 2004–2006 (informe preliminar).* 18 December. Lima: Oficina Subregional de la OIT para los Países Andinos.

Organisation for Economic Co-operation and Development (OECD). 1999. *Employment Outlook*. Paris: OECD.

Organización para la Cooperación y el Desarrollo Económicos (OCDE). 2000. "Síntesis: Estudio económico de México 2000." *OECD Observer*. Available at http://www.oecd.org/publications/Pol_brief/.

Parodi, Jorge. 2000. *To Be a Worker: Identity and Politics in Peru*. Chapel Hill: University of North Carolina Press.

Partido de la Revolución Democrática (PRD). 1998. *Anteproyecto de reforma laboral del Partido de la Revolución Democrática*. México, D.F.: Grupo Parlamentario del PRD, Cámara de Diputados, LVII Legislatura, Congreso de la Unión.

Pastore, José, and Thomas E. Skidmore. 1985. "Brazilian Labor Relations: A New Era?" In *Industrial Relations in a Decade of Economic Change*, ed. Hervey Juris, Mark Thompson, and Wilbur Daniels, 73–113. Madison, Wis.: Industrial Relations Research Association.

Payne, Leigh A. 1995. "Brazilian Business and the Democratic Transition: New Attitudes and Influence." In *Business and Democracy in Latin America*, ed. Ernest Bartell and Leigh A. Payne, 217–56. Pittsburgh: University of Pittsburgh Press.

Pier, Carol. 1998. "Labor Rights in Chile and NAFTA Labor Standards: Questions of Compatibility on the Eve of Free Trade." *Comparative Labor Law and Policy Journal* 19 (2): 185–277.

Piore, Michael J., and Charles F. Sabel. 1984. *The Second Industrial Divide: Possibilities for Prosperity*. New York: Basic Books.

Polaski, Sandra. 2003. "Central America and the U.S. Face Challenge—and Chance for Historic Breakthrough—on Workers' Rights." *Issue Brief* (February): 1–8. Washington, D.C.: Carnegie Endowment for International Peace.

Portella de Castro, Maria Silvia. 2001. *As mudanças nas leis trabalhistas e no perfil sindical no Brasil e na Argentina na década de 90*. Master's thesis, Universidade de São Paulo, Department of Sociology.

Portella de Castro, Maria Silvia, and Achim Wachendorfer, eds. 1995. *Sindicalismo latinoamericano: Entre la renovación y la resignación*. Caracas: Nueva Sociedad.

Pozas, María de los Angeles. 1993. *Industrial Restructuring in Mexico: Corporate Adaptation, Technological Innovation, and Changing Patterns of Industrial Relations in Monterrey*. La Jolla: University of California, San Diego, Center for U.S.-Mexican Studies.

Pozzi, Pablo A. 1988. "Argentina, 1976–1982: Labour Leadership and Military Government." *Journal of Latin American Studies* 20: 111–38.

"Proyecto de un acuerdo político para la transición en el mundo del trabajo." *Trabajo y Democracia Hoy* 10 (58) (2000) (supplement): 1–7.

Ranis, Peter. 1995. *Class, Democracy, and Labor in Contemporary Argentina*. New Brunswick, N.J.: Transaction Publishers.

Remmer, Karen L. 1995. "New Theoretical Perspectives on Democratization." *Comparative Politics* 28 (1): 103–22.

———. 2002. "The Politics of Economic Policy and Performance in Latin America." *Journal of Public Policy* 22 (1): 29–59.

Rendón, Teresa, and Carlos Salas. 2000. "La evolución del empleo." In *Trabajo y trabajadores en el México contemporáneo,* ed. Graciela Bensusán and Teresa Rendón, 25–91. México, D.F.: Miguel Angel Porrúa.

Rittich, Kerry. 2003. "Core Labor Rights and Labor Market Flexibility: Two Paths Entwined?" In *Labor Law Beyond Borders: ADR and the Internationalization of Labor Dispute Settlement,* ed. International Bureau of the Permanent Court of Arbitration, 157–208. The Hague: Kluwer Law International.

Rodríguez Yebra, Martín. 2002. "El peronismo quiere reformar la ley laboral de De la Rúa." *La Nación,* 8 March. Available at http://www.lanacion.com .ar/02/03/08/dp_379233.asp.

Romaguera, Pilar, Cristián Echeverría, and Pablo González. 1995. "Chile." In *Reforming the Labor Market in a Liberalized Economy,* ed. Gustavo Márquez, 79–135. Washington, D.C.: Inter-American Development Bank.

Roxborough, Ian. 1984. *Unions and Politics in Mexico: The Case of the Automobile Industry.* Cambridge: Cambridge University Press.

Ruíz-Tagle P., Jaime. 1985. *El sindicalismo chileno después del Plan Laboral.* Santiago: Programa de Economía del Trabajo, Academia de Humanismo Cristiano.

Saavedra, Jaime. 1999. "Reformas laborales en un contexto de apertura económica." Lima: Grupo de Análisis para el Desarrollo.

Saavedra Chanduví, Jaime, and Máximo Torero. 2002. "Union Density Changes and Union Effects on Firm Performance in Peru." Research Network Working Paper R-465 (September). Washington, D.C.: Inter-American Development Bank, Latin American Research Network.

Sagardoy Bengoechea, Juan Antonio. 1987. "Labour Market Flexibility in Spain." *Labour and Society* 12 (1): 55–67.

Sandoval Rodríguez, Isaac. 1997. "Relaciones de trabajo en Bolivia." Santa Cruz, Bolivia: Asociación Iberoamericana de Derecho del Trabajo y la Seguridad Social "Guillermo Cabanellas."

Secretaría del Trabajo y Previsión Social. 2001. *Modernización y actualización de la legislación laboral.* Mimeograph. In author's possession.

Senado de la República. Grupo Parlamentario del Partido Acción Nacional. 1995. *Iniciativa de decreto que reforma a la Ley Federal del Trabajo.* Manuscript.

Shugart, Matthew Soberg, and Scott Mainwaring. 1997. "Presidentialism and Democracy in Latin America: Rethinking the Terms of the Debate." In *Presidentialism and Democracy in Latin America,* ed. Scott Mainwaring and Matthew Soberg Shugart, 12–54. Cambridge: Cambridge University Press.

Siavelis, Peter M. 2000. *The President and Congress in Postauthoritarian Chile: Institutional Constraints to Democratic Consolidation.* University Park: Pennsylvania State University Press.

Silva, Eduardo. 1998. "Organized Business, Neoliberal Economic Restructuring, and Redemocratization in Chile." In *Organized Business, Economic Change, and Democracy in Latin America,* ed. Francisco Durand and Eduardo Silva, 217–52. Miami: North-South Center Press.

Smith, Peter H. 1995. "The Changing Agenda for Social Science Research on Latin America." In *Latin America in Comparative Perspective: New Approaches in Methods and Analysis*, ed. Peter H. Smith, 1–29. Boulder: Westview Press.

Smith, Russell E. 1995. "The 1988 Brazilian Constitution: Continuity or Change in the Industrial Relations System?" Latin American Labor Occasional Paper no. 23. Miami: Florida International University, Center for Labor Research and Studies.

Standing, Guy. 1997. "Globalization, Labour Flexibility, and Insecurity: The Era of Market Regulation." *European Journal of Industrial Relations* 3 (1): 7–37.

Stephens, Evelyne Huber. 1983. "The Peruvian Military Government, Labor Mobilization, and the Political Strength of the Left." *Latin American Research Review* 18 (2): 57–93.

Taylor, Robert. 1999. "OECD Backs Down as Finding Is Attacked." *Financial Times*, 9 July, 4.

Teichman, Judith A. 2001. *The Politics of Freeing Markets in Latin America: Chile, Argentina, and Mexico*. Chapel Hill: University of North Carolina Press.

———. 2004. "The World Bank and Policy Reform in Mexico and Argentina." *Latin American Politics and Society* 46 (1): 39–74.

Tomada, Carlos. 2004. "En busca de equilibrio y de honestidad." *La Nación*, 3 March. Available at http://www.trabajo.gov.ar/prensa/historicos/nacionales/files_03/columna.doc.

Tuman, John P. 1998. "The Political Economy of Restructuring in Mexico's 'Brownfield' Plants: A Comparative Analysis." In *Transforming the Latin American Automobile Industry: Unions, Workers, and the Politics of Restructuring*, ed. John P. Tuman and John T. Morris, 148–78. Armonk, N.Y.: M. E. Sharpe.

Unidad de Análisis de Políticas Económicas (UDAPE). 1997. *Consideraciones sobre la reforma de la legislación laboral*. Estudios de Milenio no. 8 (March). La Paz: Fundación Milenio.

U.S. Department of Labor. Bureau of International Labor Affairs (ILAB). 2003. *Labor Rights Report: Chile*. Available at http://www.dol.gov/ilab/media/reports/usfta/HR2738ChileLaborRights.pdf.

U.S. Department of State. Bureau of Democracy, Human Rights and Labor. 2002a. *Bolivia: Country Reports on Human Rights Practices—2001*. Available at http://www.state.gov/g/drl/rls/hrrpt/2001/wha/8299.htm.

———. 2002b. *Chile: Country Reports on Human Rights Practices—2001*. Available at http://www.state.gov/g/drl/rls/hrrpt/2001/wha/8318.htm.

———. 2002c. *Peru: Country Reports on Human Rights Practices—2001*. Available at http://www.state.gov/g/drl/rls/hrrpt/2001/wha/8263.htm.

———. 2003a. *Bolivia: Country Reports on Human Rights Practices—2002*. Available at http://www.state.gov/g/drl/rls/hrrpt/2002/18321.htm.

———. 2003b. *Brazil: Country Reports on Human Rights Practices—2002*. Available at http://www.state.gov/g/drl/rls/hrrpt/2002/18322.htm.

———. 2003c. *Peru: Country Report on Human Rights Practices—2002*. Available at http://www.state.gov/g/drl/rls/hrrpt/2002/18342.htm.

————. 2004. *Bolivia: Country Reports on Human Rights Practices—2003.* Available at http://www.state.gov/g/drl/rls/hrrpt/2003/27887.htm.

Valdés, Francisco. 1997. *Autonomía y legitimidad.* México, D.F.: Editorial Porrúa.

Valenzuela, J. Samuel. 1989. "Labor Movements in Transitions to Democracy: A Framework for Analysis." *Comparative Politics* 21 (4): 445–72.

Vega Ruíz, María Luz, ed. 2000. *La reforma laboral en América Latina: Un análisis comparado.* Lima: Oficina Regional de la OIT para América Latina y el Caribe.

Vergara, Pilar. 1985. *Auge y caída del neoliberalismo en Chile.* Santiago: FLACSO.

Vergara, Rosalía. 2005. "Abascal, el fracaso." *Proceso,* 19 February. Available at http://www.proceso.com.mx.

Von Bülow, Marisa. 1998. "Reforma trabalhista em um contexto de integração hemisférica: O caso do Brasil." Paper presented at the International Congress of the Latin American Studies Association, Chicago, 24–26 September.

————. 2000. "O movimento sindical brasileiro nos anos 90." Paper presented at the International Congress of the Latin American Studies Association, Miami, 16–18 March.

Wannöffel, Manfred, ed. 1995. *Ruptura en las relaciones laborales.* Caracas: Fundación Friedrich Ebert (México) and Editorial Nueva Sociedad.

Warn, Ken. 2000. "Argentina: President Challenges Unions on Labour Reform." *Financial Times,* 27 January, 11.

Washington Office on Latin America (WOLA). 2005. U.S. NAO Submission US 2005-01. 17 February. Washington, D.C. Available at http://www.dol.gov/ilab/media/reports/nao/submissions/Sub2005-01.htm.

Wells, Don. 1999. "Building Transnational Coordinative Unionism." In *Confronting Change: Auto Labor and Lean Production in North America/ Enfrentando el cambio: Obreros del automóvil y producción esbelta en América del Norte,* 2d ed., ed. Huberto Juárez Núñez and Steve Babson, 487–506. Puebla, Puebla, México: Benemérita Universidad Autónoma de Puebla and Wayne State University Labor Studies Center.

Weyland, Kurt. 1998. "The Fragmentation of Business in Brazil." In *Organized Business, Economic Change, and Democracy in Latin America,* ed. Francisco Durand and Eduardo Silva, 73–97. Miami: North-South Center Press.

Williams, Heather L. 2001. *Social Movements and Economic Transition: Markets and Distributive Conflict in Mexico.* Cambridge: Cambridge University Press.

Williams, Mark Eric. 2001. *Market Reforms in Mexico: Coalitions, Institutions, and the Politics of Policy Change.* Lanham, Md.: Rowman and Littlefield.

Wise, Carol. 1997. "State Policy and Social Conflict in Peru." In *The Peruvian Labyrinth: Polity, Society, Economy,* ed. Maxwell A. Cameron and Philip Mauceri, 70–103. University Park: Pennsylvania State University Press.

Xelhuantzi-López, María. 2000. *La democracia pendiente: La libertad de asociación sindical y los contratos de protección en México.* México, D.F.: Sindicato de Telefonistas de la República Mexicana.

Zapata S., Francisco. 1976. "The Chilean Labor Movement Under Salvador Allende: 1970–1973." *Latin American Perspectives* 3 (8): 85–97.

———. 1995. *El sindicalismo mexicano frente a la reestructuración.* México, D.F.: El Colegio de México.

———. 1997. "The Paradox of Flexibility and Rigidity: The Mexican Labour Market in the 1990s." In *Labour Productivity and Flexibility,* ed. Edward J. Amadeo and Susan Horton, 113–50. Hampshire, UK: Palgrave Macmillan.

Zazueta, César and Ricardo de la Peña. 1984. *La estructura del Congreso del Trabajo: Estado, trabajo, y capital en México.* México, D.F.: Fondo de Cultura Económica.

Zylberstajn, Hélio. 2005. "President Lula's Union Reform." In *Dimensiones sociales de la globalización,* vol. 2, ed. Asociación Chilena de Relaciones Laborales and Asociación Internacional de Relaciones de Trabajo, 591–610. Santiago: Quinto Congreso Regional Americano de Relaciones de Trabajo.

Index

Page numbers in *italics* indicate tables.